the
INDIE BAND
SURVIVAL
GUIDE

ST. MARTIN'S GRIFFIN
NEW YORK

THE INDIE BAND SURVIVAL GUIDE

Randy Chertkow
& Jason Feehan

the complete
manual
for the
do-it-yourself
musician

www.stmartins.com

Book design by Jonathan Bennett

Library of Congress Cataloging-in-Publication Data

Chertkow, Randy.
  The indie band survival guide : the complete manual for the do-it-yourself musician /
Randy Chertkow and Jason Feehan.—1st. ed.
      p. cm.
  ISBN-13: 978-0-312-37768-7
  ISBN-10: 0-312-37768-1
  1. Rock music—Marketing. 2. Rock music—Vocational guidance. I. Feehan,
Jason. II. Title.
  ML3795.C46 2008
  781.64058'8—dc22

                                                                    2008013009

10   9   8   7   6   5

Dedicated to musicians everywhere

CONTENTS

INTRODUCTION

WELCOME TO *The Indie Band Survival Guide,* a practical how-to manual to get your music heard, distributed, sold, booked, promoted, and seen. In the past, you could only do all of this with the backing of a major record label, but you can now do it on your own. We'll tell you how to get started and walk you through the process.

This book is for all musicians, from hobbyists to professionals. It's also for managers, bookers, labels, promoters, recording engineers, music teachers, music-video directors, filmmakers, and anyone else who works with music. In fact, many of the methods we share here are useful for any creative endeavor; you don't have to be a musician to get a lot out of this *Guide.* But our focus is on how each topic relates to music. For instance, when we explain how to create Web sites, we specifically cover the creation of *music* Web sites, even though the principles of good Web-site design we share are applicable to any site.

The information in this book is applicable to musicians of all ages, from teens starting their first garage band to retirees who have rediscovered their love of music and want to share it with the world. It will be indispensable to you whether or not you have a lot of experience with the Internet. The *Guide* will explain how to use all of the talents that you already have and supplement them with tools, techniques, and a network of people to accomplish what was only possible for major-label bands in the past.

More than anything, at the heart of this book are essential techniques for getting your music to the world.

WHO ARE "WE" ANYWAY?

"We" are lead members of Beatnik Turtle, an indie band with more than a decade of experience, more than a dozen albums, a song that was licensed to Disney for a commercial campaign, years of live shows, college-radio play, countless podcast plays (we'll explain podcasts, don't worry), theater shows at venues such as Second City, TV theme songs, music videos, Web sites, and a completed Song of the Day project where we released one song each day for a year. In case you're curious, all things Beatnik Turtle can be found at www.beatnikturtle.com.

We are two working professionals—an IT expert and an attorney—and we've brought all the knowledge and experience from our respective fields to bear on this book, just as you will learn to take advantage of your own skills in making your band a success. Thanks to our backgrounds, the two of us are just as inclined to discuss the state of the music industry or the future of independent music as we are to actually sit down and jam.

In the end, though, we are indie musicians with a band. We generated the material in this book by actually solving the problems we discuss here. In fact, this is the book we wish we'd had when we started out over a decade ago. For instance, when we wrote the section about how to submit your music to podcasts, we recorded the steps we'd been using for years, then did another round of submissions to test and refine the process.

So when we say "we," we're talking to you as one musician to another.

WHAT YOU NEED TO GET STARTED

We're going to cover a *lot* of topics, but we're going to take for granted that you know how to sing and/or play your instruments, and that you have your own music to perform. You might do cover songs, or you might write your own music, but, either way, we assume that you should already have that ready to go.

Finally, we assume you know how to use a computer and possess at least basic Web skills. We aren't going to spend a lot of time explaining what hyperlinks are or how to use a Web browser. Many of the opportunities that have opened up for musicians in the last few years are on the Web, so you'll be using it quite a bit to promote your music and get it heard by a worldwide audience. If you'd like to do some background reading, we suggest the book *Internet for Dummies* by John R. Levine, Margaret Levine Young, and

Carol Baroudi for a basic overview, as well as the book *Rule the Web!* by Mark Frauenfelder, which can help you get the most out of the Internet.

HOW TO USE THIS BOOK

This book is about *doing*.

In this book, we cover the theory behind how things work so you can navigate unfamiliar tasks (such as publicity), but you should expect to *act* on these how-to steps and suggestions, not just think about them. This book will work best if you have a notepad next to you while you read so you can take notes on what to do next.

We're big fans of *Getting Things Done*, a book by David Allen that provides an excellent system of organizing your tasks and your time. With the *Guide* in hand, you can shortcut trying to figure out *what* you should do. That's what we struggled with for the past decade. We wrote it here so you can pick up where we left off.

Lastly, the *Guide* is not a book of lists and links. Although we have important links throughout this book, new tools and services for musicians are always popping up (as well as disappearing). For this information, as well as a way to connect to other motivated musicians, head to IndieBandSurvivalGuide.com.

Naturally, as a musician you'll want to improvise on what we suggest here. Go for it. As we like to say, these tools and lessons are no substitute for artful practice.

TERMINOLOGY

Below, we provide our own definitions of a few music-business terms to avoid any confusion about what they mean when we use them:

- **Unsigned:** Refers to a band or musician that does not have a contract with a label for recording, production, and distribution. Unfortunately, it seems to imply that being signed is the goal, and that musicians who haven't been signed have a lower status than those who have. We will not be using this term, and we suggest that indie bands skip it as well.

- **Independent ("indie"):** Used to describe a band, musician, or label independent of the major labels. We don't believe that musical success should be defined in the context of business contracts. The definition we use is, independent musicians are artists who handle their own music careers. It's something to be proud of.

• **The music industry:** The music industry has changed so much in recent years that a person in the business just five years ago would hardly recognize it. While today the term still seems to refer to the monolithic music business, it's more safe to say that many industries are coming together around music. This term is in transition, but we will use it to talk about the business of music.

Because the traditional players in the music business used to be gate-keepers for the distribution and sale of music, many of their terms defined music between what was inside their system, and what wasn't. This isn't surprising: in the past nothing outside the system would get heard by anyone but local bar crowds. What *is* surprising is that these terms are still used even though musicians have gotten access to almost all of the same recording and distribution channels that the traditional players use. When people talk about bands that are signed or unsigned, we ask them what difference they hear between a song that is owned by musicians and one owned by a company. Is there some magic way to analyze the audio signal to get an idea of who owns it?

Fortunately, music is music, no matter what contracts are signed and how the lawyers have chopped up the rights. Music fans don't care about contracts, they care about the music and the musician. And that's the point: there no longer needs to be a middleman between musicians and music fans.

This book will tell you how to reach the fans who are waiting for you.

CHAPTER 1

THERE HAS NEVER BEEN A BETTER TIME TO BE A MUSICIAN

Less than ten years ago the "Holy Grail" for artists was to get a record or publishing deal. Today, many artists avoid these deals (especially record ones) at all costs.

—*"The Record Biz Today: On Which End of the Food Chain?"*
NATIONAL ASSOCIATION OF RECORD INDUSTRY
PROFESSIONALS *(June 5, 2007)*

THERE HAS never been a better time to be a musician.

The tools at your fingertips today were barely even dreams just ten years ago. Global digital distribution for music is simple to achieve, and with it you can sell millions of copies of your album from one physical copy. More opportunities than ever before exist to get your music played, and they are no longer exclusive to the major labels. The Web can get you a worldwide fanbase. And you can record your music at home with technologies and capabilities better than a professional recording studio could do a mere decade ago. The system, which used to be closed off, is now wide open for anyone who wants to participate. The traditional players in the music industry were like tollbooth operators, and the price of admission was your music. Now, you don't have to ask anyone's permission, and the cost is minimal.

We've entered a world where the musicians are in charge. The numerous middlemen who separated the musicians from their fans are falling away. In fact, musicians can stop wasting their time trying to appeal to the mainstream-minded music executives and focus on the people who really matter: the fans.

Unfortunately, the best techniques for taking your music into your own hands are scattered all over the Web, or in books and courses oriented toward audio and computer professionals. Even more answers have existed only in the heads of musicians who have solved these problems from scratch, but haven't yet shared how.

That is, until now.

You are holding a book written by two indie musicians who ran into those problems and who, by necessity, navigated and deciphered the confusing worlds of music copyright and licensing, CD replication, publicity, music-video production, and booking, to name a few. This is the guide that we wish that we had when we started our own band over a decade ago.

With this book, you'll learn how to win fans worldwide, achieve global digital distribution and sales, get your music heard on radio and the Internet, launch publicity campaigns, and get yourself and your music noticed throughout the world.

In short, you now have everything you need to do it yourself.

THE DEATH OF THE HIT-DRIVEN MUSIC INDUSTRY

THE LONG TAIL

The music industry has long focused on the hits. From the *Billboard* Top 100 charts to the focus on gold and platinum albums, success for music was marked by the number of units sold. This industry is obsessed with popularity and sales numbers. This isn't surprising, since most of the sales for the industry came only from those hits. Why bother with any other music?

But that was in the days when music could only be sold as pieces of acetate or plastic, and the only way to hear new music was to listen to the handful of radio stations in your town. At the heart of the titanic changes to the music industry is a concept called the Long Tail, a theory created by Chris Anderson, editor of *Wired* magazine, author of the book *The Long Tail*, and, incidentally, a musician.

His theory about what changed is simple: there has never been *room* for items that might sell just one or two units a week. But, with computers and the Internet, there is no end of shelf space. For example, if we look at music sales, it would resemble the graph below. Most of the music industry focused on the Head of the graph, which represents hit albums. But the gray part, the Long Tail, extends way beyond what even the graph can show.

Here's the surprising part: the combined sales of the Long Tail are *greater* than the combined sales of the Head (the "hits"). The reason is simple: so much more makes up the tail than can ever make up the head. And because people aren't limited to just buying their music from the head, they are traveling down the tail and buying what *they* want to hear, rather than what the industry has made available to them.

Are all of these so-called Long Tail songs, well, good? Naturally, not. But the amazing thing is that every single one of these tracks, good, bad, and ugly, usually sells. This key paragraph from *The Long Tail* explains it best:

> ... for online retailers like Rhapsody the market is seemingly never-ending. Not only is every single one of Rhapsody's top 60,000 tracks streamed at least once each month, but the same is true for its top 100,000, top 200,000, and top 400,000, even its top 600,000, top 900,000 and beyond. As fast as Rhapsody adds tracks to its library, those songs find an audience, even if it's just a handful of people every month, somewhere in the world.

This means that there's a market for all music thanks to high-speed Internet connections and dirt cheap hard-drive storage. The implications for your own music should be obvious: there's room for you in the pool. Hop in.

UNLIMITED CHOICES

In the recent past there were only so many radio stations, TV channels, and shelf spaces. Audiences' choices were limited. But today, choices are unlimited.

This changes everything.

And not all of it is good for the traditional media, the media that most musicians target to get their music played. A multitude of new entertainment options such as YouTube, podcasts, video games, and the Internet have diluted their audience. According to *The Long Tail*, if you were to drop a television share sheet for today's top network television show on the desk of a television executive from one of the three networks of the 1970s, he would immediately cancel the show due to poor ratings. And with even more choices being offered to audiences, these numbers will probably drop even further.

In the past, because the channels were so expensive, the gatekeepers focused on hit music or shows that maximized their audience share. Generations of people internalized this hits-only economic model and began to assume that there was "a mainstream" that everyone liked. Anything that didn't make it past the gatekeepers had no value. So how much of this was because mainstream entertainment was the *only* entertainment available?

"Music is an industry grossly underserved by the blockbuster model," Chris Anderson told us in an interview. "People don't realize how much music is out there. The vast majority of bands don't get signed to a major label and don't get sold in major record stores. Music is an example of the richness of culture and the violence that traditional distribution does to that variety."

But as he explained in his book, the traditional distribution model is now being swept away. And this trend is good for indies. Plus, because the means of production and distribution are in the hands of people like you and me, more people are making music themselves. They have realized that they can find an audience on the Internet, even a big one. And the irony is that the average person is not only spending less time consuming traditional mainstream media, he or she is actually competing against it.

With these trends dividing the attentions of the audience, the established players must change their business models. They are still focused on hits, with most of their income streams based entirely on the number of people watching and listening to their shows. As their audience continues to drop, the advertising money supporting film, TV-show, and major-label-album production is flowing elsewhere. The hit-driven producers of music—the major labels—are especially impacted.

NICHES

The limited number of channels of the past has exploded into a universe of niches. People can easily find others that share their interests no matter what that interest is, and no matter where in the world those people are. But this doesn't mean niches are small. For example, there are millions of tennis fans.

Music works the same way. No matter what genre of music you play, fans of that style can find you and hear your music. All you need to do is reach out to them. You need only go to CD Baby (CDBaby.com), the world's largest independent music store, to find that the top sellers appeal to particular niches. Derek Sivers, the president and founder of CD Baby, shared his observations about this trend:

> Imagine an archery range with a target one hundred feet away that you're shooting at with your bow and arrow. For the last few decades that target has been two inches wide. And the only way you could hit it was aiming dead at the middle. If you had perfect aim, you could have a big hit. Otherwise, you'd have nothing at all. Now it's like that target is one hundred feet across, and it's easy to hit, except somebody did a little trick and cut out the middle. It's like a big giant doughnut. It's easy to hit, but if you're still aiming at the middle, there's nothing there.

This trend is good for indies. There are people who want to hear your music. And, the goal of the rest of the *Guide* is to tell you how to effectively find your niches.

How the Long Tail Affects Your Music

Here's what it means to you:

- There is room for every artist.

- You no longer need to go through gatekeepers to get your music to an audience.

- Traditional mainstream media such as television and radio are no longer the only ways to get heard. There are more ways to win fans using a broad array of other media that don't have the same barriers to entry.

- Music hits are never going to be as big as they were in the past, because people aren't forced to select their music from a small set of options. Astronomical hits were an artificial by-product of limited choices.

- Because of the number of options that the audience has, you must compete for your audience's attention, but there are countless niches for your music.

- The distinction between being signed and being indie will not matter to fans. Instead talent, quality, publicity, and genre will be all that matters.

- Your band is a niche.

MYTHS AND REALITIES

Most people's conception of how the music industry works seems to be derived from movies and television. The movie *That Thing You Do!*, a film directed by Tom Hanks, is a perfect example. It tells the story of a fictional band called the Wonders in the early 1960s. They write a couple of songs and, after performing live, decide to record an album. After sending their record to a radio station, something wonderful happens—it gets played. The Wonders are a hit! The music labels come knocking, and in no time at all the band members are thrust into riches, fame, and fortune.

Unfortunately, although this type of story gets repeated over and over, it's just not true. While this might be shocking to some, the music industry doesn't quite work the way Hollywood portrays it.

THE MYTHS AND REALITIES OF COMMERCIAL RADIO

Possibly the most common goal that bands have for their music is to get it played on the radio. Unfortunately, commercial radio is mostly inaccessible to independent musicians. There's a reason why you rarely hear of indie bands getting discovered due to commercial radio (except in movies). You can certainly do it, but it will probably cost you a minimum of $20,000, and that's no guarantee. You're better off with a budget in the low six figures. If this goes counter to your beliefs that "payola" was made illegal, it will help to know a little bit of history before starting your commercial-radio campaign.

How Commercial Radio Really Works

Think back to when rock and roll was starting to make a splash in the 1950s. The powers that be were against that "sinful" music. They believed it was corrupting the youth. Whether it was good or bad for our children, rock and roll was certainly big money. By the late 1950s, record labels were routinely sending record albums with piles of money—and even drugs—to DJs to get their songs played on the radio. This practice came into sharp public focus when the legendary rock-and-roll DJ Alan Freed was convicted in 1962 of accepting bribes to play music. Shortly after, payola laws were passed.

These payola laws have been on the books since then, but there is still payola. Today, it's just done through intermediaries. While it isn't permitted for a record label to pay a radio station to play its music, it is permitted for them to pay a third party to help get their music played. And thus, the independent promoter was born.

These promoters aren't allowed to pay money to the radio stations either, but they find other incentives, such as providing vacation packages to radio programmers, giveaways for the stations' listening audiences, and even payments to cover miscellaneous expenses. As Eric Boehlert wrote in an exposé for Salon.com, the techniques "indies" (independent promoters, not bands) use to get around the restrictions vary:

> Indies form alliances with a station's general managers (or the corporate owners) and cut deals, typically guaranteeing a station in a medium-sized

market $75,000 to $100,000 annually in what is termed "promotional support" to buy a station van, T-shirts, billboard ads, etc.

The annual promotional payment secures the indie as the station's exclusive point man, the only one (or at least the first one) its programmers will talk to about playing a new single—an "add," in industry parlance. The indie becomes a high-priced toll collector. Once that indie has claimed a station, he (it's almost always a he) sends out a notice to record companies, letting them know he will invoice them, on average $1,000, every time the station adds a new song to its playlist. If indies don't get paid, the songs don't get played.

So, contrary to popular belief, none of the music on commercial radio is chosen by DJs from submissions made by artists. Nor is it made a hit by radio programmers "discovering great music" that's out there.

Commercial Radio and Independent Bands

With this kind of money being thrown at radio stations to play major-label music, it should be clear why you can't get commercial radio play. Few of us indies have the kind of money needed to get played.

Added to this, due to new FCC rules allowing corporations to own even larger percentages of stations in a single market, there are fewer owners of radio stations in general. Smaller stations have been absorbed into large corporations such as Clear Channel Communications. This means less diversity, and fewer truly different places to get played in commercial radio. How likely is it that a corporate radio giant is going to play your music when you have no advertising dollars to offer them in return?

Fortunately, radio is no longer the only method to introduce your music to new fans. And, as we stated above, they're losing listenership anyway. Today, plenty of other distribution channels are available to indie musicians, such as college radio, podcasts, and music blogs, to get their music heard by music fans. We'll tell you how to get your music into these channels later in this *Guide*.

THE MYTHS AND REALITIES OF MAJOR LABELS

Back when studio time was expensive and distribution and promotional channels were limited, musicians needed labels to record, distribute, and promote their music. But this has changed. And yet, some musicians dream of getting signed to a major label. This is no longer good business sense and there are a variety of reasons why:

- *The money's not there.* As record producer Steve Albini revealed in a well-known essay called "The Problem with Music," musicians in a moderately successful major-label band with a $250,000 advance (which is owed back to the label) can make as little as $4,000 per year. In the end, most albums never earn out their advance—the only money most musicians see.

- *You give up creative control.* Labels wield a great deal of control over your creative work, and worse, they can go through the entire recording process with you before deciding to withdraw their support. In many documented cases, a label coming under new management has canceled the release of a finished album before it goes out. For examples, see *The Ultimate Survival Guide to the New Music Industry: Handbook for Hell* by Justin Goldberg.

- *You give up your rights.* The label keeps rights to the recording master of your album *forever*. Even if the album goes gold, and the band pays back all of the money owed to the label, that recording will still be owned by the label. A quote from Courtney Love said it best: "The band owns none of its work . . . they can pay the mortgage forever but they'll never own the house."

To get more insight into major labels, we suggest *Confessions of a Record Producer* by Moses Avalon and *All You Need to Know About the Music Business* by Donald S. Passman.

Consolidation, Cost Cutting, and Layoffs

The major labels are in turmoil. They are losing money, cutting costs, laying off employees, and consolidating to stay alive. As stated above, the music industry's business model is broken. They are still focused on hits and selling CDs. Each year, sales of CDs decline. Unsurprisingly, these sales declines are affecting those musicians who choose to sign with the labels:

- *Artist development.* Labels are spending less than ever on nurturing new musicians and bands. In an article entitled "Music Labels Might Still Be Shorts" (RealMoney.com), Cody Willard writes, "They can't just cut costs to boost cash flow forever. There's no fat left in those labels. They sure don't spend to develop talent over the years like they did back in days past."

- *Turnover.* To compensate for lower revenues, the labels lay off employees. Musicians who do get signed can't be sure that the people they are dealing with today will still be there tomorrow.

- *Taking even more revenue streams.* Major labels are trying to get at even more of the artists' revenue streams. While the labels used to be limited to album distribution and ownership of the master recordings, they are now taking a cut of music publishing, merchandise, live shows, and even sponsorship revenue in the guise of providing a one-stop holistic approach—something that a band can handle more profitably for themselves.

The Major Labels' Effect on Indie Musicians

The good news for indie musicians is that those people being laid off are experienced and talented music professionals, skilled personnel who are increasingly hiring themselves out to indies, charging by the hour or per project. When we decided to get the help of a publicist for our CD release, we found one who had worked at Sony BMG promoting major groups for years, deeply experienced with getting albums in front of lots of reviewers. And we didn't have to give up the rights to our music to take advantage of that experience.

Even veteran artists are catching on to these trends. The ones who are popular enough to get out on their own are doing so now. Many of them are bypassing the labels and going to banks and investors to raise the funds to record their albums. Artists who can show a steady income stream from prior releases have been able to raise serious money. The real question is, what role will the labels play now? According to Aaron O. Patrick in the *Wall Street Journal:*

> Big record companies say they aren't threatened by the efforts to produce music without them. Bands "are not equipped with the necessary

specialist skills to take care of business" such as hiring producers, designers, photographers and publicists, says Max Hole, an executive vice president at Universal Music Group International, the overseas arm of the world's largest music company by market share. "We are experts in providing these services and skills, which allows the artist to create and make music."

We find Mr. Hole's suggestion that a band can't find a photographer, publicist, and designer to help them put together their own albums absurd, especially in the age of the Internet. And they're not going to ask you for the copyright to your music in return for their services. Furthermore, some tools, such as a digital camera or a copy of Photoshop, are easily in your grasp. Whether the traditional players acknowledge it or not, we've entered a new era, one where musicians can do it themselves.

THE NEW ERA OF MUSIC

Today's music world has entirely new concepts and terms that drive it, with audiences that have a completely different view of music from what they have had in the past. You will need to take these changes into account to plunge forward into this world. We're going to talk about this new era below.

PRE-NET AND POST-NET

The heart of this new era for music is the Internet's capability to instantaneously transmit music among people all over the world. Other factors include better encoding for small music-file sizes, peer-to-peer file sharing, faster computers, and broadband connections.

In the *pre-Net* era, limited resources meant limited access for audiences. It meant few channels of distribution, with control concentrated among few players. These players decided what music would be distributed and where. It was a world of one-way communication—of broadcasting.

In the *post-Net* era, barriers between artists and their audiences have fallen away. Post-Net audiences are fickle, and they expect to get most of their information and entertainment for free. Trends come and go quickly in this world. It's easy for something to "go viral" because people spread the music they enjoy to people they know. In the Internet world, this can mean millions of people taking an interest in a short time.

Perhaps the most interesting and relevant change in the post-Net world is the cynicism of the public regarding the traditional media, especially when it comes to the music business. Today's audiences crave authenticity, a fact that isn't lost on the major labels. For instance, singer-songwriter Marié Digby rose to "Internet phenomenon" simply by making homemade videos of herself playing cover versions of popular songs on YouTube. Views soon totaled 2.3 million. This led to her getting played regularly on radio and MTV and ultimately signed by a label—Walt Disney's Hollywood Records. Or did it? A *Wall Street Journal* article reveals the amount of work in making Digby *appear* to be authentic:

> ... a press release last week from Walt Disney Co.'s Hollywood Records label declared: "Breakthrough YouTube Phenomenon Marié Digby Signs with Hollywood Records." What the release failed to mention is that Hollywood Records signed Ms. Digby in 2005, 18 months before she became a YouTube phenomenon. Hollywood Records helped devise her Internet strategy, consulted with her on the type of songs she chose to post, and distributed a high-quality studio recording of [her song] "Umbrella" to iTunes and radio stations.

Given what we know about pay-for-play on commercial radio, it should come to no surprise that a label was orchestrating Digby's rise to "phenom" status. The surprising lesson to take from this is what lengths a major label will go through to make their artists appear indie. According to the article, Digby's MySpace page had "None" listed under "Type of Label." After inquiries from the *Journal*, it was changed to "Major." It's clear that Hollywood Record's approach catered to post-Net expectations of authenticity.

Indies, on the other hand, don't need to manufacture it. They actually *are* authentic.

We will be using the terms *pre-Net* and *post-Net* to discuss differences between these two eras. We'll be comparing them often because many commonly held pre-Net conceptions still need to go.

PRE-FILTERS AND POST-FILTERS

In the pre-Net world, there are two layers of filters.

Pre-filters are the gatekeepers who decide what music will go into distribution channels such as stores, TV, radio, and film. Examples of these are music executives, agents, and A&R representatives. In the pre-Net world, it was tough to break into this system, and only a minute percentage ever did.

Post-filters are the reviewers, newspapers, Web sites, and other sources that people trust to filter through the sea of information and find the gems that match their tastes.

While the pre-filters still exist in the post-Net era, they can be ignored if someone wants to post their work for the world to see. There are no pre-filters on YouTube, for example. Anyone can post any video he or she wants. But of that morass of videos, which ones are actually entertaining? That's where post-filters come in. Many people depend on sites such as Milk and Cookies (milkandcookies.com), which only posts links to videos that users in their community found amusing, to point out the good ones.

Also, even the role of post-filters has opened up. In the pre-Net era, only a few people were empowered to review new works for the public. In the post-Net world, anyone can blog his or her opinions or post a review on Amazon.com. The traditional reviewers, who were at times influenced by the major players, suddenly had unbiased, genuine competition from people who wanted nothing more than to share their opinions. This authenticity is the true currency of the Internet.

There are many types of post-filters:

- *The traditional reviewer.* An individual who gives his or her personal opinion as to what is worthwhile. Some examples are music writers and movie reviewers. In the post-Net era, it also includes bloggers and Web sites that post reviews.

- *Community-based filters.* Community-based filters are Web sites that let their own communities suggest and vote on what they consider to be the best content. With a large enough community, this can be a powerful way to filter. Some examples of community-based filters are Digg.com and reddit. com, which we discuss in the "Your Web Presence" chapter.

- **Editor-based submission filters.** This combines elements of traditional reviewers with community-based filters. A Web site that has editor-based submission filters will accept submissions from anyone, but an editor will sift through these and post what he or she thinks is worthwhile. One example of this type of post-filter is Slashdot (slashdot.org).

- **Aggregation filters.** Since so many opinions are now to be found, some sites aggregate reviews to give a more accurate picture. For instance, Rotten Tomatoes (rottentomatoes.com) takes reviews from known movie reviewers and quantifies their opinions into a combined approval percentage for each film.

- **Word of mouth.** The most important kind of filter there is. One that becomes even more powerful online.

- **Advertising and marketing.** Although these are less effective than the other types of filters, advertising and marketing can have a powerful effect on what rises into people's consciousness.

Since pre-filters can now be avoided, the post-filters have become all-important. They are the primary way that people will find out about your band. As Jim DeRogatis, music editor for the *Chicago Sun-Times* and cohost of National Public Radio's *Sound Opinions*, says, "No matter how obscure a name I throw at you or you throw at me, the fact that we'll be able, in no time at all, to sample that band for ourselves is incredibly liberating. But you'd never know about [these groups] if I didn't mention it to you." As an indie musician, you will need to target these post-filters. We will talk about how to influence them to cover your music in upcoming chapters.

DO IT YOURSELF

As an indie, making your music successful is now your responsibility. Unfortunately, it's not enough to just post an MP3 on your MySpace page. Everything that a label would have done for you is now in your hands. You need to get yourself noticed, booked, distributed, played, seen, and publicized.

Luckily, you have outstanding tools, services, and resources at your fingertips to help you do it yourself. You have global distribution, unlimited promotional opportunities, and countless new ways to get your music to millions of people all over the world. Stop worrying about a music *industry* and start focusing on music *fans*. They're out there. You just need to win them over. That's what the *Guide* is all about. Read on to find out how.

PART I

GET PREPARED

CHAPTER 2

YOUR NETWORK

LABELS USED to be the only way to get your music recorded, distributed, and promoted. The entire game was all about winning over a few key people—businessmen, usually—who decided which bands got heard and which sat in obscurity.

That is no longer the case.

Rather than spend your time, money, and energy on "getting signed," you can now focus on winning over the people who really matter: the fans. Of course, the responsibilities, roles, and costs that labels would have handled fall on you now. That's a lot to take on. Not only do you have to create all the music, you also have to design logos, book gigs, design a Web site, and arrange publicity, to name just a few things. Although you can do it all yourself, it's hard to do it all well.

But doing it yourself doesn't mean doing it alone.

In fact, doing it yourself in music isn't the same as doing it yourself in other areas. Even small labels don't do everything "themselves." They get graphic artists to design logos, album covers, and posters. They get Web designers to create Web sites. They get publicists to convince the press to write about their bands.

You've heard the saying before: "It's not what you know, it's who you know." Or, as one of our friends puts it, "It's who you get to know." This is as true in music as it is in any other field. At the end of the day, despite all the advances in technology that have empowered the artist, it's not technology that will get your music noticed, booked, distributed, played, seen, and publicized. It's people. People make things happen.

These are all real problems that you'll need to solve. Now your goal is to find the right people to help you do it.

THE ARM'S-REACH LESSON AND NETWORKING

Networking scares most people. Maybe because they associate it with unpleasant tasks such as "finding a job." Or because it can feel like a phony way to befriend someone. But networking doesn't have to be hard, and it shouldn't start with strangers at all. The people that you already know—people within your arm's reach—may be the ones who can help you achieve your band's goals.

We discovered some surprising talents among the people whom we already knew that helped our band succeed, talents we didn't possess ourselves. For example, when we wanted to make a music video, one friend directed, others acted, and we even got the use of a friend's professional video equipment. When we wanted to improve our Web site, we found graphic artists and Web programmers in our existing social network. Similarly, people within our arm's reach have given us opportunities. We performed at a college outdoor festival set up by a friend who worked there. We got great press for our TheSongOfTheDay.com project when a friend mentioned it to his buddies who wrote for a popular Chicago blog.

These opportunities arose because we made our goals and obstacles known to our friends, coworkers, and families. If they didn't have the answers, we asked them if they knew anyone else who might. When they did know someone who could help, we asked them to introduce us so we could follow up. When people helped us, we made sure to repay them in some way—by giving them credit, assisting them in solving some problem of their own (even if it wasn't music-related), or simply by sending a thank-you note.

We didn't realize it at the time, but we were networking. While the traditional concept of networking put us off, it turned out it isn't that difficult when you begin with the circle of people you know. And as you expand your network, problems get easier to solve. The key is to understand what types of networks are available to you, how to use those networks effectively, and how to reciprocate so that people feel appreciated.

TYPES OF NETWORKING

There are two general types of networking: skill networking and opportunity networking. A single person might be in both networks, but thinking about each type of networking differently will clarify your approach.

SKILL NETWORKING

In a band, each member possesses skills beyond music. You might have a visual artist, a Web designer, and a booker all within your band. Obviously, when possible, you should provide these skills for yourselves. But you'll probably need more people to help out with all the other roles that a label traditionally filled. These roles include:

- Manager

- Booker

- Distributor

- Web designer

- Webmaster

- Graphic artist

- Publicist

- Photographer

- Recording producer

- Recording engineer

- TV/film camera crew

- TV/film editor

- Store clerk (for shows and events)

- Attorney

- Accountant

If your indie band doesn't fill these roles from its skill network, essential tasks just won't get done. And yet, there are some that you just can't skip—especially when it comes to promoting your band and getting your music heard. The goal of skill networking is to find those who can help you fill in the gaps you can't manage yourself.

OPPORTUNITY NETWORKING

Some people within your arm's reach will have access to opportunities for getting your band and music out there. In general, the people in your opportunity network will have one thing in common: they'll have an audience. Some of these people include:

- Music journalists
- Bookers
- Venue managers/bar owners
- Podcasters
- Radio hosts/DJs
- Bloggers
- Video-game designers
- Film/TV/video directors and music scouts
- Companies .
- Theater artists/sketch-comedy troupes

You might have some of these people in your arm's reach, but these networking opportunities are typically harder to access at first. They require time and energy to cultivate. Sometimes they require credentials. The good news is, once you establish the necessary relationships, they will start coming to *you* with opportunities.

HIDDEN SKILLS AND OPPORTUNITIES

Many people have hidden skills or opportunities that you may not be aware of at first. For instance, when we were putting together the artwork for our second album, *Santa Doesn't Like You*, we lacked the software and know-how to get it in the format that the CD printing house required. We were stuck, until one of our friends—a neighbor, actually—revealed she was a graphic artist and had the necessary software to create the files. We'd had no idea she could do this. She was just someone we hung out with in our building from time to time. When we mentioned the problem, she offered to help. Since she was a friend, all she asked for in return was to get a credit in the liner notes so she could use it as part of her portfolio. We were happy to do that for her, and we got the album art done in time.

You can also access networks online in innovative ways. When Brad Turcotte of Brad Sucks wanted a new logo, he turned to Worth1000.com, a contest site that challenges both professional and amateur artists to create (often humorous) photos, images, text, and videos each week. Turcotte contacted the site owner to arrange a "Design a Brad Sucks Logo Contest." For only $50 in prize money, he got the full rights to a logo he was pleased with. Hiring a graphic artist the normal way would have cost him much more than that.

WORKING AND GROWING NETWORKS EFFECTIVELY

As George Hrab, a successful indie musician, puts it, the secret to networking is "to find really talented people and be really, really, really nice to them." If you can't pay them, you should find other ways to show your appreciation. Movies always end by rolling the credits. This is good advice for any indie band as well.

CROSS-PROMOTION

One way to acknowledge people who have helped you out is to expose *their* work to *your* fans. This can be as simple as linking to their Web site or mentioning them in a blog entry. For example, we have a special "shout-out" section at our TheSongOfTheDay.com site that lists every podcast that has played one of our songs. It's our little thank-you. The most recent plays get a mention on our front page, with direct links to the episodes so that fans of our music can check them out. This results in more and more requests to play our music—not just from the same podcasters, but from others who saw what we offered in return.

CELEBRATE AND ACKNOWLEDGE SUCCESSES

Theater groups throw a cast party at the close of every run. We suggest doing the same for everyone who has helped you out whenever your band reaches a milestone such as completing a tour, releasing an album, or getting some great press. We've thrown parties, held barbecues, and taken people to dinner to show our appreciation and to celebrate. Usually, we end up talking about the next projects we want to work on, and because everyone's excited about what we've just achieved, they all usually offer to stay on board.

If you can't throw a party, at least send an e-mail to everyone involved and acknowledge everyone who's played a part. Of course, it still helps to mention your next project....

THE WARM HANDOFF

Sometimes, people in your network can introduce you to people whom you don't know but want to meet. It can be a big help to have a common connection refer you.

For example, for years we wanted to be part of the Chicago leg of the International Pop Overthrow (IPO) festival—a roving festival that showcases power pop-rock bands. We went the traditional route of sending in our CD and press kit to the festival organizer and never heard anything back. Months later when the festival came to town, we discovered our friend Yvonne Doll and her band, The Locals, managed to get in. When we told her we were hoping to be a part of the festival, she said she'd introduce us to the festival organizer, David Bash. The day after her show, she introduced us to David, who asked for a CD. The very next day he contacted us to fill in for a last-minute cancellation in the schedule. We had a great show and thanked Yvonne for the warm handoff. We've since played the festival every year it's been in Chicago and have also been included on a couple IPO compilation albums.

MANUFACTURING YOUR OWN OPPORTUNITIES

Sometimes you need to manufacture your own opportunities and expand your reach. The best thing to do then is to set your sights on someone who might be able to help you or provide an opportunity for your music, and contact them. This is what most people think "networking" is.

Sure, you might get a no or no response at all, but it's always worth trying because, often, people can surprise you. Although this can be the hardest way to expand your skill and opportunity networks, it can also be the most rewarding when it connects.

Our band did this when promoting *The Cheapass Album*—an album of songs based on game titles from the trendy board-game manufacturer Cheapass Games. At the time of the release back in 2004, we discovered a niche podcast created by Scott Alden and Derk Solko, the people behind BoardGameGeek.com (a Web site that gets over six hundred thousand unique visitors a month). It was immediately evident that the podcast didn't have a theme song. We didn't know Scott or Derk, but we decided to make our own opportunity and offer to do a theme song for their show if they were interested. A few days later, after we sent them our albums, they agreed to let us write a demo and give it a listen.

Within a few weeks, they adopted the song for their podcast. We kept in contact with them and later took it a step further by doing more music, helping them with voice-over bumpers, and creating some off-the-wall public-service announcements. They talked about us in many episodes, which kept our name, our music, and our Web site in front of hundreds of listeners. They even interviewed us in one episode. Scott and Derk became a big part of our opportunity network, and we all became good friends. Their podcasts have been downloaded thousands of times, and they continue to be downloaded years later by new visitors.

NETWORKING WITH OTHER BANDS AND MUSICIANS

As a musician, you're already a member of one of the most helpful networks you can access. You're holding a book by two of them right now. But we're not the only musicians willing to share what we've learned. When musicians cooperate and share resources, productive things happen:

- **Booking cartels.** Bands and musicians with a complementary sound can join forces for booking purposes. Being able to offer an entire night of entertainment to a venue or bar makes their job easier and can get you more gigs in the long run.

- **Musician exchange programs.** Team up with like-minded musicians in another city online. Each band can book a gig in their respective town and share the same bill. Both bands establish an out-of-town presence.

- **Substitutes.** Ever had a gig you just couldn't make? It's quite hard to find a substitute unless you know other bands and musicians in the area. Finding an appropriate substitute when you can't meet your commitment can save your relationship with the venue.

- **Cross-promotion.** Bands and musicians that work together can introduce their music to each other's fans.

- **Recommendations and referrals.** If you need to find someone who can help you or need someone to hire, other musicians can often refer you to a trusted person or service.

- **Shared roles at gigs.** Bands can help each other out at shows. For instance, we once ran another band's store while they were playing onstage, and they did the same for us while we performed.

- **Going beyond your arm's reach.** Each band has its own skill and opportunity networks and will often share and share alike. This can be a great resource for referrals of trusted freelancers and other services.

- **Newbies.** Don't forget that, as you progress, it's a good thing to offer guidance and assistance to other bands and musicians just starting out and add them to your own network. You never know if they'll return the favor someday.

Remember that you don't need to be in the same location to collaborate with other bands and musicians; it can happen online as well. Message boards, blogs, social-networking sites, and our own site, IndieBand-

SurvivalGuide.com, can help connect you to other bands and musicians. Often, a solution or an opportunity is just a few clicks away.

YOUR FAN NETWORK

At the start, you and your band members will form the center of your skill and opportunity networks, but eventually your music will form your most powerful network. The network that should be your focus at all times: your fans. Winning these people over one by one is what the *Guide* is all about.

In the past, fans were little more than those people who liked a band's music, bought albums, purchased merchandise, and came to shows. In other words, they were simply consumers.

That is no longer the case.

Thanks to the Internet, fans have also become empowered. They now feel entitled to a relationship with the bands they like. They are no longer limited to watching bands play onstage, they are now a part of that stage. They e-mail, they download, they comment, they make mash-ups, they shoot videos, they record podcasts, they chat, and they blog. Fans want a place to meet, discuss, collaborate, and interact with you and other fans. Your fans form the most important and critical network your music will ever have. And it can grow or wither based on your involvement.

FANS AS CONTRIBUTORS

Fans today want to interact and participate—not just listen. Many are creative and can help you fill in gaps in your skill network. And when they do, good things can happen for both you and your fans.

Jonathan Coulton is an independent musician who makes a living writing and performing his own music. In September 2005, he challenged himself to write, record, and release a musical "Thing a Week" for free on his Web site, Jonathancoulton.com. Midway through the release of the songs, a fan named Len Peralta e-mailed him and asked if he might create artwork to accompany each of the fifty-two songs. Coulton agreed. Soon, under Coulton's active encouragement, fans began making videos, animations, and machinima (movies "filmed" using video games) based on his songs. Coulton even asked fans to send in hand claps so he could include them in his final "Thing a Week," a cover of Queen's "We Will Rock You." One fan created a Coulton card game. Coulton and Peralta later went on to sell the artwork as a book at Lulu.com and even created a coloring book. And then there's the fan who created karaoke versions of Coulton's songs ...

A similar thing happened to Brad Turcotte, sole member of Brad Sucks (bradsucks.net), a band composed of "one man with no fans." However, his "nonexistent" fans have created tons of remixes of his debut album, *I Don't Know What I'm Doing*. After posting the original source tracks of his album on his Web site and encouraging his fans to remix them, Turcotte soon found himself overwhelmed with the response. Fans sent in *hundreds* of remixes—and they're still coming in. Turcotte decided to turn to his fan network for designing a logo and a week later picked out one that he liked. Then he did the same for album art—not just for his second album, but also for a "best of" compilation album culled from all the remixes his fans had created. He's even let fans come behind the curtain by making demos of his upcoming second album's songs available for their comments and feedback.

FANS AS PROBLEM SOLVERS

Although both Coulton and Turcotte use their blogs and forums to share their opinions, they also use them to ask their fans for help and direction. During the "Thing a Week" project, Coulton regularly posed questions to his growing fan network to get their thoughts on whether they thought he was giving away too much music for free and whether they thought it was hampering his ability to make a living as a solo artist. Fans responded to his request. Soon, his "Thing a Week" became not only a creative challenge and an experiment in promotion, it became a public discussion of what it means to be a post-Net musician. Fans offered up advice on his Web-site design, his gigs, and his merchandise. When the importance of promotion became critical, Coulton naturally enlisted his fans to help. After all, he's only one person.

Turcotte also regularly turns to his fans for help. He asks his fans for their opinions on new Web services, software, and instruments. When

Turcotte was researching digital download stores to use for his Web site, he asked his fans if they knew of others. They responded with alternatives (although he eventually built one of his own!).

FANS AS PROMOTERS

One of the more famous experiments in networking was Stanley Milgram's "six degrees of separation," which states that everyone is connected to everyone else within six people. What it means to you and your music in this connected world has been summed up by Eben Moglen, one of the primary lawyers and voices behind the free-software movement: "The result . . . is that twelve-year-olds do a better job of distributing music than the music companies. The music company continues to take ninety-four percent of the gross for promoting and distributing music, and the twelve-year-olds who take zero off the top do a better job."

But as thought provoking as this is, Moglen's twelve-year-olds will only promote music that they've heard of. So rather than wait for a junior-high street team to start promoting your music, you need to ask your fans to help promote you. Fortunately, people love to promote things they know and like. And some of your fans may be well connected and can help get you access to opportunities. Building an enthusiastic fan network to help spread the word about you is powerful. The best "advertising" is trusted word of mouth.

Turcotte gave his music away for free to enable his fan network to become active promoters. Although he made his first album available for free download, people still bought his CD. Since CDs are harder to share than the MP3 files, he embedded the MP3 versions of his songs on the CDs to make it easy for his fans to continue to share his music. And as we mentioned above, he later released his source tracks for free to enable fans to remix his songs. This further introduced his music to others, since the creators of these remixes actively promoted *their* remixes of *his* songs to other people.

Similarly, Coulton asked his fan network to spread the word, and they did with so much enthusiasm, it surprised him. Fans would share his music with friends, play his music at parties, and create CDs to give as gifts. Some realized they had press connections and opened those opportunities to

Coulton. Others simply added a link to Coulton's Web site in their signature lines when they posted in forums or discussion groups. This type of promotion adds up.

FANS AS ORGANIZERS

Your fans can even help you organize events or even help book your band. For example, fans are always demanding that Coulton tour in their hometowns. When he realized he had to travel halfway across the country to Seattle at the last minute for a personal matter, he blogged that he'd have one night free and could play a show if something was set up. Fans in Seattle—who didn't want to pass up a rare opportunity to see Coulton live—immediately took up the challenge and, within twenty-four hours, had arranged a respectable venue. All Coulton had to do was contact the place to cement the details. Twenty-four hours later, he was onstage playing to a packed house.

FANS AS CONSUMERS AND SUPPORTERS

Your fan network will be the greatest source of revenue for your music. This can come both from playing live as well as from album and merchandise sales. It can also come from donations. Beyond selling their music, both Coulton and Turcotte have online "tip jars" for those who have enjoyed the music they've given away for free. One of the side benefits of socializing with your fans is that it makes you and your band real people. There's a human face to the music. When you offer up albums and merchandise for sale or set up a tip jar, and your fans feel connected to you, they're likely to support you by reaching for their wallets. Additionally, your involvement and interaction help make it clear that the money they are spending is actually going to the artist, not some label.

YOU'RE NOT ALONE

As we said previously, the rest of the *Guide* will be showing you how to do the things that a label would do. As you discover what you need to do, don't be overwhelmed, and always remember that doing it yourself doesn't mean doing it alone. As Derek Sivers of CD Baby suggests, "Whatever excites you, go do it, and whatever drains you, stop doing it as soon as possible.

Because for everything you hate doing, there's someone else that loves it. Your goal should be to find those people and have them help you." It's your band members, friends, family, and fans that can help you make your music a success.

CHAPTER 3

YOUR BRAND

PRE-NET, YOU had to build awareness of your music among those people you could physically meet or those who could see you play live. Post-Net, you have the ability to share your music with more people than those pre-Net bands could ever dream of. Your arm's reach is no longer limited to where you're located.

Today, the people who have met you or seen you play live are likely to be a minority of the people who listen to your music. The majority will now be those who discover you online. To these people, your band will only be known through your music, name, and the identity you convey through your Web site, logos, photos, blogs, videos, avatars, and so on. Another way to say this is that they will only know you through "your brand." While you can't meet everybody, your brand will.

Because of this, whether you like it or not, you have a brand to manage. Ideally, you should not even start putting your music out into the world until you've come up with a clear and consistent brand identity. Skip this step, and you'll have a haphazard brand that you don't control. If you have three different logos, a new slogan each month, or otherwise portray an inconsistent online presence, it will confuse people.

You should take the time to accurately brand yourself. We'll talk about how to establish an effective brand in this chapter.

BRAND BASICS

WHAT'S A BRAND?

A brand is a communication of your band's identity. The key to effective branding is ensuring that your audience sees the identity you want to project.

Whether you're a solo musician or a large group, there's simply too much information about you and your music for new fans to easily digest. Branding is about distilling your identity into its key components. Some of these components are your name, your images (logo, album artwork), and your text (your story, your tagline). These components make up your Brand Toolbox, but before we talk about these, we need to first understand what makes an effective brand.

BRANDS THAT WORK

There are four ingredients to an effective brand:

- *Accuracy.* Your brand should not be at odds with your actual identity. In other words, it should set accurate expectations and give people a clear sense of what your band and its music is about.

- *Impact.* Your brand should convey its message quickly and easily. When it comes to words, this means brevity (e.g., "Have a Coke and a smile" or Microsoft's "Where do you want to go today?"); when it comes to graphics, it means having an image that "pops." It should be memorable. The cooler your logo, tagline, and so on, the more likely your fans will promote it and purchase branded merchandise.

- *Repetition.* The key to an effective brand is to use it repeatedly. Repetition is necessary since it takes time to cement your identity in the minds of your fans. This can only happen at the individual level, so your brand only gets stronger each time a person encounters it.

- *Consistency.* Because repetition is the key to strengthening your brand, consistency is critical. Changing elements of your brand on a whim ruins the associations you've built up over time in people's heads. Your past branding work goes to waste every time you make dramatic changes.

ALWAYS BE BRANDING

Given these four ingredients, it's crucial you brand everything: your Web sites, your albums, your videos, your MP3s, your press kits, your posters, and so on. Your brand is what fans will identify you with. After all, why else would anyone buy a T-shirt from a *musician*? Your brand gives merchandise its value.

FINDING YOUR BRAND

You'll want to make sure you build a brand that's on target right from the start. You need to be comfortable with the words and images representing your band, both today and years down the road. Your brand should be rooted in your identity. At the heart of this is your music (style, attitude, lyrics) and your story (where you're from, your influences, your motivations, your goals). The best branding comes from these things because they're genuine. Plus, the more specific your brand is to you and your identity, the more distinctive it will be. Since branding is a long-term endeavor, the more in tune your brand is with your band's unique identity, the more durable it will be over time. Distilling your music and identity into a brand takes thought, but we assure you that the time and energy you put in now will pay dividends in saved time and energy in the future.

YOUR BRAND TOOLBOX

Your Brand Toolbox consists of your name, your images (logo, photos, artwork), your text (story, tagline), and your music. You'll be using these components over and over for your Web sites, your albums, your videos, your MP3s, your press kits, posters, and so on. You should have them ready before you even think of creating your first press kit or releasing your first track online.

YOUR NAME

More than anything, your band name will be the unique identifier of your music. If people hear your music, the first thing you want them to know is who you are. It's all about name recognition, so obviously you'll be associating your name with everything you do.

The second thing you want them to know is where they can go to find out about you. From a branding perspective, given the importance of the Web, it's an advantage to have a Web address that's the same as your band name. And by having your band name in your web address, you'll have the further advantage of an e-mail address that promotes your brand with each message.

If you don't have a Web address that matches your band name, you'll need to include your Web address each time your band name is used. If you haven't picked a name, you're in luck and we have some advice on how to pick one.

PICKING A BAND NAME, POST-NET

Your band name should represent the type of music you play and your energy and style as performers. You want a name that's memorable and unique.

When picking a name, we recommend following these steps:

1. Check a Band Database Check your name against a band-name database to ensure that it's unique. We recommend Bandname. com, although directories at Yahoo! and elsewhere might also be worth checking.

2. Perform a Web Search Use a search engine to ensure that your name isn't associated with something else that might confuse your brand. Don't name your band Google for instance. Also, if you can, make up a word, or choose a name that absolutely nothing else has so you can track any mentions of your band. For example, we know that Beatnik Turtle is an unusual name, but we're the only ones with it.

3. Check Your Trademark Office Check your trademark office to ensure that no one has trademarked your name. Note that owning a domain name does not automatically make you the owner of that trademark.

There are a variety of databases you can check. For instance, in the United States, you can search the U.S. Patent and Trademark Office Web site (uspto.gov) and use the Trademark Electronic Search System (TESS). Perform multiple searches, including one for the actual domain name you intend to use with the *.com* or other suffix, as well as similar spellings and variations of the name.

You should know that the USPTO is just one database and it's possible that another country, or even a state, may have something registered on file that's similar to your band name.

That is why record labels typically hire a professional trademark searching service or attorney, which is often too expensive for indies simply trying to pick a band name. For more information about trademark law and how to register your name as a trademark, see the "Your Rights" chapter.

4. Check a Domain Registrar Check your name with a domain registrar such as GoDaddy.com. If the name is available, reserve it immediately. ♥

YOUR IMAGES

Images are worth a thousand words, particularly online. If you have someone in your band with some artistic ability, take advantage of that in crafting your images. Otherwise, turn to your skill network for help. To get started, you'll need a logo, an official band photo, and a general color palette. You may also need a mascot and/or an avatar.

IMAGE BASICS FOR MUSICIANS

When working with your brand images, keep these basics in mind:

Color Formats

- **RGB:** This is the color standard for computer monitors. Red, green, and blue are blended to create all the colors of the spectrum. Files saved in RGB format are appropriate for anything that will be displayed on a monitor, including anything intended for the Web.

- **CMYK:** This is the color standard for printing. It's the format that printers and merchandise manufacturers use. Cyan, magenta, yellow, and black are blended together to achieve full-color printing. If you intend to print any of your brand images—on a T-shirt, for instance—match the RGB number of each color to a CMYK number so that the resulting ink color matches what appears on your screen. See Textbox on page 41 for more information.

• **Black-and-White Line Art:** Some print media, such as newspapers, print only in black and white. Giving them your CMYK color logo and letting them do the conversion to black-and-white line art may have disastrous results. A black-and-white, line-art version of your logo will also come in handy if you print a CD with one color on the silk screen.

• **Grayscale:** Grayscale printing allows shading, which is useful for photos that will appear in newspapers and other black-and-white media. Color images convert more easily to grayscale than to black and white, but those created specifically for grayscale will work better.

Image Structures

Computers save images in one of two ways:

• **Rasterized:** Rasterized image files use a rectangular grid of pixels to capture the image information. The more pixels, the higher the quality and file size of the image. Digital photos are rasterized. Issues arise with rasterized images when resizing. In general, you can reduce a rasterized image in size without problems, but if you expand the size, you'll lose sharpness since the file replicates pixels to fill the extra space.

• **Vectorized images:** Vectorized image files use geometric objects such as curves and polygons to represent the data. Resizing vectorized images poses no quality issues since the image is mathematically re-created to fit any scale. Create your logo, mascot, or any other line-art image in a vector-image editor such as Adobe Illustrator.

The Importance of Using Layers

Many art programs such as Adobe Photoshop and Illustrator, and GIMP, allow you to create layers. Layering is the art world's equivalent to multitracking. Each layer is a complete and separate picture. This means you can make layers visible or hide them as you work, before "mixing it down" or flattening them all into a final JPEG or GIF image. This flexibility allows you to test out different ideas quickly and easily. If you don't like one element, you can simply hide that layer from view. For instance, the source file for our Beatnik Turtle mascot is composed of layers. We have the standard turtle as the basic layer, with additional layers for each type of hat he wears. This makes creating different versions with different hats a snap.

Your Logo

Just as you want your band name associated with your music, you will want it associated with a logo. We recommend either setting your band name in an unusual typeface or using a combination of typeface and symbol. Whatever you create, it should be distinctive enough for a T-shirt or other merchandise. Line drawings and other symbols work better than photos because they can scale to small or large sizes cleanly. There's a reason the logos of major brands use drawn images.

The logo you choose will often suggest both the appropriate matching color palette and font. A dynamic logo isn't easy to create, so enlist the help of a talented graphic artist in creating it. And make sure everyone in the band approves of the final version—you don't want to change it drastically once you start using it.

Your Band Photo

Although your logo will represent your band and its music, people will still want to see the people behind the band. Your band photo will be used as the representative shot of your entire group in your press kit, in articles the press writes about you, on your Web site, and on other promotional materials such as posters and flyers.

Your band photo needs to be a group shot of all the members. Naturally, it should be clear, in focus, and well composed, since this photo will represent your band to the world and will likely be printed in newspapers, magazines, and blogs when you get publicity.

Often, someone within your skill network will have the equipment and skills to help you and won't mind giving you the full rights to do whatever you please with the photo. However, if you end up hiring a professional photographer, keep in mind that they usually own the copyright. We discuss permissions in the "Your Rights" chapter.

Your Mascot

Your mascot refers to a character that represents your band. For instance, the Grateful Dead had its Dancing Bears, Iron Maiden has Eddie the Head, and Beatnik Turtle has, well, its Beatnik Turtle. Your mascot is not the same as your logo, although your logo can incorporate your mascot. Having a mascot for your band is not necessary, but it's useful for creating album artwork as well as for merchandising because it gives you more branding images to work with when creating products. Like your logo, it's best if your mascot image is line art, since the image will be resized depending on how it's used. Your mascot's colors should also match your color palette.

Your Avatar

You will be using your brand extensively on the Web. Services such as YouTube, MySpace, bulletin boards, and so on allow you to upload a profile image, or avatar, to represent you. It can be used for other image identifiers such as the ID3 image tag embedded in an MP3. In general, these avatars are small, so your logo might not be clear enough. You can either create a special, stripped-down logo or use your mascot image. The main point is to create a profile image that can consistently be applied across Web presences. That way when people see your videos on YouTube, your comments on a bulletin board, or chat with you over instant messenger, the avatar is the same.

Your Color and Font Palette

Locking in a color palette and limiting the fonts you use not only gives your brand a consistent look and feel, it's also a subtle and powerful way to evoke a mood that mirrors your music. Using the same colors and fonts will only strengthen this connection between your music and the identity you wish to convey to the world.

As you create your logo, mascot, and other brand images, you should define and limit yourself to a set palette of complementary colors. And make sure you use the same colors in each instance. The green in your logo should be the same shade of green you use in your mascot, on your Web site, on CDs, and so on. Of course, the colors you see on-screen are not necessarily the same colors that print out on paper or on a T-shirt. To match colors on-screen with those in print, it's a good idea to define your color scheme using Pantone colors.

PICKING A CONSISTENT COLOR PALETTE FOR SCREEN AND PRINT

Getting all your colors to match between screen and print is not difficult. The Pantone system matches print colors (CMYK) to screen colors (RGB) and provides an RGB number to use in your art software. Pantone's color-matching system is widely used by printing houses, T-shirt printers, and other merchandise manufacturers. To ensure a consistent color scheme:

1. **Go online and download** a Pantone color chart. (www.pantone.com/downloads/inkjetsolutions/downloads/pdfs/ColorChart.pdf).

2. **Pick each color you** want in your palette and note the RGB number and the CMYK number.

3. **Use the RGB numbers** to set the colors in your art software.

4. **Give the matching CMYK** numbers to your printer and merchandise manufacturer.

Taking this step at the outset will save you time, energy, and aggravation down the road. ●

As with your color palette, consistency and repetition calls for you to define and limit the fonts you use as well. Consistent fonts among your logo, Web site, press material, merchandise, and albums help tie all your materials and merchandise to your brand. You'll probably use three primary fonts: one for your band name, one for your tagline, and one for standard text on your Web site and in print materials.

Your Banners and Promos

Some Web sites may want to link directly to your site from one of your branded images. You should make these links available from your Web site. Some sites even give their visitors the embed code, similar to the embed codes on YouTube, so that they won't even need to copy the images to their own sites.

YOUR TEXT

Your text is composed of the following: a description of your sound, your story, your slogan, your contact information, and your writing voice.

A Description of Your Sound

You will need an accurate description of your music. This is never easy for any band. However, one of the best ways to describe your music is to talk about it in relation to well-known bands that you've been influenced by, or bands you sound similar to.

Some musicians resent having their music compared to that of other groups, but doing so accomplishes two things. First, by accurately referencing a few similar bands, you help set expectations for those people who have just discovered you and are curious about your sound. But make sure you actually sound like the bands you mention. You should aim to cultivate people who already like the type of music you make. They'll make better fans. Second, by making these comparisons, you're leveraging the marketing efforts of those more popular bands. When people search for those bands—whether through search engines or through dedicated music services such as iTunes or Last.fm—your music might come up as a recommendation. Even better, because your band does actually sound like the comparison band, the people who discover your music this way will be just the sort of people who are most likely to become new fans.

Ideally, you should also compose a description of your music that does not rely on comparisons. This one should emphasize your style, genre, and instrumentation. Again, it's better to go for an accurate description of your music rather than anything off-the-wall or tongue-in-cheek. Once you create these, keep them handy. You'll be using these just about everyplace you publicize your band.

Your Story

You need an interesting and compelling way to introduce your band to people. You can't just write down the story of how you met. You need an angle. Once you find this, you need to be able to tell this story in multiple ways and in varying lengths. You should have a one-page version of your story as well as a one-paragraph version. Most important, you need an elevator pitch, a compact description of your band that must quickly categorize who you are and what you sound like—all within the time it takes to ride an elevator between floors. Ariel Hyatt from Ariel Publicity told us that her favorite pitch was from the bluegrass, rock, country, blues, jazz, and Cajun/zydeco band Leftover Salmon. Their elevator pitch was that they played "polyethnic Cajun slamgrass." It was accurate, summed up their energetic live show, and did it all with three words. Distilling your band and its sound down to an elevator pitch takes thought, but if you create a good one for yourself, it can help define your identity.

Each of these versions—and parts of them—will come in handy in different circumstances when you need to explain what your band is all about, whether it's on your Web site, in your press materials, or even in person.

Your Slogan

Not every group uses or needs a slogan, but one tends to come in handy. This is especially true if you can create one that really captures the essence of your band and music. Your slogan is most likely to be used on the Web, but it can also become part of your logo, be included in your e-mail signatures, or be used on promotional materials. Web services such as YouTube, MySpace, and Twitter typically provide fields for short taglines that are perfect for slogans. If you don't have one, you'll have to leave these empty or make up something on the spot, leading to an inconsistent Web presence.

Your Contact Information

Your band's contact information—phone number, e-mail address, and any other methods for contacting you—will appear in your press kits, on your Web site, and perhaps elsewhere online. Changing it more often than absolutely necessary will result in out-of-date information leading to missed opportunities and connections. Additionally, you should use an e-mail address at your Web domain (e.g., joe@beatnikturtle.com), instead of using a Gmail, Yahoo!, or AOL address, since doing so reinforces your brand and leads recipients back to your Web site.

If the members of your band split the roles of booking, publicity, and managing, then you'll need to make everyone's contact information available for all. But this arrangement can get confusing for those trying to contact you. Instead, we recommend designating one person as the main contact to simplify matters. One way to handle this is to set up your account to forward any incoming e-mails to multiple members of the band. It also helps to have a business card so that if you talk to people in person and they want to contact you, you can easily hand them something with your contact information on it.

Your Writing Voice

Just as your color palette and fonts evoke a mood or style, your writing voice reflects your band's identity to the world. This becomes a question of style and consistency. First, you need to make sure that whoever is writing for your band has a style that fits your music, and one that everyone in the band is comfortable with. Ideally, the writing in your brand materials should evoke a singular tone and remain consistent throughout your story, Web site, newsletters, Web presence, blogs, and any other text you share. In Beatnik Turtle's case, we chose a voice for the band that was a little tongue-in-cheek. Since our lyrics are typically upbeat and humorous, we felt our writing should be as well.

Additionally, this tone should be consistent throughout your branding materials. If you're a solo artist who is writing for yourself, this should come naturally. With a band, however, this becomes a challenge. The band itself needs a singular voice—not individual voices. You don't want a voice that's at odds with the music and the message you want to evoke.

Of course, your writing voice can change depending on the audience you're addressing. For instance, we adopt a more professional tone in our press and booking materials since we want potential bookers and music journalists to know that we take them and the opportunities they can present for our band seriously. We also write more formally on our BackStage Blog so that our readers understand that we are sharing genuine information.

Related to your writing voice is your spokesperson, the person who represents the band with the press or other media. Again, if you're a solo artist, you speak on your own behalf. However, when there are several band members, it often helps to have one or two people in the group do the majority of the speaking. It doesn't have to be this way, but if designated people do the talking, it's easier to stay on message. We'll talk more about speaking to the press in the "Get Publicized" chapter.

YOUR MUSIC

You should prepare a few tracks in MP3 format for your Brand Toolbox since your music is distinctive and forms the basis of your brand identity. Have some of your top songs—the ones that represent you the best—handy and available to send out to the press, or anyone else who will be needing them.

MIXING AND REMIXING YOUR BRAND TOOLS

Think of it like this: the materials you create for your Brand Toolbox are the equivalent of the multitracked source files you create when you record a song. The public doesn't typically hear these individual tracks. Instead, the multiple tracks are mixed down to stereo for iPods or home audio systems. It's the same here: you'll be returning time and time again to all the source files of the images and text you've made to create different but consistent versions for your Web site, your Web presence, your albums and merchandise, and your promotional materials.

For instance, you may end up mixing your logo with your slogan to create a Web banner in Photoshop and then flatten the result into GIF format for your Web site. Then, you might take this banner, resize it, combine it with your contact information, and make a letterhead out of it for a Word or OpenOffice document. Later you might create a grayscale version for a show flyer. Eventually, you'll have quite a library of alternative versions, so when that newspaper writes a last-minute article about your band's show and asks you for logo in grayscale at a certain size and resolution, you'll be able to get it to them immediately.

Best of all, by working in this manner, you're not making up your brand on the fly. Given that consistency and repetition are the keys to an effective brand, this process ensures that the mixes you make for public consumption are consistent with your brand.

MIXING DOWN YOUR BRAND—RECOMMENDED FORMATS FOR IMAGES AND TEXT

Since your brand source files are for your eyes only, you'll need to make mixdowns of your brand images and text for distribution.

Images
Choose the appropriate format, size, and DPI (dots per inch) of your images to maximize clarity and sharpness depending on where you intend them to appear.

Format
- **Screen/Web:** For the Web, GIF and JPEG are the universal formats to use. The GIF format is best for line drawings and other simple graphics, while JPEGs are best for photos and other complex images. Most art programs allow you to optimize your GIF and JPEG settings for the Web to minimize file size, but, as most of our audience has broadband Internet access, we use the settings for maximum quality (with correspondingly larger file sizes). Over a broadband connection, these images still download quickly.

- **Print:** For print applications, the format depends on the recipient.

  - PRESS: When the press wants photos, they typically ask for TIFF or BMP versions, which are uncompressed and therefore large. When the press wants a logo, mascot, or other line drawing, GIFs usually suffice, although they will sometimes request these in TIFF or BMP format as well.

• PRINTERS/MERCHANDISERS: For printers and T-shirt or other merchandise manufacturers, the source file will usually work, depending on what software you use. If not, they'll tell you whether they need TIFFs, BMPs, JPEGs, or GIFs.

Image Size and DPI

• **Screen/Web:** Use 72 DPI for the optimal balance between quality and file size, regardless of the image size needed, which is usually measured in pixels. For example, avatars are generally 80 pixels by 80 pixels or 100 by 100. Album art for the iTunes Music Store needs to be 300 by 300. Either way, keep the DPI at 72.

• **Print:** Make your band photo, logo, and other brand images available in print-ready form at your Web site for the benefit of the press. Flyers and posters should be available as well. To ensure that these print clearly, create these versions at 300 DPI at the physical size you intend them to print. For instance, a flyer should be eight by ten inches. When creating images for a T-shirt or CD, the manufacturer will inform you of the exact standards they require.

Text

All of your text, such as bios and other information, should be available to the public in Adobe PDF format as well as on standard Web pages so the press can copy and paste when necessary. The text source files—Word documents, OpenOffice documents, and so on—should only be available to you for editing. ♥

ACCESSIBILITY

At the end of the day, you'll have source files and mixdowns of your branded materials. As a band, you'll want to be able to access both at a moment's notice. However, only the mixdowns—the finished logo in JPEG or GIF format, the band bio in PDF format (see "Mixing Down Your Brand," above)—should be made publicly available. For convenience, we recommend that you save your source files privately online for easy access by all members of the band, either at a password-protected section of your Web site or on a storage and sharing service such as Box (box.net) or Amazon's S3 (aws.amazon.com/s3).

Mixdowns should, of course, be made public. After all, this is the brand you're promoting. Bookers, the press, and fans may want to have access to these branded images and text. We'll talk more about setting up a Press/Booking page and its importance in the next chapter.

CHAPTER 4

YOUR WEB SITE

BESIDES YOUR musical instruments, your Web site is the most important tool that you have as a musician. It's the Web that took the decision of whether you will get heard out of the hands of music executives and back into your hands.

Hundreds of millions of people are on the Web, and if you have a Web site, any one of them could be discovering your music at this very moment. Your Web site is your best promoter, salesperson, agent, publicist, distributor, disc jockey, news reporter, and more. It's the center of your fan network and a store that never closes. Even if people meet you or see you play live, if they can't find you later on the Web, you might as well not exist.

Web technology changes quickly and is a broad topic that could fill many books, so we're going to stick with concepts that don't change, and others that are specific to music Web sites.

DON'T RELY SOLELY ON MYSPACE

Thousands upon thousands of musicians have chosen social-networking sites such as MySpace to represent their brand and music to the world and then called it a day. And why not? It's quick, easy, and free. While there are a few advantages to doing so—simple tools to stream music, write blogs, and post videos—they don't approach the real benefits of having your own Web site, under your control.

You should definitely have a profile on those sites. In fact, we're going to tell you the best way to use them in the next chapter—but don't rely on them exclusively. Here's why:

- *Limited songs.* These sites limit the number of songs you can make available.

- *Lack of creative control.* Social-networking sites force you to conform to their limited options for format and design. Their priority is branding themselves, which is why you're limited to *their* choices, not yours.

- *Advertising, advertising, advertising.* Your content must compete with their advertising.

- *Goofy domain name for your brand and merchandise.* You will have to print *their* Web site name on *your* T-shirts, stickers, posters, and other branded materials. Additionally, your e-mail address won't be from your own Web site.

- *Poor Web statistics and trackback.* Aside from the "number of views," these sites provide poor Web statistics for gathering information about when visitors arrived, how long they stayed, what they read, what they listened to, and who referred them to your site. All this information is critical to understanding your audience. Having access to these stats is extremely important, as we describe below.

- *Poor place to host critical information.* These sites are a poor place to host important information about your band such as press releases, stage-plot and microphone layout, or to effectively promote your albums and merchandise.

Although these are significant disadvantages, this is only a partial list. Social-networking sites are intended for just that; they are not meant to be a substitute for a fully featured Web site.

STARTING A NEW WEB SITE

DOMAIN NAMES

The first thing you'll need is a unique Web address, or domain name. As we said in the "Your Brand" chapter, your domain name is extremely important because it conveys the most information about your band. When we say "beatnikturtle.com," we've given you everything you need to know to access our music, videos, podcasts, show information, photos, press materials, and more.

If you haven't registered a domain name, be careful about letting your Web-hosting company do it for you. Some Web-hosting companies will register your domain in *their* name, which means you may have a legal battle on your hands if you need to move to a different Web host. Avoid this at the start by registering the name yourself with a reputable domain registrar. That way you control your domain and can take it with you if the Web host you originally choose doesn't work out.

Domain names are inexpensive and should cost between $8 and $20 a year to maintain. Once you have your domain, your Web-hosting company should advise you on how to configure it for their services.

WEB HOSTING

After you get a domain, you will need a Web host for your site. Web hosts typically charge a monthly or annual fee to host your site, make it available for the public, and provide e-mail addresses with your domain name.

Because you will have a music Web site, your needs are slightly different from those of most Web-site customers. Bandwidth, which is the amount of data that gets transferred to and from your Web site, becomes expensive if you get popular. So review any Web host's bandwidth charges carefully, and use hosts with high limits.

You can use any Web-hosting company, but a few are geared toward musicians. Often Web hosts that specialize in music sites provide functions other Web hosts don't—tools and resources that make designing and updating content for your band Web site quicker and easier. Some of these include easy-to-use flash music players; RSS-enabled blogs, news pages, and forums; robust gig calendars; integration with social-networking and media-sharing sites; mailing-list programs; and other important features we'll be discussing below. Obviously, if you're going to pay for a Web host, quality tools and resources are an extra benefit that can save you time and energy that are better suited for music making, music promotion, and winning over fans—not being a Web developer. So it's worth giving specialized Web hosts a look.

Two Web hosts that specialize in sites for musicians are Hostbaby (hostbaby.com) and Sites4Performers (sitesforperformers.com) (disclaimer: we're affiliated with Sites4Performers as we help them design their features to meet the needs of indie musicians). Both provide many useful tools for musicians such as mailing lists and music players as well as high bandwidth limits streaming music needs. Hostbaby.com is associated with CD Baby; CD Baby will even waive their CD registration fees if you subscribe, which can save you money—especially if you have multiple CDs.

WEB DESIGN TOOLS

Now that you have a Web host, you need to design your Web site. There are two main methods of creating a custom Web site: Web-site creation software and content management systems.

Naturally, if you decide to work with a Web designer from your skill network, you should defer to whatever tools that person is comfortable with.

Web-Site Creation Software

If you use a software package on your own computer, use a full-featured package such as Adobe Dreamweaver. The advantage to using tools like this is that you have complete flexibility in your design. The downside is that updates to your Web site can be difficult, since you are limited to making changes from home, or even just from the designer's PC. This doesn't seem like a big deal until you realize that changes happen often, including adding a news story, adding a new show listing, or even just fixing some spelling mistakes. This quickly becomes a pain, so we recommend a CMS instead, which is what we use.

Content Management Systems

A content management system (CMS) can be thought of as a Web-site creation program that exists at your Web site—not on your local computer. Because of this, you can update your site using any Internet browser. Most of these systems, such as WordPress or Movable Type, have WYSIWYG editors that work just like a word processor, which you can use to write text for your site without learning HTML. Most allow you to keep a blog, as well as make updates easily whenever and wherever you'd like to do so—at home or from any Internet connection. And because it's so accessible, multiple band members can update. You don't need to rely on one band member to do all the work. Since you should be updating your Web site often with news, fresh tracks, and upcoming shows, these features are advantageous.

The best part of a CMS is that it separates the site's design from its content, allowing you to update each separately. With a few clicks, your designer can change the look of your Web site without affecting the content you posted. And your less technologically savvy band members can post new entries without fudging the design.

Web hosts often feature built-in CMS software. And, typically, Web hosts specializing in music sites feature CMS software designed specifically for the needs of bands, which will make creating your site easier. If you go with a standard Web host, one flexible and free tool is WordPress found at WordPress.org. Originally designed as blogging software, WordPress is also a CMS and can make Web sites. It's used by many bands, including some of the bands mentioned in this book.

PLANNING YOUR WEB SITE

KNOWING YOUR WEB SITE'S AUDIENCE:
AUDIENCE PROFILES

Before you can design your Web site, you need to decide what content you'll offer. Most band Web sites we surveyed were either designed around the assumption that only fans visit or, worse, designed as ego-trip billboards that focus only on the people in the band. Instead, you need to determine who your audiences are and design it for *them*.

For example, imagine that bookers or talent buyers are visiting your site. Can they immediately tell what you sound like? Is it apparent whether you've played other gigs? Can they easily find your stage-plot and microphone layout? Most important, can they find your contact information right away? If your Web site can't meet this audience's specific needs, you should adjust the design and content accordingly.

Thinking from each audience's viewpoint doesn't only affect the type of content you provide and where it's located, it also affects your navigation structure. After all, you don't want audiences finding themselves in the wrong section of the Web site, lost and with no idea what to do next. They should always be able to find what they want.

Fortunately, band Web-site audiences aren't too complicated to unravel. But remember, catering to each of the audience profiles is only half the story. The other half is to steer them where you want them to go.

DESIGN YOUR WEB SITE TO CONVERT VISITORS

Visitors come to your Web site for their own reasons, but the site should also actively steer their decisions and make it as easy as possible for them to do what you want them to do. You want a new visitor to join the mailing list, participate in your forum, and buy your albums and merchandise. You want the press to find information about your band to help them write a great (and accurate) article about you. You want a booker to contact you with that gig. This means that your Web site should balance its content and design between giving each audience what they want and leading them to take those actions you want them to take.

Conversion can be encouraged in the design by limiting choices and making them simple to spot and navigate. Conversion can also be driven by content. For example, if one of your goals is to build your mailing list, repeat the "join the mailing list" message in your news updates, blog entries, and elsewhere on your site, where appropriate.

PROVIDE CONTENT FOR EACH OF YOUR AUDIENCES

To help you, we've put together a table of the seven audience profiles a typical band Web site should be designed for. We've outlined what each of these audiences wants out of your Web site, and what it is you want out of them. Lastly, we've outlined a few of the key Web-site sections in play at each instance.

Additionally, we've put together a table of site feature content for a typical band Web site. This table is useful as you set out to create the content and should be used in conjunction with the "Putting It All Together" table to help reinforce the idea that content needs to speak to various audiences.

PUTTING IT ALL TOGETHER:

YOUR AUDIENCES, WHAT THEY WANT, AND WHAT YOU WANT THEM TO DO

Audience	Expectations	Conversions	Site Features
All fans	Finding tour dates. Finding upcoming shows. Discovering latest projects. Buying your albums and merchandise. Listening to your music. Viewing photos and videos. Participating in the fan community.	Joining the mailing list. Subscribing to the blogs. Participating in the forum. Buying the albums and merchandise. Coming to shows. Telling friends about the band.	News. Blog. Forum. About the Band. Music. Photos. Videos. Store. Calendar. Mailing List.
Fans coming to a show	Finding an address, directions, map, and phone number for the venue. Finding the time of the performance and the acts going up before and after. Determining the cover charge and any drink minimum.	Coming to the show. Bringing friends. Promoting the event. Discussing the event in the forum.	Calendar. News. Blog. Forums. Mailing List.
Bookers and talent buyers	Locating the band. Contacting the band. Learning about the band's performance history. Reading fan and venue testimonials. Downloading flyers, bios, and other text and images.	Hiring the band.	Testimonials. Booking Information. Calendar. Music. Photos. Contact Us.

Continued...

Audience	Expectations	Conversions	Site Features
The press and journalists	Downloading the press kit and press releases. Contact the band for interviews. Finding images and credit info for the article. Reading testimonials.	Writing articles about the band. Reviewing the latest album. Featuring the latest project. Contacting us.	Press Information. News. Music. Photos. Contact Us.
Sound people	Determining the style of music and instrumentation. Preparing for any special sound needs. Viewing stage-plot and microphone layout.	Contacting us. Making the band sound right onstage.	Sound/ Performance Information. Music. Contact Us.
Potential song licensees	Listening to songs. Requesting high-quality versions. Determining licensing requirements. Finding noncommercial use requirements. Determining podsafe status.	Contacting us to license our songs. Requesting high-quality versions. Commissioning custom music.	Copyright Information. Music. Contact Us.
Web surfers who stumble onto your Web site	Finding instant gratification.	Listening to music. Watching videos. Buying albums and merchandise. Joining the mailing list. Subscribing to the blogs.	Music. Photos. Videos. About the Band. Store. News. Blog. Forum.

SITE FEATURE CONTENT FOR WEB SITES

Content	Description
About the Band	Basic information about your band: name, style of music, similar bands, members and bios, instrumentation, hometown, and band history.
News	Latest news on your band. Place the latest story on the front page with older stories cycling to a separate news page. If possible, offer an RSS feed.
Blog	Offer one or more band blogs with more personal perspectives on the band.
Show Calendar	Upcoming shows as well as a catalog of past shows you've played.
Music	All the music you've made available to the public as well as samples of those available for purchase. Ideally, provide an embedded player to listen immediately.
Store	All albums and merchandise available for sale with photos and descriptions of each, or links to the appropriate vendors such as CD Baby, iTunes, Spreadshirt.com, etc.
Album Information	Information on each of your albums including lyrics, liner notes, and possibly guitar tablature or full sheet music.
Photos	Albums of photos of your band, recent performances, and other events.
Videos	Music videos or videos of the band performing.
Information for the Press	The band bio, press releases, press-ready photos, logos, and other images, contact info including the band press representative's e-mail and phone number, and press clippings.

Continued...

Content	Description
Information for Bookers	Band contact info including the band representative's e-mail and phone number, booking information, stage and microphone plot, and press-ready photos and images.
Testimonials	Quotes from fans, bookers, venues, and satisfied customers from corporate events, festivals, weddings, and parties.
Stage and Performance Information for Sound People	Stage and microphone plot, band instrumentation, and any other information a sound person might need.
Forums	A place for fans to meet up, arrange shared rides to your performances, coordinate grassroots promotion, and so on.
Mailing List Information	Information about your mailing list and an easy sign-up process.
Contact Us	Usually a Web contact form, but can be as simple as a band member's e-mail address.
Site Map	A map of the entire site to help people find what they want.
Legal Information	Any legal information such as the copyright or Creative Commons license, privacy-policy statement (for your mailing list), and so on.
Links	Links to external sites such as individual band-member pages, other bands, favorite venues, and so on.
Band-Only Area	Password-protected section to store Brand Toolbox source files for access anywhere.

GIVING THEM A REASON TO RETURN OR KEEP CONNECTED

While it's often possible to get people to come to your Web site, the hard part is getting them involved—to come back repeatedly or to stay in touch via your mailing list or RSS feed. Think about the Web sites you check regularly. What do you like about these sites that keeps you coming back? What made you subscribe to their feed, join their mailing list, or discuss things in their forums?

Usually, the secret ingredient is fresh, updated content that people *want*. News sites constantly post new stories. YouTube constantly features new videos. Blogs such as BoingBoing.net always have a new blog entry. Daily deal sites such as Woot (woot.com) and Tanga (tanga.com) always have a new product.

As a musician, here is what you can offer at your music Web site to keep people coming back:

Updated Band Content

Writing new blog entries and keeping people informed on what you're do-ing as a band is a big part of getting people invested and cultivating your fan network. Fans, after all, want to feel involved.

You can document life in your band by writing, taking photos, or shooting videos. Many bands post daily tour blogs when they're out on the road. Some solo musicians use their blog as a personal journal, shar-ing their thoughts not only on music but also about their day-to-day life.

Naturally, the more entertaining these updates, the better. Our friend Pete Shukoff, of the band Nice Peter, is a natural at this. He frequently up-dates his blog with humorous observations about what's going on in his life. He'll discuss anything: drunken audience members at shows, playing "You Are My Sunshine" twenty times to the delight of seniors at the old folks' home (they didn't know any of his own songs), or interesting graffiti he's seen scrawled on venue bathroom walls while touring.

Episodic Project Releases

Jonathan Coulton's episodic project, "Thing a Week," promised fans one new song a week from September 2005 to September 2006. The lure of weekly updates kept people coming back for more, and his forums took off and became extremely active. Fans were always eagerly anticipating the next "thing" to come along.

We did something similar at TheSongOfTheDay.com by releasing a new song for every day of 2007. Visitors returned daily to hear each new song. Over the year, more people kept visiting, and interest in our band and its music grew.

Brad Turcotte got people returning to his Web site by posting the source tracks to the songs from his debut album. Each month he would post one of the tracks, then fans would download and remix them. Turcotte actively promoted any remixes people made of his music, creating an incentive for people to join the forums and share their results.

One added benefit of an episodic project is that it tends to generate material for your blog and news feeds. Coulton would regularly blog about the new "thing a week" he was writing and has kept this level of involvement by blogging regularly since. Turcotte maintains an active blog as well, posting not only about his music and upcoming projects, but also on topics related to his music, such as the software and equipment he uses, as well as commentary on the music industry—which leads us to a third method.

Updated Nonmusic Content

You can use your Web site to cover topics beyond the scope of your band, too. These topics should be related in some way to what your band is all about, but by widening your focus a bit you can piggyback on the popularity of a larger topic (we'll talk about the concept of piggybacking in the "Get Noticed" chapter). For instance, if your music speaks of social or political activism and your band feels passionately about an issue, then dedicating a section of your Web site to that issue would be a natural fit.

The Brobdingnagian Bards (thebards.net) did this years ago when they used their site to collect and catalog the lyrics and tabs of traditional Irish folk songs. Adding this section to their band's Web site was natural since the band was rooted in traditional Irish music. This section not only helped them catalog songs for their own repertoire, it also became a destination among search engines—sending people directly to their site whenever they searched for information about an old Irish folk song. This piggybacking worked in their favor given that their own music aligned with the music people were searching for. Many new fans discovered the Brobdingnagian Bards simply by searching for their favorite Irish song and listening to free song samples of their music. An album purchase was just a few clicks and sample songs away.

We did this when we released our first *Indie Band Survival Guide.* We wanted to share everything we had learned from nine years as an indie band with other indie musicians. Because no books spoke directly to us as indies, and because we felt strongly enough about the subject to research and write the initial *Guide* over two years, we felt it would be a natural complement to our band's Web site.

There are more ways to encourage people to return to your site beyond news of a new album for sale or a show next Saturday. The more regular, relevant content you can offer at your site, the more reasons people will have to stay tuned to your Web site and, ultimately, your music.

WEB SITE DESIGN AND CONTENT

Knowing what your audiences want and knowing what you want them to do will help keep you focused as you start branding, designing, and creating content for your Web site.

Rather than try to teach a mini-course in the subject of Web design, we simply recommend one book: *Don't Make Me Think: A Common Sense Approach to Web Usability* by Steve Krug. It will help you create an effective Web site with a design, navigation, and structure that's intuitive and accessible. If you're tackling your Web site on your own, this book is well worth your money and time. Even if you have a Web and graphic designer in your skill network or one that you're ready to pay, understanding the concepts in this book will help you relate to what your designer will be doing.

A few general concepts to consider as you're putting together a design are:

• *Always be branding your Web site.* All aspects of your Web site need to be branded. You need to keep your identity in front of your audiences at all times while they visit your site.

- *Lead with your best music.* In our opinion, it's so difficult to even get a person to listen to an independent band's music in the first place, you shouldn't shoot yourself in the foot by leading with anything but your best music. You are better off winning a new fan than worrying about phantom lost sales.

- *Make it a multimedia experience.* People now expect interactive and engaging content on the sites they visit.

DESIGN CONCEPTS
Billboards

One of the best ways to design and lay out your Web pages is to think of them as billboards. People don't spend a lot of time on Web sites, so if you have a message to get across, use images and just a few words. Your entire Web site should be easy to understand, easy to navigate, and easy to use.

For example, when we initially launched a radio player that streamed hours of Beatnik Turtle music, we had a news story about it (text), hyperlinked to the feature (again, text), and promoted it in our newsletter (once again, text). But what got visitors to finally click on it was a big, bright banner with a drawing of a radio and the words BEATNIK TURTLE RADIO—CLICK HERE! right in the middle of the page.

Your Front Page

Web designers usually leave the front page until last. It's the hardest page to create because it performs many functions beyond being the hub of navigation. Some Web sites try to cram all of their content on the front page. We're embarrassed to say that we subscribed to this misguided idea for years. But we've learned some things since and we have the following suggestions:

- *Brand.* Have we emphasized this enough? Beyond having a branded Web banner, logo, color scheme, font, etc., your front page needs to clearly inform the visitor what your site's about and what they can expect from it.

- **What's new.** Your latest news update and/or blog entry should be clearly visible since this is where you'll be telling audiences what you're currently doing and what you're planning to do.

- **Make your music player readily accessible.** You're a band, so make your music the focal point of your site. Your music player should be readily accessible on the front page—either embedded or one click away. Don't make people search for it. (We'll discuss everything you need to know about music players below.)

- **Focus on one or two additional content items.** This took our band years to figure out. At first we thought we needed to include all our content on the front page so visitors would know how much there was to do at our site. But this only confused and frustrated our audiences. We've learned to emphasize only a few key content items—things we want visitors to see if they only have a few seconds to look around. For us, this means our albums (displayed in a column along the right side of the screen) and our latest video. Both are presented as billboards—images with big play buttons (YouTube does this naturally)—not text.

- **Ditch the splash page.** Many bands insist on a splash page welcoming people to the site. Although it may seem cool to have a page like that, it's totally unnecessary. It violates an important rule of human nature: instant gratification. Throwing up a splash page acts as a roadblock, creating one more click between people and their destination.

Your Contact-Us Page

No matter what content you put up, you have to have a contact-us page. Almost all of Beatnik Turtle's best opportunities have come through the site this way. Gigs, music-licensing opportunities, press articles, interviews, and songwriting commissions have all come to our attention via the Web form and e-mail address on this page. We can't imagine what we would have missed out on if we hadn't made it easy for people to contact us. You may include a phone number, too, if you're comfortable releasing it. For instance, when ABC Family/Disney wanted to license one of our songs for a commercial, they left multiple voice-mail messages with all of the numbers we had posted in addition to e-mailing because they were under a deadline.

You should have the contact-us link at the top or bottom of each page and built into your template so that any new pages feature it automatically. If you use a Web contact form rather than a direct e-mail address, verify that it works properly. We've had more than one Web contact form fail on us. It's hard enough creating opportunities for yourself; you don't want to block the ones that come knocking. We've configured our Web form to send all submissions to multiple members of the band.

Your Store Page

Your store page should contain all of your albums and merchandise. This page should be easy to navigate with links to all the services handling distribution of your music and products. To encourage sales, you will want to include direct links to songs sold at digital distribution stores (iTunes, Rhapsody, Napster, etc.) and wherever your CD is sold (CD Baby). Direct links to your merchandise is also a must. We'll talk in detail about getting your music in these stores in the "Get Distributed and Sold" chapter.

Donations, Sponsorships, and Memberships

Donations are an alternative way for fans to support a band, particularly if you offer free music on your Web site. We recommend putting the donation link near where users download songs. Of course, some bands put their tip jars on every page of their site.

When accepting donations, it helps to give fans something in return as a thank-you. Some musicians e-mail free songs, others send buttons or stickers. Some musicians take a cue from National Public Radio and public television by offering sponsorships with different levels of benefits depending on the amount donated. Jonathan Coulton did this at his site by offering his fans a chance to post a short message on his site. A donation buys you a fifty-word message alongside an icon of a banana ($5), monkey ($10), or robot ($25).

Most bands use PayPal (paypal.com) for this function because it offers embeddable tools to seamlessly integrate donation boxes into your Web-site design. If you have an account on PayPal, search their help center for "donations" for instructions. You can use other methods for accepting payments, such as credit-card-merchant accounts, but PayPal boasts a trusted brand name and a streamlined payment process for users.

Finally, some bands sell memberships rather than sponsorships. Members get access to parts of the band's Web site that has special songs, or other content. Most Web-hosting solutions will have an option to password-protect parts of the site that can be used for this. An alternative is to use services such as aMember (amember.com), which is a tool that costs money, but nevertheless allows you to control access to parts of your Web site. It handles a log-in system for your users, expires users who haven't renewed their membership, and more.

Your Photo Album

When we designed our first Web site in January 1998, we sat behind our friends and watched as they tried to use it. Their initial complaint was that it had no photos. When we revamped the site, we made sure to include a photos page. When we watched people use the new site, *it was the first thing they clicked on.* Not the music. Not our bios. The pictures.

You should take new pictures of the band frequently. And you don't want to lump all your photos on one page. You want an effective solution for organizing images that handles time-consuming tasks such as creating thumbnail images and slide shows. Your Web host or your CMS might offer a solution, but alternatively, specialized programs allow you to host your photos on your own server.

Although you'll have a dedicated photo-album page, you'll want to incorporate your best shots in other areas of the site: blog entries, news stories, and so on. We'll discuss further in the next chapter photos and photo-sharing sites that you can embed in your site.

Your Mailing List

Joining your mailing list should be convenient and simple because the goal is to cultivate and grow a fan network. Include a link to your mailing-list form on each page and build it into your standard template, just like your contact-us link.

Feature the mailing-list link wherever your visitor takes a conversion action on your Web site such as downloading a song or joining your forum. At that point, you'll know they're interested in your band and music, so it'll be especially likely that they'll take the time to sign up for your newsletter as well.

Almost all of the mailing-list software available will deliver a special welcome message to new subscribers. Don't use the default text for this message; this is a rare opportunity to send a direct message to an interested fan, and to feature your albums, merchandise, and other conversions on your Web site. If your program allows you to write welcome messages in HTML, you should even include pictures and images.

We discuss mailing-list software and newsletters further in the next chapter.

Integrating Web-Presence Gadgets and Tools

Social-networking and media-sharing sites often allow you to embed features on your Web site. YouTube allows you to embed videos; Twitter allows you to embed your latest update; Flickr allows you to embed your most recent photos. As you design your site, be sure to anticipate using these tools. We'll talk more about these social and media sites and integrating some of the widgets they provide in the next chapter.

Testing Your Site

Designing your site to speak to the various audiences is difficult. If you didn't use a Web host specializing in music sites or take advantage of a Web designer, your site will probably need tweaking. You need to test it—from each of the seven audiences' perspectives. Pretend you're a booker, a journalist, a fan, and so on, and see if you can find the information they would each be looking for quickly and easily. Browse your site as one of these audiences and purposefully put yourself in the wrong place on your site. Can you easily find your way back to the information they need? A general rule of thumb is, if it takes more than two clicks to get back to where you should be once you've gotten lost, you need to redesign.

After you've test-driven your site, get your friends and family to try it out. Stand over their shoulders as they click around. Don't lead them or answer any questions they have, because you won't be standing over the shoulder of any visitors to your site. Can they find your music easily, or do they get lost? Do they learn what your band is up to, or are they distracted by other things? Are they confused and frustrated? If your friends and family are, you can bet others will be as well. And others won't have the patience to keep clicking to find what they need. Take this feedback and make the necessary changes. Then test again, until you get it right.

CONTENT CONCEPTS AND TECHNIQUES

As you build your site, keep the following techniques in mind. Many of these will also apply to any content you create—including your press materials, posters, and flyers.

Draw Them a Map

One of the most useful lessons we've learned about writing content for our Web site came from the book *The Tipping Point* by Malcolm Gladwell, an examination of how and why trends are started. We call it Draw Them a Map. In *The Tipping Point,* Gladwell tells the story of an experiment performed at a college campus attempting to boost the rate of students getting tetanus shots. The researchers showed the first group photographs of the devastating effects of tetanus and gave the second group a written description. The expectation was that the grotesque visual images would better inspire students to get their shots. Counterintuitively, both groups came in at an almost identical (and low) rate. The researchers decided to run a second experiment, but this time gave one of the groups a map to the student health center, even though every student knew where the health center was. This time, more students in the group with the map got their tetanus shots.

What's the lesson here? We've drawn four from it, and we use them whenever we write for our Web sites:

1. Get to the point. The content is less important than the message you want to convey. You can write paragraphs about why people should buy your album, but the only important sentence is *Click here to buy our album right now.*

2. Direct people to act. Insert a concrete "call to action." Write "Call 555-2983 and book Beatnik Turtle today," not "If you are interested in booking Beatnik Turtle, you should call us at 555-2983." Direct readers to act how you want them to.

3. Keep it simple. Anything you tell readers to do should be convenient. If you want them to buy an album, don't make them click ten times to do it.

4. Be explicit even when it's obvious. The map in the experiment was unnecessary yet effective. On your Web site, it may seem unnecessary to write "Click on the button to buy the album" if the button says "Buy now," but it can eliminate any shred of confusion (and it acts as a call to action).

AIDA

An old marketing acronym reinforces these ideas: AIDA. It stands for four concepts that marketers use when drafting advertising or marketing material:

Attention
Interest
Decision
Action

Take your readers through all four of these steps if you want them to respond to a call to action.

Make your message flashy to get their attention. Once you've got their attention, get them interested in what you want them to do, whether it's listening to your latest track or buying a ticket to your next performance. Then, give them a reason or two to make the decision you want them to make, such as a discount on merchandise or that time is running out. Finally, make your call to action: *Click here now.* Every advertisement, billboard, TV ad, radio spot, and movie trailer follows this formula. Obviously, AIDA helps direct your Web-site audiences to actions you want them to take, but it's also useful for posters, flyers, and any other marketing materials that you create.

Repetition and Convenience

Repetition is also important when influencing people to take action. If you want people to do something, keep repeating that message. Of course, this doesn't have to be done with words. For example, we have images of our albums throughout our site, each of which links to its respective ordering page. Featuring album artwork is one form of repetition. Try to think of as many different ways as you can to repeat your call to action.

Salting

Would you like to learn a technique that will make people take notice and pay attention to whatever you say? What if you could do it right now, in one easy step?

You would? Great. This technique is called salting. Effective salting piques a reader's curiosity. Once you've "salted" their desire to know something, you're the only one who can quench their thirst. This technique is useful for sales, but it can also be handy for conveying information you want people to retain.

Radio stations use this technique all the time before going to a commercial. They announce which songs will be coming up after the break so listeners stick around. Magazines do this by asking questions on the front cover, promising the answers within.

Use Images for Every Story

Include an image wherever text appears. The Web is a visual medium. And less is more. The adage "a picture speaks a thousand words" rings true because people love looking at photos first rather than the captions. Create your content, your blog entries, and news stories with this psychology in mind. Use graphics and photos to break up long blocks of text.

ROYALTY-FREE IMAGES

It's often helpful to have a set of royalty-free images and photos handy. Here are some suggestions:

- **Photo and clip-art libraries.** You can buy archives of stock photos or clip art on CD or DVD.

- **Clip-art subscriptions.** You can subscribe to services that will give you access to thousands of images, such as www.clipart.com.

- **Government archives.** Anything created by the U.S. government, such as space photos taken by NASA or other U.S. departments (.gov), is in the public domain and copyright-free thanks to taxpayers.

- **Photo-sharing sites.** Many photo-sharing sites, such as Flickr and Photobucket, allow you to copy photos, but most of them don't allow you to use their images for commercial purposes, such as your band. Note that if you use images from members of these sites, depending on the license they have, you might have to ask permission. See the "Your Rights" chapter for more information. ♥

GETTING INTO SEARCH ENGINES

People will find your Web site in a variety of ways. They may learn your domain name at a performance or get it off your CD or other branded material. But many will discover you either through referrals or searches. You want your site to feature prominently in searches at Google and other major search engines whenever anyone searches for your names, your band name, your albums, or your song titles.

SUBMITTING TO SEARCH ENGINES

Once your site is launched, submit it to search engines to make sure they pick it up. See "Submitting to Search Engines" below for submission URLs. Although there are more search engines than these, most simply license and repackage the results of the others.

SEARCH ENGINE OPTIMIZATION

Search engine optimization, often called SEO, is the art of engineering a Web site and its content to achieve higher rankings in a search engine.

The higher the ranking, the more likely you'll be at the top of the search list when the appropriate search terms are entered. Getting a high ranking in search engines can mean serious money so, unfortunately, you'll be competing against experts who get paid to optimize their client's Web sites for the highest rankings possible. The good news is, search engines don't want to be manipulated and are constantly sifting through the results for sites engineered to be popular without actually being relevant or genuine. Simply creating a genuine band Web site with frequently updated content often helps. After a while, your site should naturally rise to the top of the search results for your band and your music.

SEO is an ever-changing topic. Search engines continuously modify the mechanisms they use to calculate rankings. They adapt their algorithms in an endless battle to keep SEO companies from exploiting their systems. So, techniques to keep your band's Web site on the cutting edge of SEO don't belong in the *Guide*. However, a few general principles stay constant, and if you follow them, you will improve your ranking.

The following should be kept in mind as you design your Web site:

- *Title each web page.* Be sure to title each page you create. The title gives search engines the best clue to the topic of the page. Even more

SUBMITTING TO SEARCH ENGINES

Search Engine	Submit Link
Google.com	http://www.google.com/addurl/?continue=/addurl
Yahoo.com	http://search.yahoo.com/info/submit.html
Live.com	http://search.msn.com/docs/submit.aspx

important, when your page does come up in a search, it's the page title that is displayed and highlighted as a link. People looking over their search results will only have this to go by. So, your page title should entice people to click it.

- **Remember text.** Search engine results are based on text, not images. Although it's important to have images and to be brief with text, be sure to include all search-relevant text on your site. For instance, we display lyrics for all of the songs on TheSongOfTheDay.com, which has gotten us a lot of searchers who ended up there based on a snippet of text that happened to be a lyric.

- **Intrasite linking.** When external sites link to your site, it increases your rankings. Although you can't control what external sites do, the linking between pages within your own site can affect your page ranking as well. Cross-link where appropriate.

- **Flash, video, and graphics don't count.** Flash, video, and words in graphics aren't readable by search engines and therefore don't appear in the search rankings. A site that uses a lot of these tends to do poorly in search results. Always offer alternative text for every image file, and create text captions for your flash animations and videos so that the search engines know what they're looking at.

- **MP3 search engines.** If you're comfortable sharing your music without restrictions, make your MP3s downloadable to the user's PC, not just available as a streaming feed. Doing so will allow those files to be picked up in MP3 search engines. These search engines link to your MP3 files directly. Our Web statistics show that MP3 search engines send us far more visitors than text search engines. And when MP3s are properly tagged, those listeners will know where to find your band's site if they want to know more about your music.

TRACKING WHO'S TALKING ABOUT YOUR BAND

You can also use search engines to discover who's talking about your band and music, and who's linking to your site. This can be useful information.

To track mentions of your band and find out the rank of your Web site, you will need to do the following:

1. **Search on your band name.** Search on your band name to track the overall number of search results, and to find all pages that mention your Web site. Make sure to search on common misspellings. Enclose multiple words in quotation marks, and use the OR operator, which works in most engines. For example, we search on *"beatnik turtle" OR "beatnick turtle."*

2. **Search on other terms associated with your band.** Additionally, you'll want to search on other terms associated with your band such as the names of your albums and songs.

3. **Use the following search engines**

• *Standard search engines* Search Google.com, Yahoo.com, and Live.com. Each engine also offers real-time alerts (google.com/alerts, alerts.yahoo.com, alerts.live.com), which will notify you when new mentions of your search terms are indexed. We often use these to find mentions of our band name.

• *Blog search engines* Although the standard search engines search blogs, we also recommend Google Blog Search (blogsearch.google.com) and Technorati (technorati.com), a specialized blog-search engine.

4. **Check your PageRank.** Check your Google PageRank by installing the free Google Toolbar (toolbar.google.com). The higher your PageRank, the higher up your page will appear in the search results.

Tracking your band regularly will give you valuable information—information you can use to fine-tune your SEO strategies. We'll be using this technique in the "Get Publicized" chapter to track the progress of your media campaigns and to reach out to those who are talking about you in order to network and explore other opportunities for your music.

WEB TECHNOLOGY FOR MUSIC WEB SITES

Next we're going to cover all of the key Web technologies that you will be using on your band's Web site. These include RSS, flash music players, MP3 encoding, ID3 tagging, Web statistics, and more. Rather than go into great detail about each of these topics, we're going to tell you what you need to know from a musician's standpoint, with more specific information available from any of a number of Web-design books and Web sites. While some of these topics might seem obscure or technical, we actually use all of these technologies for Beatnik Turtle *every single day*. No band Web site should be without them. It's even better if your Web host provides these features as part of their package.

REALLY SIMPLE SYNDICATION (RSS)

The Web is drenched in information. In the early days, when you wanted to keep up with a Web site, you had to bookmark it and remember to return regularly. Developers created "what's new" pages and encouraged visitors to "check back often." With the advent of blogs, podcasts, media-sharing sites, news aggregators, and other frequently updated Web sites, developers evolved a new communications standard to make it easy for people to follow their favorite sites. The most popular standard invented to solve this problem is called Really Simple Syndication (RSS). Another standard is called Atom, but it's not as widespread, so we recommend sticking with RSS.

Although the term *syndication* implies the broadcast of information, RSS doesn't quite work that way. An RSS file is simply a text file: a date-organized list of entries. Let's take a blog as an example. Once you publish a new post on your RSS-enabled blog, the software automatically appends a new entry to the RSS file. This entry contains the title of the entry and the content of the post, or perhaps only an excerpt. When the RSS file is updated, it doesn't alert those who have subscribed to the RSS feed. All your blog software does is add the new entry to the file and call it a day.

The real work is done by the programs that subscribe to the feed. Blog readers and podcast players will typically periodically check all the RSS files they are subscribed to and pull up the latest RSS file. By comparing the new RSS file with the previous ones, they figure out which entries are fresh and pull the new information to the subscriber's reader or player. For instance, if you subscribe to TheSongOfTheDay.com's daily podcast feed through iTunes, the next time it launches, it will conveniently download the latest podcasts to iTunes.

Because RSS makes it simple to inform fans of updates, your blog, news, forums, and all other regularly updated content should be RSS-enabled. We'll discuss how in the next chapter.

One RSS service that you may want to explore is FeedBurner (feed burner.com), which makes it simpler for your users to subscribe to your feeds.

PASSWORD-PROTECTED WEB PAGES

One advantage to having your own Web site is that you can protect parts of your site so that only you, or people you approve, can access files in that section. Password-protection methods vary and depend on your Web host and possibly the technology that you use for your Web site.

The following material should be password-protected and reserved for your band's own use:

- *Brand Toolbox image-source files.* Source files of your Brand Toolbox for easy access and sharing between band members. This usually consists of layered Photoshop and Illustrator files, but can also include special images you use only in certain circumstances. Final, mixed-down images should be available for any visitors to your site.

- *Brand Toolbox text-source files.* Word-processor files (Word documents, OpenOffice documents, etc.) with your press releases, bios, and so on should be protected because they are easily edited. Final versions should only be distributed in Adobe PDF format.

- *Song files.* Songs that you don't want released to the public, but want to have on hand for press campaigns or for exclusive release to other music sites, should be protected as well.

SOUND ENCODING

Sound encoding is the process of turning analog sound waves into digital information. A particular encoding method is called a codec. There are many different codecs that you can use. Of course, the most famous and universal codec is the MP3. Below, we'll discuss everything you need to know to prepare music for distribution on your Web site.

Sound-Encoding Formats and Terms

Before we talk about the formats, we need to introduce some terms to help you understand how they work. Audio formats can be either uncompressed or compressed:

- **Uncompressed.** Uncompressed formats keep sound information in its raw form, without trying to shrink or otherwise modify the file. Uncompressed formats leave the audio data unchanged, but result in large file sizes.

- **Compressed.** Compressed formats use mathematical or audio-approximation techniques to shrink the size of an audio file.

There are two types of compression you can use:

- **Lossless compression.** Lossless compression shrinks the size of an audio file without degrading sound quality. It does so in a variety of ways. For example, it might encode four seconds of silence by inserting a time marker that essentially tells the player to play silence for four seconds, ditching the actual silence you recorded. These techniques result in a smaller file size and don't degrade sound quality.

- **Lossy compression.** Lossy compression reduces the file size by removing or approximating some of the original sound information. For example, these methods may drop certain sound frequencies that are beyond the range of human hearing. Whether you notice the effect of the compression on the sound quality of the recording depends on the type or amount of lossy compression applied to the file. Applying lossy compression to a file that's already been compressed will lead to greater sound degradation.

Now that you know the types of compression, we can discuss the most common codecs useful for Web distribution:

- **MP3.** MPEG-1 Audio Layer 3 was created by an organization called the Motion Picture Experts Group. This is the most common music codec, the one people are most likely to be able to play on their computers or portable players. There are both lossless and lossy compression versions of this format, but the most common ones are lossy. You can adjust many settings while encoding an MP3 file that alter the sound quality of your music, and in a later section we'll recommend how to best do so for Web distribution. Additionally, MP3 files contain a layer of information that allows text to be embedded that audio players can display, such as the song title, band name, copyright, and lyrics. It even allows an image such as an album cover. Inserting this information is called ID3 tagging, and we'll discuss this below.

- **WAV.** The WAV codec is one of the best formats to use to preserve sound quality. The most common forms of WAVs are uncompressed. Uncompressed WAV files are usually quite large and thus are not ordinarily used on the Web to distribute music. They are more appropriate when sound quality is critical, such as for TV, film, or podcast purposes. Media projects that incorporate music are often themselves compressed, which can make the final version sound bad and unfortunately reflect badly on the band rather than the producer of the program. It's usually up to you to convince the producers to use the WAV file instead.

- **AAC.** Advanced Audio Coding is Apple's proprietary audio codec. It's used by iTunes and is not universally handled by all players as are MP3 and WAV. AAC allows tagging much like an MP3. It also allows Digital Rights Management (DRM) technology to prevent unauthorized use.

- **WMA.** The Windows Media Audio format is Microsoft's proprietary audio codec and is the second most popular format. It can support a range of encoding quality and is playable on many devices, but not all. Like Apple's AAC, WMA allows the use of DRM to control distribution.

- **OGG.** The Ogg Vorbis codec is a high-quality open-source standard. Many of the other formats, such as MP3, ACC, and WMV, are patented, but OGG technology is free to developers and users alike. OGG files have encoding settings that can affect the size and quality, similar to MP3 files. They also allow ID3 tagging.

- **FLAC.** The Free Lossless Audio Codec, or FLAC, is a lossless compression format. The tools to compress audio to a FLAC format are free, and open-source versions exists for them. Sites such as etree (etree.org), the live-music archive, use FLAC exclusively to get the highest-quality audio with the smallest size.

OUR RECOMMENDED METHOD FOR ENCODING MUSIC FOR WEB SITES

We're going to share the Windows encoding method that we used for releasing more than 365 songs over the Web. This method ensures the most reliable playability and quickest download times across multiple platforms:

1. Export a file from your final mixdown with the following settings:
   a. Stereo
   b. 16-bit
   c. 44.1 kHz
   d. WAV file

2. Install the free audio tool Audiograbber from audiograbber. com-us.net.

3. Download the free Windows binary version of the LAME encoder from lame.sourceforge.net. Unzip the files into the same directory as Audiograbber, by default, C:\audiograbber.

4. Start Audiograbber and click the MP3 button. Change your settings to the following:

Grab To: MP3 file via intermediate WAV file. Keep the WAV file.
Use ID3v1 Tag.
Enable the Internal Encoder Tab.
Choose the LameEnc DLL.
Choose Constant Bitrate, and set the slidebar to 128.
In the Quality box, select Joint Stereo and Normal.
In the Bitstream flags, click only Original.
In the Encoder priority, choose Normal.
Click OK when your screen has these settings.

5. After you have changed these settings, drag your WAV files from a file window into Audiograbber. Audiograbber will begin converting them into MP3s at these settings. You can also use the browse button on the MP3 screen. ●

Preparing Your Music: Optimal MP3 Encoding for Your Band Web Site

While there are many ways to encode your music, you want everyone to be able to play your files, and the MP3 standard is the most widely used and playable standard. While you may prefer certain MP3 encoding settings for your own music collection, you should take into account special considerations for your music Web site. Unfortunately, many different settings and methods to encode an MP3 file are incompatible with some players. It's critical to encode your songs in a format that is playable by as many different setups as possible.

See "Our Recommended Method for Encoding Music for Web sites" above. These suggestions were born out of trial and error as we encoded hundreds of our own songs. If you're a techie or audiophile and want a detailed technical explanation of how each of the MP3 encoding options work, visit IndieBandSurvivalGuide.com.

ID3 TAGGING

An additional benefit of MP3s is the ID3 tagging feature. That allows you to embed text in your MP3 files to display the song title, band name, copyright, and lyrics in music players. It even allows an image such as an album cover. As we noted previously, this function allows you to brand your MP3s properly.

There are two versions of ID3 tags: ID3v1 and ID3v2. ID3v1 is older, cruder, and limited in scope. ID3v2 is a much more useful and descriptive format and is the most common standard today. We used to fill in both ID3v1 and ID3v2 tags on all of our MP3 files to be safe. Occasionally, though, some media players would display the more limited ID3v1 tags, ignoring the ID3v2 tags, resulting in truncated titles and less information than we'd actually embedded. Therefore we recommend using only ID3v2 tags (www.id3.org/Frames) since all modern media players support the newer standard.

Plenty of free software programs, including iTunes and Windows Media Player, allow you to quickly and easily tag your MP3 files. You can also purchase ID3 tagging software to help you manage large numbers of songs. If you have to handle a lot of song files, we recommend purchasing the software we used for tagging all the songs we posted at TheSongOfTheDay.com: Tag & Rename from Softpointer (softpointer. com/tr.htm).

Make sure to fill in the tags as consistently as possible. Be careful to spell your band name, album, and song title correctly. Since this is a branding opportunity, we recommend including your Web site address, the copyright information, and any other relevant information. Lastly, you'll want to insert an image for media players to display. Usually, musicians opt for inserting the album artwork, but you can use your logo or another branded image instead. For example, for the songs we released at TheSongOfTheDay.com we used our Brand Toolbox to create an image with our mascot, band logo, the logo of TheSongOfTheDay.com, and our tagline.

MP3 FILE-NAMING STANDARD

Always name your audio files consistently, because you never know where they might end up, such as a huge folder of song files. Make sure the file name emphasizes your band's name. We suggest putting your band name first: Band Name—Song Title.

Due to the way most computers read files, omit punctuation marks such as question marks, apostrophes, and quotes. For maximum compatibility, replace spaces with underscores. Also, the shorter, the better. And make sure you've spelled your band name and song title correctly!

- **Bad Examples**
  PizzaTheRockOpera.mp3
  PizzaTheRockOpera-BeatnikTurtle.mp3
  pizzatherockoperabeatnikturtle.mp3

- **Good Example**
  Beatnik_Turtle-Pizza_The_Rock_Opera.mp3

PLAYING MUSIC FROM YOUR WEB SITE

Once you've encoded your music into MP3 format, tagged the file, and named it, it's time to make it available on your Web site. One of the reasons MySpace.com and similar social-networking sites have done so well with musicians is the ease of uploading music and using their audio players. Unfortunately, the players are typically inflexible and limit the amount of music you can make available.

Today, multiple technologies are available for playing your music from your Web site, and we are going to cover each method, as well as giving practical examples of how to use each.

Uploading Your Music

Now that you have your MP3 files ready, you will need to upload them to your Web site. First, create a directory on your Web server called "music" or "MP3" that can be accessed from a browser. (It needs to be inside your Web directory, which might be called "public_html," "Web," or "www." Ask your Web host for specifics.)

Once the files are uploaded, protect the directory from being listed so that visitors can't download all of your MP3 files at once. See the documentation from your Web-hosting provider for information on how to do this.

There are three ways to upload your MP3 files to your Web site:

- *File transfer protocol (FTP) or secure shell (SSH).* Your Web host should give you an FTP or SSH account for you to upload files to your server. To use these methods, you must use a program on your computer. We recommend WS-FTP (ipswitch.com) or the free and open-source WinSCP (winscp.net). For Macintosh, Transmit (www.panic.com/transmit) and Cyberduck (cyberduck.ch) are both good choices.

- *Web-based upload solution.* Your Web host may provide an uploading solution for you to transfer files to your Web site through its CMS. If one is available, you'll need to follow the instructions they provide.

Downloading, Streaming, Sharing, and Podcasting

Each method of delivering music to visitors has its advantages and disadvantages. We use all four of the following methods to distribute our music to people based on the circumstances.

- *Downloading.* Downloading lets users copy the file onto their computer. Once it's downloaded, the file is available to them for their own use.

- *Streaming.* Streaming works like radio. Although the sound data gets sent to the user's computer, streaming players are usually configured to prevent the user from saving the file locally. However, determined people can always get around this limitation, so do not depend on this to protect your music.

- *Sharing.* Sharing a file is similar to downloading, but allows a user to get the data from multiple sources in addition to your Web site.

- *Podcasting.* Podcasting lets users subscribe to a feed and automatically download songs when you publish them. This is only appropriate for songs that you wish to give away. We cover this in the next chapter.

Downloading

The simplest way to share music from your Web site is to upload MP3s to your Web site and provide direct links that visitors can use to download the entire file. This simple method of distribution has a few advantages. First, visitors can keep the file and add it to their iTunes or Windows Media Player playlists. Second, if you post direct links to your MP3s, they'll be indexed by MP3 search engines. We get a large number of plays from these engines.

While this method is simple, it can confuse some users. When visitors click on the link, QuickTime will most likely launch in their browser and play the file. To the uninitiated, it may appear as if the song can only be listened to, and they might believe that they can't download it. Users can right-click the link (or shift-click on a Mac) and choose to save the file locally, but not every user knows this technique. So, some people won't figure out how to save the file. To avoid confusion, remind visitors that they can "right-click or shift-click to save."

Online Playlists (Streaming)

Another method is to create an online playlist and post it at your site. This allows visitors to stream your MP3s rather than download them. In principle, online playlists work the same way as almost any audio player you might have on your computer, except that the MP3s are being accessed from your Web site rather than locally. Although this is a streaming method, it's easy for people to open up the playlist and download the songs directly if they want to. Some sites still use this format, although we don't recommend this if you can use any of the other methods that we list below.

The two major formats you can use for this are:

• **M3U.** This format was originally developed for Nullsoft's Winamp player and has been adopted as a fairly universal standard. Most every MP3 player handles playlists created in this format. There are two types: M3U basic and M3U extended format. We recommend using the M3U extended format because this includes information about the songs that the player can display, such as the song title, artist, etc. Some players will pick up the ID3 tags and display them. Some, though, may not.

• **PLS.** The PLS format is compatible with many players including Nullsoft's Winamp player and iTunes. It is not compatible with Windows Media Player, however, because Windows doesn't associate the file extension PLS with any media player. Because of this, we do not recommend using this standard.

If you want to know how to make an M3U playlist for your site, we have a sample at IndieBandSurvivalGuide.com

Flash Music Players (Streaming)

We recommend using flash players above any other delivery mechanism for music. Most players let you control exactly how you want to deliver your music (downloading or streaming), change the look and feel (brand your player), and link directly to your store pages (which encourages sales). Your visitors need Adobe Flash Player installed on their computer for any flash players to work, but this software is nearly ubiquitous and available for all major platforms (Windows, Mac, Linux). Still, a few people might not have it and may not be able to hear your music.

Flash players vary. Some are simply play buttons (like the one we use at TheSongOfTheDay.com), while others rival any audio player software you might have on your computer—boasting playlist functionality, EQ controls, volume, balance, and other standard features. Here are three recommended flash players: Wimpy player (wimpyplayer.com), JW MP3 player (jeroenwijering.com/?item=jw_mp3_player), and XSPF Web Music Player (musicplayer.sourceforge.net) (an open-source and free solution).

PLAYING VIDEO FROM YOUR WEB SITE

Hosting videos from your Web site may raise your Web-hosting rates—especially if any videos you post become popular. You can use a variety of formats for your videos, with some of the better-known ones being QuickTime, WMV, Real, MP4, AVI, DivX, and Flash. Unfortunately, each of these has its own associated player, and not all of your visitors will have the means to play it. This can frustrate viewers. To resolve this, you may want to encode your video in a variety of formats.

Web-hosting sites such as YouTube (youtube.com) and Blip TV (blip.tv) have become an extremely popular way to solve video-hosting problems. Not only do you take advantage of their bandwidth, their sites are so prevalent, in many respects they have standardized video. Every Internet surfer can play a YouTube video, for instance. We'll talk about these video-hosting sites in the "Your Web Presence" chapter.

WEB STATISTICS

One of the biggest advantages of having your own Web site is full access to Web statistics. Your Web host will likely provide some Web statistic programs by default, but free options you can install include AWStats (awstats.sourceforge.net) or Webalizer (mrunix.net/Webalizer). Additionally some solutions are for sale, such as Mint (haveamint.com).

Many people ignore their stats, but that's a big mistake. Statistics are an incredibly powerful technique for understanding how people actually use your Web site and for gauging interest in your band "out there." Also, Web stat analysis is crucial for publicity purposes. There is no more important technique for tracking your media campaigns—your statistics will clue you in to who's talking about you and who's sending visitors your way, identifying the blogs, podcasts, news sites, and other Web sites directing traffic to you.

Statistics Are People

Hundreds of millions of people are on the Web, and any one of them might be discovering your music at this very moment. While these people may only show up as numbers in your Web stats, they are people nonetheless. As you review your stats, it helps to visualize a venue you've played at. If a thousand people listened to one of your songs on the Web, for example, imagine all of those people standing in that venue, listening to you play. We've found this technique helps put your statistics in perspective, and while you might not get the same rush out of reading your stats as you would if you were playing live for a massive crowd, it still means your music is being heard by a thousand people.

Web Terminology

Once you start getting into the back end of a Web site, there's a new set of terminology to learn. These terms have specific meanings that aren't always straightforward, so we're going to define them here so that we can use them in our discussion later.

- **Hits.** A hit is a request to the Web server where your Web site is hosted. Many people still equate hits with popularity. This is not the case. Whenever a person browses one of your Web pages, each image, frame, and page element counts as a hit from a visitor. Ignore this statistic. Although it used to be the major statistic people tracked because of the way browsers originally worked, it's useless today. Visits and Unique Visitors are more useful statistics.

- **Visits.** A Visit is a complete session spent at your Web site by one user. It can last seconds, minutes, hours, or days and is determined by the continuous presence of a Unique Visitor at your site.

- **Unique Visitors.** This is the number of distinct visitors to your Web site. This is usually calculated per month. For example, a single Unique Visitor might visit every day, but would only be counted as one Unique Visitor that month, even though the visitor was responsible for thirty Visits.

- **Visits per Visitor.** Dividing Visits by Unique Visitors, you get an average Visits per Visitor. This tells you how often people return to your Web site. You want this number to be as high as possible since it means you have regular visitors. If this statistic is close to one, your Web site does not bring people back.

- **Pages.** This is how many separate Web pages are requested from your Web site, total. This is also expressed as Pages per Visit, which can be an interesting statistic. If the Pages per Visit stat is close to one, your visitors are looking at just one or two pages before exiting.

- **Bandwidth.** This is the amount of data people have transferred from your site. Because of the file size of your MP3s, you can use this to determine if the average visitor is listening to your songs. This is also expressed as Bandwidth per Visitor.

- **Visit Duration.** This is the average amount of time that a user spends on your site.

- *Referrers (or Referring Sites).* Referrers tell you who has linked to your Web site. This can be used to identify each site that links to you and also how many people have clicked those links. This is one of the most useful statistics. You can see, for instance, if the music blog that reviewed your latest album actually sent any new listeners your way.

- *Referring Search Engines.* This statistic tells you which search engines sent visitors to you.

- *Search Terms.* This statistic tells you what search terms are sending people to your site and how many visitors each one sent.

- *Viewed Files.* This statistic will display a list, usually sorted from high to low, of the number of times each file is requested from your Web site. This shows you what your most popular files are. This statistic can help you gauge how many times one of your MP3s was listened to by visitors.

Nothing Is as It Seems

Unfortunately, nothing about Web statistics is straightforward. Web stats can be both inflated or deflated depending on factors you can't control. The biggest factor is something called caching. Caching occurs when large Internet service providers (ISPs) make a copy of your Web site to their network so that they can serve it to their users more quickly. Some of your visitors will visit these cached pages instead of your site itself, and as a result your Web server won't be able to count them, even though, in essence, they were visitors.

Additionally, the Unique Visitor statistic is based on unique IP addresses. However, unique IP addresses don't necessarily mean unique people. Multiple visitors can come from the same IP address (e.g., different people visiting your site from the same office network), while one visitor may come from multiple IP addresses (e.g., while checking your site from home and at work).

These statistics can only give you a general sense of what's going on at your Web site. They shouldn't be read as absolutes.

Referrers

Possibly the most useful information you'll get from your stats is a list of all the Web sites that have referred visitors to you, and how many visitors each sent. We watch these statistics every day for our own Web sites and visit each new page that pops up to see what they're saying about us and why they're linking. This is called trackbacking. Using this, you can find out trends related to your band *as they are happening*.

Contrary to popular belief, not all Web sites are cataloged in search engines, and some of them may be talking about your band. Using your stats to trackback can often fill in the gaps searching doesn't capture. For example, forums and message boards might link to your site. These sites are often located behind a log-in screen that search engines can't get past. (We recommend signing up for accounts on these sites to see who's talking about you.)

Also, some bloggers may spontaneously link to a file or image on your site in passing while discussing something unrelated and without typing a single word that you would ever search for. The referrer page is the only way to find out about these links.

Trackbacking is also the best way to find out how well your media campaigns are working. Once you get media coverage, one way to gauge its impact is to see how many people are coming to your site from stories that link to you. This can help you refine your media campaign. In fact, trackbacking can even help you find media coverage that you didn't know you had. Many times, the media don't even inform you when they've published a piece—even if you did an interview with them. Fortunately, any coverage you get on the Web often provides a link to your site, and the referred visitors will clue you in to when and where you've gotten publicity.

Finding 404 Errors Using Statistics

A 404 error occurs when you have a bad link on your site or when a visitor is sent to a page that does not exist. Most stats engines provide the number of 404 links that your site has, and which links are 404 so that you can fix them.

Search Engine Tracking

Your Web statistics are the only way to track how many links you get from each search engine, as well as which search terms people used to wind up on your site. Web statistic tools not only track standard search engines but also social-bookmarking sites such as StumbleUpon, Digg, and others.

Your Global Audience

As we mentioned in previous chapters, fans can and do come from all around the world. Your Web statistics can track this and tell you which country each visitor came from. In one month alone, TheSongOfTheDay. com had visitors from New Zealand, Morocco, Poland, Vietnam, Brazil, United Kingdom, Finland, Spain, India, Chile, Israel, Canada, Macedonia, Sri Lanka, Iceland, Saudi Arabia, Australia, France, and others: seventy-eight countries in all. The world is listening, and the impact of global listeners will only grow as the Web does. It's good to know where your fans are.

Clickpath Tracking

Your basic stats help a lot, but they won't tell you the paths people take while they visit and click around your site. This information is valuable for measuring how well your design and content is leading visitors through your site. Basic Web statistic programs cannot capture this. You also need a clickpath tracking program.

With a clickpath tracking program, you will be able to find out such things as:

• What links your users are clicking

• How long they remain on each page

• The individual paths each user takes as he or she travels through your site

• The most common entry and exit pages

• The times of day that people tend to visit

Clickpath tracking solutions vary in power and accuracy. The better ones use cookies and embedded graphics as mechanisms to track users as they surf your site. Some programs can even recognize returning visitors and assign a name to them if they join your mailing list or otherwise enter their e-mail address on the site.

The information clickpath tracking programs provide can be invaluable. Using Google Analytics (www.google.com/analytics), for instance, you can track your conversion rates by entering specific actions for it to watch for such as the purchase of an album or the download of a song.

FREE CLICKPATH TRACKING

If your Web host hasn't already integrated these solutions within your site, we recommend the following free clickpath-tracking software. As with Web statistic programs, you can always use more than one to analyze what's going on at your site:

• **Google Analytics** (google.com/analytics/) We highly recommend Google Analytics. They offer detailed instructions on implementing their program on your Web site.

• **TraceWatch** (tracewatch.com) Although TraceWatch is not as easy to install as Google Analytics, it is still worth implementing. Instead of consolidating the data, it lists each visitor to let you see how *individuals* are clicking through your site. This can tell you how easy your site is to navigate. But unless you're an experienced Web-site administrator, you will need help from your skill network to get it working. ♥

Don't Rely Solely on MySpace (Reprise)

Based on all the information these statistics can provide about your site, and more important, how your band and music is being received in the world, you should take a moment to feel sorry for the bands that rely solely on MySpace or other social-networking sites for their main Web site. Those sites are better used to help bolster your branded presence across the Web, not replace it. We'll talk more about establishing your Web presence in the next chapter.

LEARNING MORE

There's a lot to having a Web site, but as we've seen there's plenty of tools and resources that can help. We keep track of all these tools at IndieBand SurvivalGuide.com. It's a free and open community for indie musicians and we'll discuss it more in the next chapter.

CHAPTER 5

YOUR WEB PRESENCE

THE WEB allows you to reach people in new ways beyond playing live shows—whether it's through social networks, message boards, podcasts, blogs, or even virtual online worlds. You'll be able to target your message and get your music in front of the people most likely to enjoy it based on their interests and tastes—not just their locale. Even better, the Web makes them easy to find. Millions of potential fans out there should know about your music, and you need to put your band and your music where they are.

The Web started out as a new way to *broadcast* information to people. Today it has grown into a *conversation*, where you can interact with anyone who shares the same interests. But more important, it's become a *collaboration*, enabling people all over the world to socialize and work together. This chapter will explore each of these activities— broadcasting, conversing, and collaborating.

While we're going to mention a lot of Web sites and technologies by name, keep in mind that the Web is fluid, and some sites that we mention might disappear even before this book goes to print. Rather than dwell on particular sites, we'll instead focus on the concepts behind them. Our goal isn't just to show you the latest useful tools; it's to prepare you to recognize and take advantage of new ones when they come out. Also, keep in mind that some of the services that you use and rely on today might disappear in the future. To help keep you up-to-date, we will maintain a listing of the current useful tools for musicians at IndieBandSurvival Guide.com.

BEFORE YOU START

Before you begin broadcasting, conversing, and collaborating, a few things to keep in mind when establishing your Web presence are setting up your profiles, doing self-promotion, and dealing with user agreements.

KEEP TRACK OF YOUR LOG-INS AND PASSWORDS

Because you will be joining many different sites for your band, you will need a way to keep track of the Web sites, log-ins, and passwords, and perhaps even share it with other members of your band. We recommend doing this in a spreadsheet, or on Google docs online (docs.google.com), although you should password-protect the files themselves. For a secure solution, we like Password Gorilla (fpx.de/fp/Software/Gorilla), a free tool that allows you to track all of it in one convenient place with a single password.

ALWAYS BE BRANDING: YOUR ONLINE PROFILES

As we learned in chapter 3, an effective brand is consistent and re-peated. As you build your Web presence, you'll create accounts at multiple sites, each of which will ask for personal information. So, you'll be making heavy use of the images and text in your Brand Toolbox.

Given the number of tools out there, you're going to want to divide the jobs of maintaining each one among your band members. We recommend having your branded images and text ready to go at your Web site so anyone in the band can access them. Some of what you'll need includes:

- *Avatar.* Upload the same avatar representing your band anytime you register an account. In our case, we always use our turtle mascot.

- *Tagline.* Many sites ask you for a pithy saying or short description of yourself. We suggest making a tagline out of your elevator pitch.

- *Description or bio.* Many sites allow a more detailed profile. Our advice is to keep it short. Use your elevator pitch or short bio (with a link to your Web site for more information).

- *Link.* Most profiles allow you to link to your Web site. We recommend copying and pasting your Web site address from your browser's address bar, since there's nothing more embarrassing than mistyping your own Web site's URL.

- **Footer or signature line.** Some sites allow you a footer or signature line that displays when you make posts or leave comments. Use this footer as another opportunity to promote your band. With these footers, we get a lot of visitors from posts that we make.

- **Your contact information.** Keep your contact info consistent. You'd be surprised at how many people contact you using your profiles.

SELF-PROMOTION (AND STEALTH-PROMOTION)

If you believe in your music, you shouldn't be ashamed to promote it, especially when you're first starting out and your music needs the biggest boost. There's nothing wrong with self-promotion, but when you promote yourself, you want to do it appropriately. That means that you shouldn't just push your music at people. As Chris Anderson says in his interview for the book *Blogging Heroes,* "Bloggers shamelessly self-promote, but they do it in an appropriate way. They e-mail people they know, regarding things that really are of interest to those people, and ask for links [back to their own blogs]. They're not just begging for a random link—they're actually adding value, because this link is in fact complementary to something the blogger they're e-mailing has already done."

This isn't just true for blogs, it's true for anything that you do online that you wish to self-promote. In fact, we recommend the following:

- Carefully target the people that you wish to get your message to.

- Think of their point of view when you promote yourself; for example, give them links to a song of yours that relates to a topic that they cover in their blog.

- Remember, real people are behind the posts, blogs, and messages on the Web. No one likes another sales pitch. You might want to wait until you've exchanged some e-mails before even bringing up your music.

- Do some research on whom you're contacting or the group you're targeting. This means actually reading their posts and blogs.

- In your messages to those you target, be sure to focus on *them*. Talk about recent entries in their blog, podcast, or profile as it shows that you are aware of their work. That way, they're more likely to pay attention to you.

- Don't forget that all of the general concepts covered in the "Your Network" chapter apply to self-promoting online as well. Also, we go into more detail on promotion in both the "Get Noticed" and "Get Publicized" chapters.

That said, keep in mind that on some sites you won't want a branded online profile. Instead, you'll just want to be yourself or an anonymous user. Sites that ask for user submissions of news stories or links to interesting Web sites, such as Digg.com, Slashdot.org, or BoingBoing.net, typically frown upon blatant self-promotion. For example, those with editors often reject stories about an "amazing" new song or video if they sense these submitted by the band itself. And sites such as Reddit.com, which make judgments by the site's online community, can often be harsher in public about you and your story than any editor.

Record labels don't let this stop them. They still shamelessly self-promote, by using pseudonyms or paying third parties to post stories on their behalf. For sites such as these, we recommend creating pseudonym profiles yourself. Eventually, your fan network will promote you spontaneously by submitting stories, links, and posts about your music. In the meantime, you'll have to be your own fan.

For example, we wrote a song dedicated to the Battle of Denmark Strait and the HMS *Hood* for our Song of the Day project. We made a simple post to a message board about the song with a link, saying that it was a tribute song. The members of the message board loved it, but we only got a handful of hits from this low-traffic forum. To our pleasant surprise, one of the people on that board posted the link to a Web site about model warships, and another about ships in general. Those additional posts got us hundreds of additional plays. This was for about ten minutes of work.

USER AGREEMENTS

Most every Web site where you create an account will have a user agreement. When you signed up for these sites as an individual, you probably didn't bother reading them. Unfortunately, with your band and its music at stake, you need to start paying attention to these, since some may require you to give up certain rights.

You must make sure that these agreements don't overreach and hamper any plans you have for your music, videos, or other content you upload. For example, the user agreements for music sites can be especially aggressive about copyrights, sometimes dictating that you give them the right to sell your music on compilation albums or to use it in other ways you might find objectionable. We routinely skip Web sites that have user agreements that claim rights to the material that we upload.

If you are uncertain about the meanings behind any agreements, you should consult with your attorney.

BROADCASTING

In this section, we'll talk about technologies you can use to broadcast information to your fans. Technologies in this category include e-mails (your mailing list), blogs, podcasts, video blogs, photo sharing, and more. Broadcast tools are often incorporated or embedded directly into the design of your Web site.

MAILING LISTS

Do you know who your fans are? You should, and your mailing list is the best way to do so. People who sign up for your list are most likely the loyal fans that come to your shows and buy your albums. Much of your success depends on your ability to inform and motivate them.

You should ask for contact information whenever possible. While your Web site should elicit contact information at multiple points (when visitors download a song, purchase some merchandise, etc.), you should mention the mailing list whenever you interact with them. Have a piece of paper out and add newcomers to the list when you see them in person, such as when you run a merch table.

Collecting a mailing list serves many purposes, but here are some of the most important ones:

- It tells you who your fan are.

- It lets you broadcast and announce your latest albums, videos, and news directly to your fans.

- It lets you broadcast show information to fans to boost live-show attendance.

- It boosts sales by allowing you to advertise and pitch your albums and merchandise.

- It helps with branding by reminding your fans about your band.

Of course, anytime you're dealing with a lot of information, it helps to have software to do the heavy lifting. You may need to track thousands of names, or even tens of thousands (or, if you're successful, millions, although at that point you'll need more than software).

You should build an e-mail list and a traditional mailing list as well. Both come in handy at different times for different purposes. We'll talk about both below.

PRIVACY POLICY

Many people are concerned about giving away their private information. With identity theft and spam on the rise, it's not hard to understand why. To set people at ease, you should post a policy for how you plan to handle the personal information you collect from them and adhere to it.

We suggest that you keep it simple and set a policy that all personal information you collect from others will only be used to keep the band in contact with those who sign up. Promise you won't sell or otherwise give any information to any third parties for other purposes. The idea, after all, is to build trust with the fans that are willing to give you their information so you can contact them.

You should create a page at your Web site where you announce your policy. It doesn't have to be in legalese. Plain English will do. You should link to this page from all pages related to your mailing list.

SAMPLE PRIVACY POLICY

Here's the most important part of our privacy policy, simple and to the point:

> We guarantee that if you join the Beatnik Turtle E-mailing List, we will not sell, transfer, or spam your e-mail address. We guarantee we'll never, ever knowingly transfer your e-mail address to any third party. Beatnik Turtle promises to use your e-mail address only for Beatnik Turtle–related information and announcements.

Keep in mind that, once you post a privacy policy, you have to abide by it. If you later decide to change it, you should notify every person on your e-mail list of this change and give them a few days to opt out before enacting the new policy. ♦

One way bands inadvertently violate their own privacy policies is by sending e-mail to their lists by using the *To:* or *CC:* field to send e-mails to multiple members of their mailing list. These fields expose everyone's e-mail address to everyone else on the message—and anyone the initial recipients forward the message to.

To avoid this embarrassing mistake and breach of your agreement, put the band's e-mail address in the *To:* field and place everyone else's in the *BCC:* field. By doing so, you'll know if your e-mail went out correctly once you receive it. Plus, if people accidentally hit *Reply All* in response to your newsletter, they'll only end up writing your band address, not everyone on your mailing list.

Privacy laws vary from state to state in the United States, and Canada and the European Union have some of the most restrictive privacy laws. So, depending on where you reside, you'll also need to be aware of and meet the requirements of these laws.

E-MAIL LISTS

An e-mail list will be one of your primary methods for broadcasting information directly to your fans. You need consistent and regular contact with your fans. In fact, as Ariel Hyatt of Ariel Publicity (arielpublicity.com) says, "No list, no band." Fortunately, it's simple, inexpensive, and fans expect to sign up for it.

Unfortunately, e-mail is not as reliable as it once was, thanks to spam. Most e-mail spam filters are aggressive. Your newsletter, which likely contains hyperlinks and images, will probably trigger some of your fans' spam filters even though they've legitimately signed up for it. Although this may occur here and there, enough newsletters should reach their intended recipients to use this method to broadcast to your fans.

To increase the odds in your favor, encourage those who sign up to add the incoming e-mail address of your newsletter to their spam white list, so it's sure to go through.

Additionally, you'll likely want to reproduce the content in your newsletters on your blog or elsewhere on your Web site. Since your site should be RSS-enabled, this will doubly ensure your fans are getting your message.

Although e-mail is inexpensive, you shouldn't bombard your fans' in-boxes with newsletters whenever you have news. Doing so will surely annoy even your biggest fans. We suggest limiting your newsletters to no more than twice a month. Of course, special announcements, such a last-minute gig or major media coverage, are exceptions. However, they should really be special, and make sure the subject line of your e-mail conveys the unusual circumstances—be clear that you aren't normally going to overwhelm your fans' mailboxes.

Branding Your E-mail List

You should brand every newsletter that you send. Each one should have a consistent look and feel and should appear as a natural extension of your Web site. We actually named our newsletter (*TurtleShell*) and created it out of items from our Brand Toolbox. Once we'd created a template for the newsletter—the design, structure, fonts, use of images—we stuck to it.

What to Write About

Sometimes, what to write about is the hardest hurdle to overcome for your newsletter.

Here's a list of ideas:

- List upcoming shows

- Mention new songs, albums, or merchandise

- Trumpet recent successes (a well-attended show, a positive music review, etc.)

- Link to media coverage you've received

- Highlight recent mentions in blogs or podcasts (and be sure to cross-promote)

- Feature photos from recent shows, both of the band and of the fans

- Announce upcoming projects (see "The Stay-Tuned Strategy" in the "Get Noticed" chapter)

- Quote interesting or funny questions or comments from fans

Whatever you decide to write, make sure it's fresh news. It shouldn't be anything too old or something you've mentioned in an earlier newsletter. Also, be sure to use your band name frequently in your stories. Although it'll be your fans reading, repeating your name always helps with name recognition.

What to Include

In addition to fresh content, each newsletter should contain the following:

- **Subject line.** Typically your subject line will be the name of your newsletter. If it's a regular mailing list, you'll want to denote the edition (the month or issue number). For *TurtleShell,* the subject line is: "TurtleShell—The Beatnik Turtle Newsletter—[Month, Year]." Of course, if the reason behind e-mailing your list is to announce something special, it helps to tell people this here.

- **How to subscribe/unsubscribe.** Include information on how recipients can subscribe and unsubscribe to your newsletter and provide links. Telling readers how to subscribe is important in cases where one fan forwards your newsletter to another person who isn't on your mailing list but then wants to join.

• *Basic information about who you are.* Beyond branding the entire look and feel of your newsletter, we suggest including your Web site address, contact information (you may want to create a separate forwarding e-mail address for replies to your newsletter), who you are (the elevator-pitch version), and links to where fans can purchase your music and merchandise (your store page).

• *Copyright information.* Don't forget to add any copyright information about the newsletter. We suggest using a Creative Commons license to make it clear that people can share or post your newsletters if they like, as long as they attribute you, and as long as it isn't for commercial purposes. Of course, by the same token you'll need to clear any copyrighted graphics or photos you plan to use.

With the exception of the subject line, we suggest including the rest of this information in the footer. In our design, we adjusted the footer font to be slightly smaller than that of the body text. Additionally, to ensure consistency, we built this footer into the template of the design. Once we'd written it, we never needed to deal with it again.

Writing Good Copy

Writing newsletters can be time-consuming. However, keeping your fan network up-to-date is vital. It keeps your name in front of them, reminds them that you're doing things, and keeps them involved. Don't make this into an overwhelming task. And since we'd all rather be making music than studying for our journalism degree, stick to the following rules of thumb:

• *Be brief.* Keep your articles short. Write headlines and blurbs that effectively convey the main message.

• *Who, what, where, why, when, and how.* Begin each story by answering all of the above questions in the first paragraph, like a good newspaper article.

• *Use pictures.* Try to include pictures with every story.

• *Direct people to act.* Insert a "call to action" in your stories if you want your fans to do something. Don't assume they'll "get it" from the context.

For example, "Buy our new album today by clicking on this link." Or, "Come to our show on Saturday." See the "Get Noticed" chapter for the most effective ways to do this.

- *Salt your stories.* Throw in a teaser promise or question at the top of a story to arouse curiosity and draw the reader through to the end. For more on salting, see the previous chapter, "Your Web site."

- *Check spelling and grammar.* Obviously.

- *Get an editor.* Pass your newsletter to at least one other person with a knack for words to look it over for obvious mistakes before hitting *Send*.

E-mail List Software

E-mail list software simplifies subscribing, unsubscribing, drafting, and sending bulk e-mails to fans. You do not want to do this manually or use your personal e-mail account. Fortunately, you have many options when it comes to this kind of software. First, your Web host may provide you with a ready-made system that can easily be integrated into your Web site. If not, Web services, desktop programs, and open-source programs that run on a Web server can do this for you. We've used PHPlist (phplist.com), which is free, and runs off our own server. We've had some people recommend the pay service Ezine Director (www.ezinedirector.com), but quite a few services are out there. We'll list the features you will want in an e-mailing list program if you are going to evaluate one:

- *Subscription form that integrates with your Web site.* The e-mail list program should provide a sign-up form solution that embeds easily into your Web site.

- *Automatic unsubscribe.* Your program should let users unsubscribe automatically via a link in the newsletter. You do not want to manually manage this.

- *Dead e-mail address function.* You'll want the program to automatically remove dead or bouncing e-mail addresses.

- *Template function.* The program should allow you to create templates. This saves time and allows you to brand consistently.

- **Archive content.** The program should keep an archive of all the messages you've sent.

- **Ability to send text and HTML versions.** Some people don't want newsletters full of photos and images and prefer the text-only version. Sophisticated e-mail list programs allow subscribers to decide what type of e-mail they'd like to receive, automatically converting the HTML newsletter you create into text for those users.

- **Click tracking.** The program should perform click tracking so you can tell whether readers are clicking on links within your newsletter.

- **Postal mail integration.** Ideally, you'll want this program to be your one-stop shop for managing all the mail you send, whether electronic or postal. It should be able to manage both and have the ability to interface with printing programs so you can use it to send postal mail, such as postcards.

- **Multiple and separate list capabilities.** Your program should handle multiple lists and let single users subscribe to multiple lists at once. This may be useful later if you create more than one newsletter.

Using Your E-mail List Software

Mailing list software combines the features of a word processor, database, and e-mail program in one package, handling all aspects of creating, managing, and administering your list.

Customizing Your E-mail Software

Mailing list software should be highly customizable and easy to integrate within your Web site. For example, add a "Join Our E-mail List" box in the sidebar of all your Web pages. Also, anytime visitors perform a conversion— buy merchandise, download a song—you should ask them to join while you have their interest.

Another way to entice people to join your mailing list is to offer something free for signing up or provide something exclusive to those who receive the newsletter. We decided on the latter for Beatnik Turtle by giving them one free song each month.

Be sure to customize the default confirmation message. Typically, when someone signs up on your list, the program e-mails them a confirmation e-mail. This message is customizable and should be branded and, more important, offer links to your albums and merchandise, perhaps with a special discount for having subscribed to the newsletter.

Postal Mailing List

Now that we have e-mail, it's become rare for musicians to use postal mail to communicate with their fans. After all, it's relatively expensive and time-consuming. However, you may want to take this step for special occasions. For example, a CD-release show may warrant a mailing.

If you do a postal mailing, we suggest using postcards. It's cheaper and more likely to be "accidentally" read by the recipient (even if it's floating through the air as it heads into the trash). It also forces you to be brief and think "billboard" when you create it. To make your postcards as effective as possible, give them some value by making them coupons for a discount ("Bring this postcard to the show for $X off the new CD") or a free gift (a button, poster, special CD, etc.). Encouraging people to bring in their postcards in this manner will give you valuable feedback as to whether this expensive way of contacting your fans was effective.

BLOGS

Blogs have changed the nature of how people communicate and interact with each other and have even changed the nature of journalism itself. Originally coined from the terms *Web* and *log*, early blogs were essentially online diaries. Although such online diaries still exist, blogs soon evolved into a communication form to rival the popularity and quality of print media.

It seems that everyone has a blog. In fact, many expect every business and organization to have one. This includes your band. But that's not the only reason you should consider starting one of your own. Most communication with your fans is impersonal. For instance, your news stories, newsletters, and press releases will tend to be factual: we have a show, we got some media coverage, our new album is out, our drummer exploded. These are not typically places to be casual. In your blog, you can (and should) promote your latest albums, releases, merchandise, and anything else that you've been up to, but do so from a personal angle. The strange thing that happened on your tour, the wild events of last night's show, the T-shirt manufacturer's misspelling your band name and having to do a second run, all make great blog fodder, though they may not be suitable for your news section.

As we said in the previous chapter, Nice Peter's blog is a great example of how to use blogs to humanize yourself and entertain your audience. They start to feel as if they're part of what you're doing.

Better still, because of the informal tone, members should feel comfortable blogging. Most blog software allows the creation of multiple author accounts and automatically identifies the author of each post.

Creating a Blog

There are two ways to create a blog: a self-hosted blogging program you can install on your own Web site, or a Web-based blog-hosting service that will serve up your blog for you. Before we go into these two options, let's look at the must-have features of your blog:

- **Rich text editor.** Your blog should have the option of working like a word processor when editing entries, with buttons for bold, italics, etc. You should have the option of blogging without knowing any HTML.

- **Embedded HTML.** YouTube, Flickr, and other sites allow you to embed their videos and images into your blog. Make sure your blog allows embedded HTML.

- **Sound player.** You'll want the blog to feature a built-in music player. If you link to one of your songs, a player should be embedded right there in the post.

- **RSS-enabled.** Make sure that the blog you choose generates RSS feeds.

Self-Hosted Blogging Programs

It's now simple to set up and update a blog. In fact, your Web host should provide blogging software for free. Of course, if your host doesn't or provides blogging software that is not RSS-enabled, you may want to install one yourself. If you've decided to use a CMS to create and manage your Web site, the CMS will likely feature a built-in blogging module that will allow you to add one to your site quickly and easily.

Blog-program features vary, so before you integrate one into your site, confirm that it contains the must-have features listed above. We suggest using WordPress (wordpress.org), which you can also use to create the rest of your Web site.

Web-Based Blog-Hosting Services

The other method of creating a blog is to register with a blog-hosting service such as LiveJournal or Blogger. Many hosts are free, but even those usually offer a pay version that adds extra features such as more storage space. The advantages of using a blog host are that they take care of the software backend for you, and they tend to have built-in blogging communities who will come and read your blog if it matches their interests.

However, because your blog is such a powerful way to personalize yourself, it should really be hosted on your Web site and be incorporated into the design. For branding purposes, if you use a blog-hosting service based elsewhere, you should embed it within your Web site. That way, you're not sending people away from your music, albums, mailing list, and merchandise to read your blog.

SOME BLOG-HOSTING OPTIONS

• **Livejournal.com** LiveJournal is more than a blog; it's a set of online social communities. Thus, we keep a LiveJournal account even though we have our own blogging software.

• **Blogger.com** Blogger.com is owned by Google and is a solid blogging engine.

• **Wordpress.com** Wordpress.com uses WordPress but allows you to just create an account and start blogging rather than needing to set it up on your server. ●

GETTING INTO BLOG SEARCH ENGINES

You should get your blog into the blog search engines such as Technorati. com. Although you can let it "find you," we recommend informing sites like Technorati initially when you launch your blog to get it in their system.

BLOG PINGS

Blog pings will inform blog search engines that you've updated. You should add the following blog pings to your blog software so that what you write will immediately appear in their search tools. There are numerous services, but we recommend these three at a minimum:

http://rpc.pingomatic.com/
http://rpc.technorati.com/rpc/ping
http://api.feedster.com/ping

PODCASTING

We'll discuss other people's podcasts in detail in the "Get Played and Heard" chapter (including how to get your music played on them). In this section, we want to explain podcasting as a method to broadcast to your fan network.

Although every band should have a blog, starting a podcast is optional. Creating and recording a podcast episode is more time-consuming than writing a blog entry. That said, if anyone knows how to produce one, it's musicians, since most of us are familiar with recording. You may want to reserve this method for special occasions such as while touring (there's always a lot of time to kill while traveling in the van) or as a lead-up to special events.

You may want to create one of two general types of podcasts. In a talk-radio-style podcast you can talk about what's going on behind the scenes with your band or cover other topics that interest you—while interspersing your music throughout. In a music-only podcast, you simply feature music you're willing to share. You can podcast live performances, alternative mixes, or demos. For TheSongOfTheDay.com, we did both types, a daily music-only podcast featuring a new song, and a weekly talk podcast where we discussed the songs we'd created that week—that is, until work and time pressures led us to drop the weekly podcast since the editing took so much time. George Hrab combines both talk and music in his *Geologic Podcast* (http://geologicpodcast.com), often adding new songs in between sketches and talk segments. For some musicians, podcasting can lead to entirely different projects, such as Grant Baciocco of the Throwing Toasters, who has gone on to produce the multiple-award-winning podcast *The Radio Adventures of Dr. Floyd* (http://www.doctorfloyd.com).

Like blogs, podcasts should be RSS-enabled. Without RSS, you're merely posting an MP3 file to your site for download. Delivering music to your fans via RSS allows those who subscribe to get the latest episode downloaded automatically to their computer or MP3 device. Every time they see a new episode, they will think of your band.

If you create a podcast, all the rules of branding still apply. Include an opening theme (or an abbreviated version of one of your signature songs) and an outro to end each episode. The outro should state what the listener just listened to, provide your Web-site address, and state any copyright or Creative Commons information.

Creating your own podcast goes beyond the scope of the *Guide*, but several good books can walk you through the steps and show you the techniques of great podcasters.

RECOMMENDED PODCASTING BOOKS AND RESOURCES

If you want more information about podcasts, including how best to start your own, we recommend the following:

- *Podcasting for Dummies* by Tee Morris and Evo Terra
- *Podcasting Bible* by Mitch Ratcliffe and Steve Mack
- *Tricks of the Podcasting Masters* by Rob Walch and Mur Lafferty

• *Expert Podcasting Practices for Dummies* by Tee Morris, Evo Terra, and Ryan Williams

Additionally, podcast411.com is an excellent Web resource (and podcast!), run by Rob Walch, that educates people about podcasting as well as interviews other notable podcasters for insights.

Music Podcast Techniques for Musicians

Although we recommend other books to learn the intricacies of podcasting, we've learned a few things ourselves by applying our musician instincts to the medium. Some of these techniques will be at odds with what the podcasting books suggest, but they will result in higher-quality audio that will help your podcast stand out:

• *Apply your mixing and mastering skills.* Treat it just like any song. Even the simple use of EQ and compression on all of your voice tracks will set you apart from most every other podcast. Most podcasters, who have little other audio experience, tend to neglect sound quality.

• *Use WAV.* When you create the sections of your podcast (songs, talk, sound effects, etc.), work with them in WAV format. Once you've assembled the entire podcast as a WAV, mix it down, compressing and limiting for clarity and punch. *Then* encode the WAV into MP3 format.

• *Sound encode for high quality.* Apply the sound-encoding techniques from the previous chapter: encode your podcast at 128K. If your bitrate is too low, your audience will think that the podcast *and your songs contained within it* were recorded poorly. We found most podcasting books suggest bitrates as low as 96K or even 56K. This is only appropriate for talk-only podcasts. Don't do this to your music.

• *Respect your audience's time, and edit.* Trim your podcasts mercilessly. Take out silences, awkward moments, or boring ones.

• *Caffeinate beforehand.* If you talk during your podcasts, make sure that whoever is speaking does so with energy and gusto. Keep your audience engaged with what you're saying.

- **_Emulate radio shows and podcasts you enjoy._** There are good reasons you enjoy listening to what you do. Beyond the content, the best shows usually sound great, pace well, don't drag, and have plenty of energy. Copy that.

- **_Syndicate your podcast._** Don't just post the MP3 file to your Web site for people to download. Do it the way any podcster would and syndicate it automatically using one of the syndication sites such as Liberated Syndication (libsyn.com), PodPress (podpress.org), or others suggested by the recommended podcasting books.

MEDIA MANAGEMENT SITES

Media management sites host your videos, audio, photos, and other media and let you share them with the world. These external sites usually allow visitors to make comments and receive automatic updates whenever you add new media. The best media sites allow you to freely embed the media you post within your own Web site. This gives you powerful options for handling bandwidth-eating media and saving you money with your Web host. In this section, we'll cover each type of media-sharing site and how you can use it to expand your Web presence and leverage their services for your band's benefit.

Photo-Sharing Sites

If you're taking a lot of pictures of the group, you may want to use photo-sharing sites that specialize in displaying your photos on the Web, such as Flickr (flickr.com), Photobucket (photobucket.com), and Webshots (webshots.com). These sites vary in functionality, but they can help you group your photos into albums, present them on your Web site, and handle time-consuming details such as resizing to create thumbnail images without affecting the original files.

Photo-sharing sites are generally easy to use and have nifty features. You can take advantage of their storage and bandwidth and save yourself the trouble of installing and managing photo-gallery software on your own Web site. Most, however, begin charging money for additional storage space or advanced features such as when you reach a photo or photo album threshold limit.

Video-Sharing Sites

If your band creates videos, they can be a major part of your Web presence. The enormous traffic generated by video sites such as YouTube is reminiscent of the initial rush that occurred when people realized they could get music downloaded directly to their computer. The same technological advances that made it so easy to record music at home has had the same effect for video. Because of this, the days when musicians were to be heard but not seen are long gone.

Even though video is better at getting a listener's attention, it has shortcomings. For one thing, video has a lower replay value. People are more willing to watch a video they've never seen than to listen to a song they've never heard, but if they like the music, they will listen to that song over and over. Videos are lucky to get watched more than once. The goal is to use the video to introduce people not just to the song in the music video, but also to lure people to your Web site so they'll discover what else you offer. It's critical to brand your video so that they can find out more about you. This is especially true since you can never be sure where your video is embedded on the Web.

Most music videos follow the MTV standard by featuring a brief flash of credits (band name, song title, director, etc.) in the lower corner of the screen. But you don't have to follow this standard. We begin our videos with a splash screen featuring our logo, band name, and the title of the song. We also end it with quick, branded credits to thank everyone who participated in making it. You can also add a "bug," which is a small logo that sits in the corner of the screen throughout the video. TV stations use bugs so viewers are reminded what channel they're watching, and you can use the same technique with your logo or mascot. Keep in mind, however, that video sites often have their own bug, so make sure to place yours in another part of the image, otherwise it will be covered up.

Video sites use compression, which can affect the quality of the video and reflect poorly on your band. To get the best-quality video, the format that you choose to upload is critical, as is the height and width. All of these affect the final presentation, sometimes drastically. Since these sites compress video in different ways, you should refer to them to see what they suggest for best results. You can also go to IndieBandSurvivalGuide.com, where we have information on the best formats and techniques for uploading music videos to these services.

An additional disadvantage is that these services include ads. Worse, these embeddable players often suggest other videos within the player itself. YouTube's player, for instance, displays related videos after yours is done playing. These are clickable and can send your hard-earned visitor to YouTube to watch other videos. This doesn't help keep your visitors on your own Web site, which is preferred.

Be aware that if you upload a video with any copyrighted content that you do not own (including a cover song), you need permission. If you do this at a video site, such as YouTube, you will be violating the user agreement, and should they find out, your account might be suspended. Even if you host the video at your Web site, you are still at risk for infringement. For more information, see the "Your Rights" chapter.

Audio-Sharing Sites

Audio-sharing sites have a mixed history. They range from the success of the early incarnation of MP3.com to outright scams that do nothing more than try to take a musician's music as well as his or her money. Because of this checkered history, you should take particular care to read the agreements of all audio-sharing sites you sign up with. Do not risk losing the rights to your music.

Nevertheless, some audio sites are worth working with. For example, Last.fm (last.fm) allows users to share a list of what they play on their computer. If users search on your band name, they will find other users that have played your music, as well as be given suggestions about similar groups to look for. If you fill in a band profile, your band logo will get associated with your page. We will talk about these sites in detail in the "Get Played and Heard" chapter.

SOCIAL BOOKMARKING SITES

Managing bookmarks nowadays is a big job, and it's not surprising that a lot of sites have grown up around tracking and filtering links. Some merely keep track of your own bookmarks, but the better ones are geared toward sharing bookmarks with the community, using "the wisdom of the masses" to help filter links for quality and context. You can set up accounts on all of these types of sites as they're free, easy to use, and might help drive traffic to your Web site.

There are two types of social bookmarking sites: nonvoting and voting.

Nonvoting Sites

By far, the most popular nonvoting social bookmarking sites are Del.icio. us (del.icio.us) and Ma.gnolia (ma.gnolia.com). Both sites allow you to enter your favorite bookmarks and tag them with one-word descriptions. Links can have multiple tags. Since these links are social, if other people post the same link, you'll see how many others have bookmarked the site, who they are, and how they tagged the site. We recommend signing up for an account at both of these sites.

You can also use these sites to track how many people are bookmarking *your* Web site and who they are. Since most people's links are public, you can find out interesting information about your fans' personalities and tastes in music by looking at the other links that they post. Finally, you can also use these sites to search on terms such as *music, indie band,* or others to find useful links or Web tools.

Voting Sites

Vote-based social bookmarking sites let their user communities decide which links are worthwhile. Anyone who registers can post new links. Then it's up to the other users to decide whether to vote for them. The links with the most votes make it to the "most popular" pages of these sites, which subsequently get a lot of traffic.

Not everyone who uses these sites votes. Voting is not a requirement. In fact, the links that make it to the top pages of these sites often get far more visits than the number of votes would suggest. Only those who care enough to do so will add their votes, and even fewer will add comments. But if your Web site ever makes it to the front page, it'll generate a lot of traffic.

These voting-based social bookmarking sites usually have a music category as well as a video category. If you write a song with a great hook or one that ties in somehow to a current event or Web meme, the community may take notice and vote on your page. The same goes for a compelling video. The best part is these sites generate quality hits—visitors tend to be people genuinely looking for music to listen to and music videos to watch. Also, these sites allow comments on every link, so read them for some unvarnished opinions about your music, video, or site. The largest and most active vote-based social bookmarking sites are Digg (digg.com) and Reddit (reddit.com).

A special class of voting sites will install a voting toolbar in your browser. These sites function like voting social bookmarking sites with the convenience of voting buttons at the top of every page, as well as an additional button that will take the user to a randomly chosen, highly rated link. The more popular the link, the more likely that the toolbar will send users there. These toolbar sites also allow users to comment on the links, although users can't read those comments until after they've visited the recommended site. The comments posted generally are as honest as any you'll see about your music, video, or site.

The most popular toolbar-based site is StumbleUpon (Stumbleupon.com). Their toolbar is easy to install and use. We suggest that you give it a try before submitting your site, to get a feel for it. It can represent a lot of traffic, so we believe that it's well worth your time to explore this tool. To our pleasant surprise, we ended up getting more than twenty thousand visitors to TheSongOfTheDay.com this way shortly after we launched the site, after a fan submitted it to StumbleUpon. Keep in mind, however, that such random visitors generally check out the link and then leave. It takes a lot to get them to stick around at your site rather than head to the next random link. However, when you generate these types of numbers, at least some will end up sticking, happy to have discovered your band.

We recommend creating an account on all of these sites so you can post links to your songs, sites, or videos. They are easy to use to drive new visitors to your site. Here are a few methods to encourage people to vote on your links:

- **Salt and compel.** Make the subject of your submission compelling, intriguing, risqué, outrageous. Ideally, it should pose a question. The subject line of the links are clickable, so if the subject doesn't pique people's curiosity, no one will click on the link, let alone vote for it.

- *Keep it short.* Make sure your description is short and to the point. Long descriptions are often ignored.

- *Get support.* Have a few friends vote on the link when it first appears. This will give it some initial momentum. Most of these sites will drive any recently voted link to the top of the "new links" pages.

Actually, posting links at these sites works best if they appear not to be from your band. Of course, it's great when your fans spontaneously promote links on your behalf, but sometimes it helps to plant the seed and see if it grows. In this case, you will want to create an anonymous, unbranded account for yourself so you look like a regular user.

Social Bookmarking Sites and Web Statistics

Once you start posting your links on these sites, monitor your Web statistics daily to keep track of how your campaigns are doing. Social bookmarking sites should appear as "referrers" in your stats. You'll be able to tell how many people each particular site sent. Using your clickpath tracking program, you'll see when these people arrived and how many ventured on and explored your site. (See the previous chapter for more information on Web statistics.) This information will help you tailor your efforts in future campaigns for maximum effect.

WIKIPEDIA

Wikipedia is a massive, collaborative encyclopedia that anyone can edit. Surprisingly, even though anyone can change it, the site has developed a large and dedicated community of editors who make it their business to uphold standards of quality and consistency.

Since Wikipedia is an electronic encyclopedia created by the masses, it covers far more topics than any traditional encyclopedia could. One such area is popular culture. Wikipedia has entries on many bands. Since Wikipedia entries tend to get high page ranks in search engines, these entries are valuable. Our Wikipedia entry is a nice contributor to traffic for our Web site.

Some things many people don't realize about Wikipedia include:

1. It's an encyclopedia, not a promotional tool. The Wikipedia community frowns on autobiographical entries and especially on blatant self-promotion.

2. The Wikipedia community will question any entry that seems insignificant or doesn't live up to its encyclopedic standards: fact-based, no opinions, plenty of citations. Many entries about indie bands are routinely removed if they fail these tests.

3. If a Wikipedia entry is created about your band, you don't own it. In fact, your own input about your entry, either in edits you make or on the discussion page that accompanies your entry, will tend to work *against* you. We advise you to not take part, or to at least avoid advertising that you're with the band.

Given this, your best bet in getting an entry on Wikipedia is to wait until you have a proven following or until you've done something significant and newsworthy. Wikipedia depends on outside sources for verifying the material, so press and media coverage of your band will help a great deal.

Ideally, a fan will spontaneously create your band's entry for you. Once you get an entry, you will want to check it periodically to make sure facts and links are correct. Since it's an encyclopedia, keep in mind that anything you add should be factual. Don't insert opinions or, worse, upcoming plans and events. This is not a Web-presence site to brand or use as a promotional tool.

CONVERSING

Now that we've covered the technologies that will allow you to broadcast to your fans, it's time to move on to those that allow two-way communication, and how to use them effectively. As with broadcast technologies, many of these should be integrated into your Web site.

SOCIAL NETWORKING SITES

Few new technologies have affected bands more than social networking sites. Tens of thousands of bands have signed up for them to showcase their music, and many bands use them in place of an actual Web site (which, as we've said, isn't a good idea).

Although we always recommend a real Web site of your own, these sites should still be a part of your Web presence. Most are free, and some are the most visited Web sites on the Internet. Some are designed around individuals, while others allow groups and bands to create profiles, as MySpace does. As with all Web-presence sites, if you register your band, your profile should be properly branded.

Also, the possibilities of these social networking sites to help you find and connect with other people who might enjoy your music are nearly endless. Members are organized in a variety of ways, among them interests, personal traits, and geographic location, with most of the information made public. Targeting the right people or groups can help create awareness of your band, promote word-of-mouth, and ultimately lead to new fans. For example, becoming an active member of a group based on a band that sounds similar to yours can expose your music to possible new fans. Instead of trying to find people who might like your music, you can bring your music to them. Groups tend to have a common message board—such as the Facebook "wall"—that encourages members to broadcast information, links, and recommendations to the entire group. Of course, this is also true for groups centered around a particular interest that your music touches on or even your band's geographic location.

Social networking sites have evolved to include applications that allow members to interact in interesting ways. For example, some sites allow the sharing of music playlists or jukeboxes. Having your fans post your music in their playlists can lead to exposure of your band to their friends. Some applications, such as Nimbit's Online Merch Table, are set up to sell songs as well (nimbit.com). Fans can embed these applications and essentially act as storefronts for your music.

But it goes beyond using these sites to broadcast your music or message. As we mentioned in the "Your Network" chapter, you should interact with your fans and potential new fans using these tools. Countless applications allow you to interact with your network, and new ones are being created all the time. Listing all the useful applications goes beyond the scope of this book, but be sure to take advantage of the applications that you find useful to promote your band.

MYSPACE.COM

In the previous chapter we went into depth about why your MySpace page shouldn't be your sole site. However, the attraction of MySpace is simple to understand. Within ten minutes, a band can have a blog, photo album, music player, show calendar, dedicated e-mail address, and more. Like most social networking sites, MySpace also connects bands directly with fans via its "Friends" feature.

The most effective way to use MySpace is to make your page a multimedia extravaganza. Your content has to compete with all the flashy advertising surrounding it. To stand out, your content needs to be more eye-catching than the ads. Your MySpace front page is essentially the only page; visitors are unlikely to visit your blog and photos unless they know you.

Although we don't recommend having your music play automatically when visitors arrive at your band Web site, at MySpace, autoplay is expected. Since MySpace visitors may not hang around for long, set your page to play your strongest song first. This is a setting in your profile, and we'll talk about this and other recommended profile settings below.

In addition to the music, you should embed any videos you've made, as well as any arresting images you've created to advertise your latest projects, albums, or shows. Have these link to your Web site where possible. If there's something you want your MySpace visitors to know, make sure it's in big letters and link it to your own site.

Setting Up a MySpace Account

When you sign up for MySpace, make sure to create a "music artist" account. The music artist account will get you the music player and a few other music features that you'll want.

You might wonder how other users have changed the look of their profile, the background, and the colors of text and links. The secret lies in MySpace's bio page. Here, they allow you to embed HTML code, which is extremely useful for branding purposes. Doing so is not as difficult as it seems, thanks to tools that help you create the profile look you want. Numerous solutions allow you to format your MySpace page. We recommend performing a search for "MySpace profile editors" to find the one that's best for you because the latest ones change often.

We don't recommend putting your actual band bio under "The Bio." Instead, you should fill this space with embedded videos, pictures, digital posters, and links to your other sites. Again, you don't have much time to get visitors interested, and your best bet is to give them a lot of multimedia to look at and click on. The Bio is one of the only places where you have some flexibility to make the page look the way you want it to so as to engage visitors.

Note that the Bio field will allow embed tags (such as for placing You-Tube videos), but not script tags, which can limit what you can do with your MySpace page.

RECOMMENDED SETTINGS FOR MYSPACE PROFILES AND SONGS

Thanks to spam, we recommend that you use the following settings in your MySpace profile to block people from posting spam to your comments area on your page. If you don't do this, your band's MySpace page might become even more of an ad space.

Privacy Settings (Under "Account Settings, Change Account Settings")

- Check the box for "Comments—approve before posting" so that no one can can post anything on your own MySpace page without your approval.

- Block event invites from "Users (who are not added to my friends)," "Bands (who are not added to my friends)," "Filmmakers (who are not added to my friends)," and "Comedians (who are not added to my friends)." ◆

What Friends Are For (On MySpace)

The "Friends" feature allows fans to be listed on your friends list and comment publicly on your page. Typically bands wantonly accept any friend request that comes their way, since the common assumption is, the more friends, the more popular you are. While we don't go out of our way to do friend campaigns, some bands do. Keep in mind that your friends can post comments on your main page, blog, and photos, so if someone is causing problems, you might need to remove him or her later. Just as your friends can post to your MySpace page, you can broadcast announcements to them individually or as a group.

Music on MySpace

MySpace limits the number of songs you can load in their player, so we suggest doing the following to make the best of what they offer:

- **Upload your best songs.** Put your strongest one first. And don't set the player to random. You don't get a second chance to make a first impression.

- **Autoplay.** Set the first song to play automatically, since that is customary at MySpace.

- **Allow embedding.** We highly recommend allowing users to add your songs to their profiles. If they want to highlight your music, you should let them. If you do this, be advised that, if you later take these songs down, you will break these links.

- **Use album art.** Make sure to upload album images for all songs that you upload so that they will display in the MySpace player.

Although MySpace allows you to block users from downloading your music, know that it is still possible to do this. Some Web sites and techniques will allow users to download and save any MP3 on MySpace.

MESSAGE BOARDS

Also called forums, bulletin boards, or discussion boards, message boards allow users to discuss certain topics in an organized and, usually, open way. Most message boards require users to register before being able to post. This generally includes an avatar, but may require more branding features as well. We'll discuss both message boards you will create for your own site and external message boards you will frequent.

Branding Suggestions

As with all Web-presence sites your band registers with, you should brand your identity. If you have multiple band members registering at the same board, you should decide whether to do so individually or to pool your exposure. If necessary, go back to your Brand Toolbox and create individually branded profiles that associate each member with your band. Use signature lines that include your Web site and tagline, since each post you make is an opportunity to promote.

Message Board for Your Band

One of the best ways to interact with your fans is to provide a message board where they can discuss your band. But a message board is only a good idea once you've cultivated enough fans to sustain it. While Jonathan Coulton and Brad Sucks have active message boards, they've spent time accumulating the necessary fans first.

Nothing's lonelier than a message board with no posts. People tend to assume that low message-board turnout means you don't have many fans, even if that's not the case. As a general rule, most read, very few post. It takes a large registered base to get any significant amount of traffic and postings. Therefore, you should create a message board only if you are really popular and want to use it as another method of keeping fans on your site.

Although having a message board provides a forum to converse with your fans, that's only one side of it. A message board also gives your fans an opportunity to network with one another. They're there to talk to you, but also to interact with others who share their taste in music. Your band is the common denominator. Interaction between your fans only strengthens the network and ties them closer to you. This works best when it evolves naturally, when the creation of a message board is driven by your fan network rather than created by you in the hopes of it sustaining itself. We recommend phpBB (phpbb.org) or bbPress (bbpress.org).

External Message Boards

Message boards dedicated to musicians are great places to seek advice, solve problems, or keep up on the latest trends within the music industry.

We belong to a few of these message boards and have learned a great deal over the years, been warned about certain scams and services, and shared some of our own insights with others.

As we noted in the "Your Network" chapter, great things can happen when musicians work together. One of the most fascinating and positive uses of message boards we've seen is musicians booking gigs for and with one another. Often bands will play in cities they're touring by simply asking other bands to let them open and creating a double bill. This type of cooperation between musicians has only been possible since the advent of the Internet, and we suspect there will be more. And there should be.

Know your audience. The musicians who frequent musician message boards will probably not be your fans. Our recommendation is to avoid promoting your music to other musicians in these venues.

We normally frequent IndieBandSurvivalGuide.com, Just Plain Folks (jpfolks.com), and CD Baby (cdbaby.org).

VIRTUAL WORLDS

As virtual environments improve, the representation of a person in these systems has evolved from crude bitmaps into detailed, lifelike figures, or avatars. Functionality for building, exploring, and communicating within these worlds has grown increasingly complex and powerful.

There are two types of virtual worlds: game-based systems and social interaction systems. While game-based systems such as *World of Warcraft* have millions of users, they are usually not good places for promoting your band (although you can certainly promote on the many message boards and on the many Web sites discussing the games). On the other hand, social interaction systems such as Second Life (www.secondlife. com) and There.com have created many opportunities for musicians to meet and interact with their fans, and to make new ones. Since you're a global musician now, meeting, connecting, and conversing with your all your fans worldwide is difficult. Virtual worlds offer one more solution to this problem.

We are at the cusp of fascinating new possibilities—an entirely new way for people to meet and interact using the Internet. These virtual worlds are still evolving, but because of the large numbers of people involved, developments have been occurring quickly, and in surprising ways. While we're going to briefly cover what has been done with these worlds to date, if you are computer-savvy, you should consider keeping updated about these environments and the possibilities that they represent by following some of the blogs devoted to the subject.

Second Life

Second Life has become an Internet phenomenon. One of the engines spurring its growth is that Linden Lab, its creator, decided to allow users to own the intellectual property rights of anything they created within the world. This means anything users create can be sold by the users for profit. This simple idea has given birth to a vibrant economy. Second Life has its own currency, the Linden Dollar, which can be exchanged into real-world currency. Some people have made large sums of real money selling virtual objects, providing virtual services, or selling virtual real estate in Second Life.

Second Life users, or residents as they are called, are represented as three-dimensional animated avatars that can be completely customized. It takes time and technical artistry to create a realistic avatar and other objects in this virtual world, but thanks to Linden Lab's decision to give users the right to sell their creations, many residents are happy to sell their creations to you for the right price.

Second Life mirrors real life. There is no game, per se. Rather, living your virtual life is about interaction, creation, and site-seeing. Business and entertainment. As a result, it should come as no surprise that there's a place here for music and musicians. Musicians have created avatars of themselves, set up stores to sell their music, and promoted themselves within this world by putting up virtual posters on virtual walls of virtual buildings. Events such as virtual CD releases and signings are frequent.

Some bands even perform music "live" in this virtual environment—inviting their Second Life fans to meet them at a certain time and place and putting on a show. Hundreds of concerts have occurred there, including performances by Suzanne Vega and Jay Z. Virtual festivals such as Woodstock Second Life have taken place as well.

To perform in Second Life, you can either stream your music (live or prerecorded) while your avatars "play" their virtual instruments, according to prescripted motions, or stream video and audio feeds of your band onto "television screens" that other avatars can watch in-game. Both of these methods use streaming-media servers to feed audio or video from your computer into the virtual world.

As technology and functionality improve in Second Life and other virtual-world platforms, other methods of in-game performance will likely be developed. Linden Lab suggests that anyone interested in running a Second Life concert should join the Live Music Enthusiasts Group that exists in-game. The two streaming services that work in-game in Second Life are SHOUTcast (shoutcast.com) and Icecast (icecast.org).

MICROBLOGGING

While blogging is primarily a broadcast method of communication, its little brother, microblogging, encourages conversation. Microblog sites allow you to post short messages about what's on your mind or what you're doing at that moment. In general, these posts are public and shared with all users on a timeline (though these services usually allow you to keep posts private as well). Microblogs also have a "friend" function that allows you to specifically follow the posts of others and, conversely, allows them to follow you.

This public and friend functionality makes this a great way for bands to keep in touch with others, promote themselves and their projects, share ideas and links with friends, and otherwise personalize their band and stay connected to their fans. But it shouldn't be reserved just for your fans. We often follow the microblogs of all our friends and acquaintances within our skill and opportunity networks as well, just to see what they're up to and what they think is important. In our case, we've used this to find new opportunities for our music, because some of our friends are podcasters, artists, musicians, or other bright and creative people.

To ensure short posts, microblogging tools restrict the number of characters you can write. For example, one of the more popular microblogging sites, Twitter.com, restricts its users to posts of 140 characters, which is the maximum length of a cell phone text message. This encourages users to post from their phones wherever they go.

As an example, if you're interested in knowing what *we're* doing at this very moment, it's as simple as checking out twitter.com/beatnik turtle. We've also embedded our latest Twitter posts, or "tweets," on the front page of BeatnikTurtle.com. We found that having this tool to help our networks stay up-to-date on what we're doing (recording, writing songs, working on the Web site, heading to gigs) humanizes us and reminds everyone that we're real people. The more your fans see you working on your band and music, the more likely they are to assist, advise, and support you (through sales or donations), since they know how hard you're working and how seriously you take the endeavor.

Beyond personalizing our band, we've used Twitter to reach out for assistance. For example, we once wanted to get in touch with the music-planning committee for a convention at which we wanted to perform. We knew that some of the people who followed our posts were associated with that convention, so we posted our query on Twitter. Within minutes, they put us directly in touch.

We've also found a creative way of using Twitter beyond its networking capabilities. Reading our friends' posts, it occurred to us that a lot of the more witty tweets might make great inspiration for songs. We soon started writing a few "TwitterSongs," all appropriately shorter than 140 seconds, and posting them to TheSongOfTheDay.com.

For example, we wrote a song called "I Am My Mom and Dad's Tech Support," loosely based on a posted lament by one of our friends. Naturally, once a TwitterSong song was posted, we'd tweet about it and include a link to the file. Many times the posters who'd inspired the songs would get a kick out of them and blog about them on their own sites. The next thing we knew, we'd get more friend requests, many people hoping their own tweets would inspire the next TwitterSong.

As with all your Web-presence tools, you'll need to properly brand your account. The advantage to microblogging is that it keeps you and your music in front of people daily, even hourly. In many ways we find this constant, bite-size way of keeping everyone updated on our band is less time-consuming and more useful than newsletters. Of course, not everyone cares for microblogs, so it's simply one more way to present your band to the world.

MICROBLOG SITES

Microblogging sites are not mutually exclusive and all vary in functionality. We encourage you to check out these popular ones:

- Twitter (www.twitter.com)

- Jaiku (www.jaiku.com)

- Tumblr (www.tumblr.com)

- Pownce (www.pownce.com)

- Utterz (www.utterz.com) Note: The others here are text-based; Utterz is audio-based. ♥

SURVEY SITES

Occasionally, you may want to survey your fans. This can provide insight into who's listening, help you assess how you're doing, and suggest goals for your band.

Questions you may want to ask include:

- What are the demographics?

- How did you hear about us?

- What other bands and musicians do you enjoy?

- Where are you located?

- What's one thing you would change about our Web site?

- If we came to your town, would you attend a show?

- Do you have any ideas to help us spread the word?

- Do you have any other suggestions for us?

Some blogs offer built-in polling. Additionally, some sites allow you to create surveys, embed them on your site, and interpret the data. To encourage people to take the poll, we suggest offering something for participation, such as a free song, remix, or live recording.

If you don't mind your fans being advertised to, then some free survey sites include Free Online Surveys (freeonlinesurveys.com), Survey Methods (surveymethods.com), and Mister Poll (misterpoll.com). If you want to tailor the look and feel of the survey for your fans, then you may wish to use the pay sites SurveyMonkey (surveymonkey.com) or Zoomerang (zoomerang.com).

COLLABORATING

The Web provides some wonderful and exciting tools to collaborate not only with your skill, opportunity, and fan networks, but also with the other members of your band.

E-MAIL

If you're anything like us, whenever you're not rehearsing, meeting, recording, or touring, you take the conversation online. Discussing the band and its business over e-mail helps keep your band in sync. While band meetings are where you might decide on larger goals, e-mail is where you will divide up the tasks, discuss strategies, or plan out the details of the next gig, rehearsal, or recording session. If you do a lot of talking with your band over e-mail, we recommend using a listserv. A listserv is a single e-mail address that will send copies of each e-mail to all members on the list.

The benefits of a listserv include:

- *It's convenient.* If you want to write everyone in your band, you no longer have to add them to the To: field manually.

- *It's inclusive.* E-mailing the listserv address automatically e-mails everyone on the list once you hit *Send*. No band members are accidentally left out.

- *It keeps a history.* All the conversations and threads on the listserv are archived. If a great idea is sent to the list, it's always retrievable.

- *It's easy to add and remove members.* Most listserv programs are simple to administer.

We've relied on an open-source listserv called Mailman (gnu.org/soft ware/mailman/) for years since we're a large band with members living and working at different locations in the city. It became even more important as we worked on TheSongOfTheDay.com, allowing us to add other musicians around the country with whom we wanted to create and record. To keep things simple, we created a new list for that purpose.

Ideally, your Web host should provide such functionality. If not, you can use free solutions such as Yahoo! Groups, Google Groups, or others. These provide an e-mail solution that works essentially like a listserv, as well as providing file-sharing and calendar-sharing features that can come in handy as well.

GOOGLE APPLICATIONS

Like Yahoo!, Google offers many free Web-based services: word processing, spreadsheets, calendars, and more. And they're all designed for collaboration. Unlike software installed on a band member's computer, they're available 24/7, anytime any member has access to the Internet. When we were busy creating, mixing, mastering, tagging, and uploading songs for TheSongOfTheDay.com, we relied on Google's spreadsheets to help our band collectively organize and manage the project. Drafts of press releases were created in their word processor and shared with other members to review and edit. Using these tools helped us manage projects that would have been much more troublesome over phone and e-mail.

SKYPE

Skype is a free program and service that basically transforms your computer into a phone. But unlike a regular telephone, Skype is a robust communication tool with digital clarity that can be used to collaborate in surprising ways. We've used it for most of the interviews we've done with podcasters. It's easy to record Skype audio and import it directly into their episodes. We've also used it to demo music to one another, talk through songs or projects with the band, and even—when the songs call for it—record vocals (giving a new definition to "phoning it in").

Skype goes beyond just audio. Skype's chat and file-transfer features have been helpful as well. Often, we'll Skype each other from our respective homes to collaborate on the bands' Web sites, press materials, or even this book, for hours on end. Being able to share files, cut and paste text, throw hyperlinks to one another, and set up a quick video chat as we're talking things out is extremely helpful.

INVITATION SOFTWARE

Any band that plays live knows that some people always promise to come to a gig only to be no-shows. When you absolutely need a minimum number of people to show up at an important performance, use invitation software to gauge the numbers. Formally requesting people's presence this way often raises the stakes and encourages those who commit to actually come to the show.

The most popular invitation site is Evite (evite.com). It's easy to set up an event, design the invitations, and send them out to a large list of people. Don't settle on the invitation templates they suggest; brand your Evite. Evite is ubiquitous, so most spam filters don't block it. Keep in mind, however, that Evite can make the e-mail addresses of your invitees visible to all. This means that, if you're using your mailing list (rather than making a list of people you know personally), you may be in violation of your privacy policy. The way around this is to either restrict your Evites to people you know personally, or to revise your privacy policy to include the use of Evite and similar services.

We've never used Evite to announce shows to our mailing list. Instead, we've found it useful for planning some of the smaller events we've done, including band events such as video shoots. Other bands we know have used it to spark interest in a particular show. Naturally, this technique should be reserved only for your most important events. If you abuse this method, it will probably stop working for you.

MUSIC COLLABORATION SITES

Some musicians—even some who have never met in person—use the Web to collaborate and create music by trading WAV files with one another to build songs. For instance, one might record a bass line and allow others to layer in the drums or vocals. We'll talk more about music collaboration sites in the next chapter, "Your Albums and Merchandise."

INDIEBANDSURVIVALGUIDE.COM

Our personal favorite music collaboration site is of course IndieBandSurvivalGuide.com. Think of it as the musician's back office. While this book can explain the how's, why's, and what-to-do's, IndieBandSurvivalGuide.com can show you where to go and who to talk to. Not only does it contain all the links mentioned in this book, it's an open, Web 2.0 community where you can keep up-to-date on all the useful resources, services, and tools that can help you get your music out there and win fans. Most important, it's where you'll find other motivated musicians such as yourself to network with.

CHAPTER 6

YOUR ALBUMS AND MERCHANDISE

BEFORE YOU need to worry about getting heard, getting publicity, and getting distributed, you'll need to record some music, possibly press an album, and create merchandise, so that you can take advantage of all the attention you'll get. In this chapter, we'll cover how to record music, how to replicate CDs, and how to create and sell merchandise.

RECORDING AND MASTERING

Unless you plan on solely playing live, you're going to eventually be recording some of your music. Recording is, of course, a broad topic that fills many books, with technology that is mutating rapidly, with new tools and techniques appearing all the time. The *Guide* will cover the recording issues you'll have to deal with no matter what techniques you're using.

For example, we'll cover whether you should record yourself or hire others to record you in a studio. We'll tell you how to minimize recording time and keep costs down. We'll also talk about the recording process in general, because most detailed recording books gloss over this topic. Finally, we're going to talk about mastering, which is perhaps the most misunderstood part of recording.

IT'S THE SOURCE THAT MATTERS

John Lisiecki, a recording engineer for Chicago's Millennium Park with years of experience recording everything from rock bands to symphony orchestras, says that most musicians forget that it's the source that matters. This may seem obvious, but we can't stress it enough: no amount of recording technology will help you if the source isn't good. This includes the following:

- **The songs.** Ever hear a great song recorded by a punk band using a tape recorder in their garage? The music is king, and the sound quality is just a detail. Our advice is to write and record a lot of songs to give your creative process momentum. Your quality will rise with the quantity.

- **The musicians.** Your band members' sense of rhythm, style, and musicianship will show through instantly when you record. If you're having trouble, just remember this rule of thumb: "In time and in tune." Anything that at least meets this standard will help make a decent song. That isn't to say that an out-of-tune song with bad timing won't be charming sometimes, but it certainly doesn't help.

- **The instruments.** The quality of your musical instruments doesn't tend to matter as much for live performances as it does on a recording. Pay special attention to the maintenance of your instruments before recording: replace strings, reeds, and the like as necessary, use top-quality wires, and make sure to lock down anything on your instruments that might make extraneous noise. For drums, pay attention to the tuning of the drums and consider using fresh heads at the start of a big session.

If you want to do some reading on recording yourself, we suggest *The S.M.A.R.T. Guide to Mixing and Mastering Audio Recordings* by Bill Gibson or *The Mixing Engineer's Handbook* by Bobby Owsinski.

HOME STUDIO RECORDING VS. PROFESSIONAL STUDIO RECORDING

The first decision regarding recording is whether to do it yourself or hire a professional studio and engineer. Quality sound-recording equipment and software have gotten inexpensive enough that a home studio is in almost every single band's reach. In fact, by the time you've paid the average professional studio to record just one album, you've probably spent the equivalent of a very capable studio setup for your house, one where you could have recorded as many songs as you'd ever want.

We will go over the pros and cons of each option below.

Home Recording

Setting up a home studio can be quite inexpensive if you just want to try recording yourself. You can get a decent-quality microphone for under

HOME STUDIO RECORDING VS. PROFESSIONAL STUDIO RECORDING

	Home Studio	Professional Studio
Cost	Greater initial outlay, but cheap to maintain thereafter.	Can pay by the hour to avoid an initial outlay, but you must pay each time you want to record.
Time	No time pressure for recording sessions, so you have time to write music on the fly and be creative. But you must spend time learning the software and recording techniques.	Time pressure for each session because you are "on the meter," but professional engineers usually do it right the first time, and you can leverage their expertise.
Convenience and creativity	You can make recording part of your creativity for ultimate flexibility. You can also work on projects whenever you want.	You can focus on the music, rather than worry about recording it.

$200. Headphones are cheap, and the recording software Audacity (audacity.sourceforge.net) is free and available for all operating systems. On Apple systems, GarageBand is a capable recording solution, perfect for getting your feet wet. You can also get a stand-alone digital-recording device if you don't have a computer or if your existing computer doesn't have the necessary horsepower for multitrack recording.

Bands that have their own studios tend to be more prolific because they can do it all "in-house." This can be an advantage for bands, because coming out with new music regularly keeps your fans engaged with you. Other advantages include:

- Producing and releasing new music whenever you feel a creative spark

- Easily creating remixes of your music

- Producing different versions of your songs, including instrumentals, loops, and samples that can be used for other purposes such as podcasts, promos, and ringtones

- Recording and editing professional-quality podcasts

- Working on audio tracks for film and video projects

- Recording live versions of your music, if you have a portable recording solution, to provide new content for your Web site

We have four different band members with studios of their own. We trade source files between members so we can work on our music in more than one location, dividing up the workload and speeding up our output.

If you decide to record music yourself but don't have experience, we recommend reading some books on the subject so you can get the best sound. At the least, you'll want to learn basic recording concepts such as microphone placement, compression, EQ, and using other audio effects.

Building a Home Studio

When it comes to setting up a home studio, Lisiecki advises, "It's the ends that matter. Everything else is a religious question." His advice is to spend your money on the best microphones you can buy, and the best monitors so you can hear exactly what you captured. The middle part (mixer, cables, recorder, and so on) can be whatever you'd like it to be, and the particulars are often debated. If you build a studio from scratch, or you want to improve your studio, remember that the ends are what you need to spend money on first.

Other details to build a successful home studio:

- The room, and how it affects the sound, will likely be caught in the microphone along with the song, so make sure that the room is either dead (carpeted or otherwise insulated) or has a sound that you can live with.

- Have a variety of instruments and inexpensive musical toys handy, because you never know when you'll want to add a tambourine, harmonica, rain stick, or some other unusual sound to add texture to a track. These little touches can make a big difference.

• Remove everything from the room that might cause extraneous noise (cell phones, telephones, snare drums that aren't locked down, dogs, etc.).

The rest of your home studio needs to be chosen based on the technologies that will best meet your needs. Fortunately, you can do this piecemeal. We recommend building a home studio slowly by just getting the pieces that you need and learning each new one as you go forward. Professional recording equipment can be overwhelming at first, so it's worth your time to learn it one piece at a time. You can replace parts of your studio that you want to upgrade as you go forward. IndieBandsurvivalGuide.com has information as well, should you decide to build your own.

Most recording books will have specific advice on recording particular instruments, and we suggest that you read up on the latest thinking when you go to build your studio. IndieBandSurvivalGuide.com has information as well, should you decide to build your own.

Professional Recording

A professional recording studio has some nice advantages. It usually has a broad selection of microphones, sound processors, amps, instruments, and rooms to get the best recording possible.

When you rent studio time, some studios won't let you even touch the knobs (or studio computer), so you'll be depending on your engineer to record your tracks. Many bands are happy to have a professional handle the engineering. Others might be happier with a hand in it, in which case they might want to consider a home studio instead.

At a professional studio, you should always stay involved during mixdown. Quite a few decisions get made during mixdown, including which effects will get added to the tracks. Also, sometimes tracks are left out of the final mixdown, and you'll want to be on hand to make these creative decisions.

The studio will probably have a contract that specifies an hourly fee you'll have to pay for your time. Make sure that the contract doesn't give the studio any rights to your music. You should own the copyrights and the master recordings. Otherwise, you'll want to go somewhere else.

Saving Money at Professional Recording Sessions

At a recording session, time literally equals money. Here are some simple methods for saving both:

- ***Rehearse for your session.*** The best way to minimize your recording time is to practice for your session the same way that you'd practice for a live show.

- ***Bring extras of everything.*** You get charged for the time it takes to go to the store for a battery for your pedal. Take care of logistics ahead of time to save money. Bring extra strings, batteries, cables, tuners, AC plugs, power strips, reeds, tools, and anything else that you might need for your performance.

- ***Prepare your instruments for recording.*** Get new drum heads, break in strings, and make sure all of your instruments are ready to go for your session.

- ***Tune your drums.*** Or find someone to do it for you.

- ***Use one tuner.*** All of the instruments in the band should use the same tuner for accuracy.

Producers

Producers fill a somewhat misunderstood role in recording. You don't have to get a producer, and many bands don't. But there are some advantages.

If you hire professional producers, sometimes they'll work for a cut of the album sales. In the somewhat-standard industry contracts, their cut comes out of the royalties before the band sees its own. If you decide to work with one, make sure that your financial arrangement is both clear and acceptable to you. And be especially careful if producers want a copyright interest in your songs or sound recordings.

Of course, in today's world, you might be able to get one willing to work for a flat fee, and we'd recommend this if possible.

The Role of a Producer

A music producer is not the same as a film producer, which is where the confusion often comes in. If an album were a film, a producer would be a director. The producers are usually in the control room during a recording and will help manage the recording session. A good producer will help realize the full creative potential of the music.

Producer Michael Freeman, who has been in the recording business for decades, explained that while a live performance is only played and heard once, a studio album is meant to be heard over and over. Pitch, meter, tuning, energy, and feeling all matter a great deal during the sessions, and bands need to be aware that it's a different process.

Freeman's advice to bands is to "find a producer that understands your music. Ask yourself, does he or she 'get it'?" Freeman said that he spends a month or more working with the band in rehearsals on the songs to prepare for the recording before even setting foot in the studio. During this preparation, they decide how they are going to play the songs for the recording, and understand the vision for the album, so that they can make the best decisions about instruments, arrangements, and recording.

Some other examples of what producers do for your band:

- Help decide what kind of sound to aim for, as well as suggest which kind of microphones and recording styles to use.

- Arrange the songs to be more effective. A producer might suggest that the song start with a chorus, rather than the first verse.

- Come up with ideas for extra parts or different sounds to give a song direction. For example, you might hear, "That's good—but what if you played it *this* way . . ." Freeman's advice on this is to at least try out suggestions that producers make, even if you don't initially like an idea.

- Supervise mixdown and mastering.

- Help manage the entire process.

Naturally, many bands do all this for themselves when recording, especially when they have their own studios. But if you do, just be aware of all the work that a producer puts in to make a quality recording. You should be prepared to do the same work if you want the same, high-quality result.

You must feel comfortable working with your producers, since you'll be including them in every creative step. They may take your recording in directions that you don't want to go. John Lisiecki says, "The best producers will help you realize your creative vision. Not theirs." If it starts becoming a question of your sound versus their sound, you may want to find other producers.

RECORDING RESOURCES WITHIN YOUR ARM'S REACH

Thanks to technological advances, a dazzling array of new resources exists for making recordings.

Samples and Loops

With the right combination of samples and loops, you can create the illusion of a full band backing you, or just enhance tracks with that little something extra that they need. While these tools have been around for a long time, many new sources will sell them royalty-free. These sources, all over the Internet, can add new dimensions to your music.

The key to using these tools is to make sure that the license is precleared and royalty-free. If not, you can end up with a legal nightmare later on. Be sure to read the agreements carefully before buying or using them.

Some for-pay sample sources include Drums On Demand (drumsondemand.com), East West Samples (eastwestsamples.com) and ACIDplanet (acidplanet.com). And for free material licensed under Creative Commons, check out ccmixter (ccmixter.org). Additionally, the Creative Commons site (creativecommons.org) allows you to search multiple sites for prelicensed material that can be incorporated into your music. Keep in mind that while many of the samples and loops may be free for nonprofit use, you might have to contact the original musicians if you want to sell tracks with their material. See the "Your Rights" chapter for more information about Creative Commons licenses.

For a current list of sample and loop resources, head to IndieBandSurvivalGuide.com.

Collaborations with Other Musicians Online

Some musicians record each other's songs by sharing source tracks with one another over the Web. This is as simple as posting individual tracks to a forum online for others to add to, or adding to other people's tracks. Sometimes, entire songs are written one track at a time. One might record a bass part. Another might record drums. And before long, there's a song with vocals and even background vocals by entirely different singers. All of this done by musicians who have usually never met each other.

Additionally, some musicians (with good bandwidth) meet online and jam in real time or write songs together. You are no longer limited to finding musicians in your area to jam with. Some collaboration sites include eJamming (ejamming.com) and Jamglue (jamglue.com). However, for a current listing of collaboration sites, visit IndieBandSurvivalGuide.com.

Virtual Recording Sessions

Thanks to the Internet, a musician can record a part for you anywhere in the world. The files are simply transferred over the Internet and merged into the song on your end.

The process usually works like this:

1. Send the musician a rough mixdown of the song in MP3 format, with an explanation of what you're looking for.

2. The musician records a track in sync with the mixdown and sends you an MP3 so you can hear how it sounds.

3. You offer notes on any necessary changes.

4. The musician records a final version and sends you a WAV file with the track.

You can also do this "live" in the following manner:

1. Send the musician a rough mixdown WAV of the song.

2. Contact them using Skype or over the phone.

3. Direct the musician as he or she performs.

4. Have the musician send you a WAV file of his or her recording.

The good news is that you can use these techniques with any musicians in the world, if they're willing. You could even start a band where none of the band members live in the same city.

Virtual Musicians for Hire

Using the methods that we just discussed above, professional studios and session players have gone virtual. This can be done for a fraction of the cost of an in-person session player. This goes beyond just getting a bass player or a drummer for a song. You can hire brass sections, wind ensembles, vocalists, or people who play rare ethnic instruments. The possibilities are endless—for a fee. And the service goes beyond musicians. You can even hire engineers to mix or master your songs.

Don't forget that if you're a skilled instrumentalist, you, too, can be a session player. These Web sites and services always need different types of musicians handy, and some virtual session players make some decent money on the side.

Note that you can get some *very* well-known studio musicians to record a track for you at a reasonable rate. There's a world of talent out there that you can tap into at such services as eSession (esession.com), Session Players (sessionplayers.com), and DrumsForYou (www.drumsforyou.com).

MASTERING

Mastering is frequently misunderstood, perhaps because it's much easier to hear its effects than to describe them. The difference between a mastered track and one that hasn't been mastered can be dramatic. We've had mastering houses offer to master one track for free, just so that we could hear the difference. They would only charge us if we liked it and decided to use it. If you can find a mastering house that makes the same kind of offer, we'd recommend it so that you can at least hear what mastering does. You'll probably be surprised.

MASTERING DEFINED

Mastering is best described as the finishing process for music recording. It normally happens after an album has been mixed down, but before it is sent to a CD printing house or sold online.

Mastering involves the following processes:

- *Powerful and targeted EQ.* The mastering house will apply EQ (boost or reduce certain sound frequencies) to the entire recording rather than just the individual tracks, which happens during mixdown. They also EQ the songs in relation to each other, so that they share a common sound. A mastering house can bring out qualities in your recording you didn't even know were there.

• *Compression/limiting.* Mastering houses usually apply some compression (normalize levels) and limiting (prevent clipping) to the whole album, rather than on individual tracks. This again helps the entire album develop a consistent sound, rather than having some tracks stand out.

• *Volume normalization.* Well-mastered albums don't have huge volume differences between tracks. During mixdown, each song is simply mixed at volume levels appropriate for itself, not in comparison to other tracks. Mastering makes the album into a coherent whole and puts all of the songs into the same dynamic range.

• *Track arrangement.* Details such as the ordering of tracks, as well as the connections and spacing between the tracks, are done during mastering. Mastering houses will often put a final volume drop-off at the end of a track to control how the album flows from one song to another.

• *Sound smoothing.* Mastering houses usually have a few vacuum-tube-based systems that can "warm up" a digital recording, which might sound harsh and cold without some analog equipment to smooth it out.

• *Crowd noise.* Because live albums are often put together in a way that eliminates waiting and silences in between tracks, the crowd noise might be added between tracks during mastering.

Most indie bands master their own work, and you can, too, if you want to learn the process. But Michael Freeman, the producer we mentioned earlier, suggests that you should never use the same person for mixdown and mastering. So a professional mastering house is sometimes worth the money.

Surprisingly, mastering is a specialty, and many mastering engineers don't do recording or mixdown work, but focus on mastering alone. They can make a good album sound great. And when your recording sounds professional, you've raised the odds of getting it noticed by fans and licensed. Mastering is useful whether you record in your home studio or use a professional one, so although many indie musicians skip this process, considering it unnecessary, they aren't doing themselves any favors.

In this day of the single, it's worth mentioning that mastering plays a significant role in making a collection of songs into an album. Creating a group of songs adds an entirely new dimension.

SAVING MONEY WITH PROFESSIONAL MASTERING STUDIOS

Hiring a mastering engineer is not cheap. It can cost over $100 an hour. Therefore, you want to get the most out of every minute of your mastering session. Use these techniques to save yourself time and money:

Finish Mixdown First

Listen to your mixdown over and over at different sessions and in different environments. Play it for different people, especially other musicians, and elicit comments. Freeman suggests that you make an instrumental mix, a vocals mix, and a mix with both and try it out in different environments to make sure that mixdown goes well.

A mastering engineer can't usually fix a track that's mixed too loudly in relation to the others—that's only possible during mixdown. Although the engineers can draw on a surprising variety of tricks, do not depend on them to fix any mixdown mistakes such as a vocal set too low. Some mastering houses will ask you to mixdown your songs with the vocals on a separate track so that they can combine these tracks and ensure that the vocals are heard above the mix. Also, you should leave yourself "headroom." If you mixdown a track close to 0dB (the highest limit of a digital track), you'll handcuff your mastering engineer. As any mastering engineer would say, let them worry about making your songs and album as loud as other recordings.

Bring the Right Formats

Confirm with the mastering house which formats they require. Make sure you bring them what they can use, whether it's WAV files, CDs, or something else. It's expensive to schedule a session, then have the music arrive in the wrong format. (Note: The right answer is *never* MP3 files. MP3 is a lossy, low-quality version of your recording. A mastering house can't do anything with an MP3 file.)

Plan the Track Order Ahead of Time

Decide on the track order before going to the mastering house, and bring a written list. Debating the order among your members while the engineer is on the clock is a waste of money.

Don't Clip the Track

Mastering houses like the before-and-after noise on a track because it gives them a sound floor to analyze before the music starts. They will clip the tracks to the exact length and get rid of the junk.

MANUFACTURING A CD

THE CD IS DYING

Musicians don't make money selling CDs.

You might be thinking, "Excuse me, but I just bought a CD the other day." Or, "I just sold a CD to a fan at a show, so you're way off."

But what you bought at the store, and what you sold to your fan, wasn't a CD. It was music. It just happened to be stored on a shiny piece of plastic, usually in a plastic case.

Why should you care about this distinction? Well, this section discusses how to duplicate or replicate (there's a difference!) hundreds or thousands of discs for yourself. What you have to decide is whether it's worth the money and effort. Although there's always a need for more music in this world, there's already plenty of plastic.

The truth is, the CD is dying, if not already dead. It's just a floppy disk full of music, a convenient way to hand someone your songs. It will certainly always exist, just as 8-tracks and records still exist. With the tremendous number of CD players in the world, the infrastructure will be around for a while. But in the end people are just not going to the store to buy larger and fancier CD display racks anymore; they're buying larger and more capable MP3 players. And while plenty of CDs are certainly still sold every day, the irony is that young people, the ones most likely to be interested in new music, are the ones least interested in buying CDs.

They'd rather just have the songs in digital form. CD sales are headed down over the long term.

Once music is pure data, released from a physical object, it becomes vastly easier to store, organize, and share, allowing people to make as many perfect copies as they want. If you live in Chicago, as we do, selling a CD to someone in the UK involves trucks, planes, and middlemen. But we make sales to the UK all the time thanks to digital music services, with no vehicles involved and a minimum number of middlemen. We can sell a million songs from just one original.

From the phonograph to the cassette tape to the CD, when music is stored on a physical object, it's necessary to choose just a few songs, grouping them together into "an album." This concept isn't necessary anymore, and while it certainly isn't obsolete, the definition of an album is going to become increasingly fuzzy. This will profoundly affect how you release your music in the future.

So if the CD is dying, how do you decide whether to make any, or how many to print if you do?

CD or Not CD, That Is the Question

The decision comes down to money and PR, and the PR reason needs to go first, because it's a perception issue that might be worth the money. Today, some media outlets want an MP3, and some still want a CD. Others will ask for the MP3 first, then ask for a CD if they like what they hear. They don't want those pieces of plastic either unless it's necessary.

Once you get past that initial gatekeeper with an amazing MP3, imagine the press holding a CD in their hand. Do you want them holding a CD-R purchased at your local office-supply store with marker written on the face? And do you want the CD cover to come from your home printer? Or do you want a professionally labeled and packaged disc?

Unfortunately, PR is exclusively about how things look. And while some in the press don't care if they're given a CD-R, many do. A professionally made CD shows that you take your music seriously because you've put money behind it. This will help them take it seriously, too.

The alternative is to do it yourself. You should consider this before going to a CD printing house. Print-on-CD printers are getting good, and you can always have the covers printed at a copy store to get that glossy, professional look. But here's where the money comes in: figure out how much it costs you per CD when you do this. Printers, ink, glossy copying costs, and empty CD jewel cases cost money, and the per disc cost may not be low. It's also time-consuming.

Once you have that per disc cost, you should figure out how many you think you can sell at what price to your fans. Your CD sales will most likely be at shows and person to person. This is where the floppy disk full of music comes in; it's where you need to have a way to hand people the music, losing a sale otherwise.

Now decide how many promotional CDs you'll need. Based on this, you need to determine whether it's worth the printing costs.

For example, we had one disc where we wanted to send two hundred promos, and even if we'd had no sales at all, we would have saved money by doing a thousands-copy run as opposed to making two hundred hand-made promotional copies. We'll have more information about the costs of using a CD printing house below so that you will be able to make an informed decision on costs.

Finally, it bears noting that if you want to get a song played on the radio, especially commercial radio, a professionally printed CD is mandatory. Please read our section on getting played on the radio before making this decision, because a radio campaign is not for everyone. Just because you'd *like* to get played on commercial radio—we all would!—doesn't mean you want to go through the enormous expense. If you are willing to spend enough to do a commercial radio campaign ($20,000 or more), a CD printing is the least of your costs, and you should just go ahead and do a print run.

The All-Important Case

Whether you make CDs on your own or have a CD printing house do it, the CD case that you use is actually important. The CD libraries used by journalists, reviewers, and radio stations are based around the size of a standard CD jewel case. Although there are slim cases, folders, and other interesting choices, none of those work well in a standard library. You will want to make it as simple as possible for these people to handle your music, so the best choice is a standard case.

Of course, every rule is made to be broken. George Hrab, an indie musician whom we've mentioned previously, has done a fantastic job packaging his CDs, making each album unique. For example, one of them comes in a tin box, another in an embossed paper sleeve, and another in a large DVD-style box. Each one stands out as a piece of art, giving his fans a genuine reason to buy the physical disc as merchandise, not just a music holder. His covers also tend to pique reviewers' curiosity enough to get them to pick one up simply because it's different. His sales have benefited from this unique approach.

An Alternative Way to Make CDs: Print on Demand

One of the latest developments affecting the book-publishing industry is print-on-demand, offered by companies such as Lulu.com. Authors can upload a PDF of their book at no cost to themselves, and when someone orders a copy, one is professionally printed, bound, and sent on its way. While each book costs more than one that is made in a mass printing, any book done this way is profitable from the first unit sold because there's no initial outlay.

A similar service is available for music CDs. In our estimates, the cost per CD is higher than doing it yourself by hand, which is why this method hasn't caught on well. But these companies handle ordering, shipping, and other services, and at the least can be used for rather expensive demo CDs or short runs of physical-sale CDs. Mainly, though, they're used for profit-only online CD sales. Since online CD sales include the cost of shipping to stock the CDs at sales outlets, these costs can become comparable to printing your own and might make the CD-on-demand option worthwhile in certain circumstances.

STEPS FOR YOUR CD PRINT RUN

A CD print run is laborious, so it helps to plan out what you need to do ahead of time. The most time-intensive parts of making a CD are art-related, so if you can't handle it yourself, get help from a graphic artist from your skill network if at all possible.

Before your print run:

1. Clear the legal status of all the music and art. (This can take the longest, so we list it first! We'll talk about this process in the "Your Rights" chapter.)

2. Choose a CD printing house.

3. Decide whether to replicate or duplicate your disc.

4. Make a CD master.

5. Obtain a bar code.

6. Create the album art.

7. Write the liner notes.

8. Get a proof (optional).

We'll talk about each step below.

Clear the Legal Status of All the Music and Art

The copyrights on all songs, loops, samples, and art on a CD being manufactured must be cleared before going to the CD printing house. They will require you sign a form affirming that you've cleared them.

Choose a CD Printing House

There are numerous CD printing houses, large and small. Most houses offer different deals with a variety of features related to printing, bar codes, mastering, and other details. These deals change often, so carefully consider the latest ones.

Small differences in money and services aside, a printing house's reputation is the most important thing to consider. To evaluate this, just check their reputation on the Web. Fortunately, musicians are not shy about complaining when they feel that they've been ripped off.

Note that, as you compare these houses, the listed costs don't represent the whole story. Here are other hidden costs to look out for:

- **Shipping.** You usually have to pay for shipping. When you print a thousand CDs or more, this can be a significant amount—CDs are heavy.

- **Glass master charges.** Some houses will charge you to create the glass master if you decide to get your disc replicated. Fortunately, once this is created, it can be used in future runs. (We discuss glass masters below.)

• *Film and preparation charges.* Depending on how the house handles printing the folder panels, and on-disc print, they may charge you film preparation charges.

There are many options for these services. We've used NW Media (nwmedia.com) in the past. Other major manufacturers you may wish to consider are Disc Makers (www.discmakers.com) or DiskFaktory (www. diskfaktory.com). And of course we'll have a complete list of manufacturers at IndieBandSurvivalGuide.com.

Replication or Duplication

Most people call the process of making a lot of CDs *duplication,* but be careful once you decide to make a CD of your own because this term has a specific meaning to CD printing houses, and you may want *replication* instead.

CD duplication is the mass printing of CD-Rs, or Recordable CDs. The art in the jewel case and the on-disc print is usually the same as in replication, but the disc itself is of a lower quality and doesn't last as long as a true replicated disc. The other disadvantage is that the discs may be unreadable in some CD players. The main advantage is that it's cheaper to make CD-Rs in short runs, usually three hundred or less.

CD replication uses a glass master, which allows the CD house to create a much higher quality product. This is the type of CD that you buy at the store from major label bands. There's no downside to going with CD replication other than that most houses won't consider doing a run of less than a thousand discs, and that sets the price quite a bit higher than a duplication run.

The decision comes down to the number of discs you want to print. At this time, it generally makes sense to do a duplication run if you're doing just a few hundred, but beyond that it makes monetary sense to jump to a thousand, even though that might be far more than you need. Since they can be used for PR campaigns as well as giveaways, the extra discs will usually come in handy.

Make a CD Master

If you use a professional mastering house, they will hand you everything you need to give a printing house. If you do the mastering yourself, note standards for delivering a master to a CD printing house vary, so confirm beforehand what yours will need from you.

These standards were created by Koninklijke Philips Electronics N.V. (Royal Philips Electronics N.V.), usually known as Philips. They are coded according to the colors of the standards book that is being used while creating the CD. The one most often used is the Red Book standard, for normal audio CDs. The Orange Book, on the other hand, is for combined audio and data CDs.

If you use a Red Book standard, note that it can introduce errors. Tracks of information that can help with error-checking can be included on a master disc via some mastering programs.

If you have any questions about this, your CD printing house will be happy to answer them, because getting this right makes both your jobs easier.

Obtain a Bar Code

You will need a bar code for your CD, especially if you intend to sell it through the digital music services. Also, with a bar code, the CD can be tracked by SoundScan and similar services. For more on sales tracking, see the "Get Distributed and Sold" chapter. If you wish to add a bar code, you need the bar code during *this step*, before you do the artwork, because it needs to be incorporated into the art itself. Getting a bar code is fairly inexpensive, and most houses will include one for free with the cost of the discs.

You can also get a bar code from an online store such as CD Baby (which is where we've always gotten ours).

A rare alternative that you may wish to consider is to sign up for a vendor UPC code. Although this is more expensive, it allows you to have multiple product codes underneath it. You can then create product codes for each disc or product that you want to sell. Unfortunately, this requires an annual fee. Information about this can be found at the official site for UPC codes: gs1.org/productssolutions/barcodes/.

Create the Album Art

The album art that you have to prepare depends on your choice of CD packaging. This can be a standard plastic case with a four-panel booklet, or just a sleeve. You also need to decide whether to use color or black and white. The CD printing house will give you the necessary templates.

Note that the album cover is the most important part of your album art, since this is the only image retained by online retailers and MP3 programs such as iTunes.

To get ideas for the art, pick up a few CDs from your own collection and look them over closely to see what elements appear on each panel. A lot of musicians get creative about what goes where. You don't even have to write your band's name on the album, but we wouldn't recommended going that far. Only a few bands can manage a White Album (or a Black Album, for that matter).

We do recommend the following:

1. Use a graphic artist from your skill network if you can't do it yourself.

2. Use a palette of colors that go well together, using CMYK values in your art program. Remember that *printed* colors are sometimes different from *on-screen* colors. This is where Pantone numbers come in handy.

3. Get permissions for any copyrighted materials that you use in your artwork. Remember that all photographs, including ones made of your own band by other photographers, are owned by the photographer, and you will have to work out the rights if you want to use them on your album.

4. Put a bar code on the back cover, usually in the lower right corner. When you obtain your bar code, it should be given to you as an EPS file.

5. If you wish, you can use the Compact Disc logo on your CD if it follows the appropriate rules for usage of that logo. You can use the logo if your CD conforms to the one of the standards owned by Philips, usually Red Book. Your CD printing house can tell you which standard has been met and should have the image available for you (it's also easy to find on the Internet). Using the Compact Disc logo image tends to make your CD look more official, but there's no other good reason to use it if you don't want to go to the trouble.

6. Make a printed proof. We suggest actually putting it in a jewel case and showing it to as many people as you can. There's nothing more embarrassing than a mistake that has been reproduced a thousand times.

7. Check and then double-check the spelling and grammar of all the text on the CD art. We have a compilation CD from a reggae label that says "Masteqrs of Reggae" on the side. Use a spell-checker.

8. Make sure to account for bleeds. Usually, most templates suggest a bleed area of one-eighth inch past the trim lines so that your image will look normal in case of small paper-cutting discrepancies. The templates will have a clearly marked bleed region that you should fill with your images, or at least a solid color.

Once this art is complete, you should carefully save the finished layered art files (not just the output file) in multiple locations and probably back it up in a safe location. You may need it again for a reprinting of your disc.

When doing the art, depending on the printing package, you can use silk screen using a few discrete colors, three color, and even full color. Follow the guidelines of the printing house carefully. The template requirements for these different options can be very specific. In particular, layering may make a big difference when discrete colors are used in silk-screening, because the layers tend to cover each other up.

Also, each panel may have different characteristics; it's not uncommon to do a full-color front panel with a black-and-white inside panel. You or your graphic artist need to take this into account. Keep in mind that not all images convert well to black and white from color, so if you need to do so, making a proof is an especially good idea.

Write the Liner Notes

When we made our first CD, we rooted through the liner notes of all the discs in our collections for ideas. If you're a meticulous writer, these notes may take you a while. Do it in a word processor first, rather than directly into the art, because you'll want to revise it, share it with others for feedback, use the spell-checker and grammar-checker, and print out copies to proof it, before turning it into eight-point type.

This part has no formal rules, of course, and you don't need to include liner notes at all if you don't want to, but most musicians have fun with them. Keep in mind that all of this information can be repurposed for your Web site.

Some things you might want to include in the liner notes, and in some cases various other places on the album art, are:

- Name of the band/artist

- Name of the album

- Lyrics

- Song titles and listing

- Song lengths/total playing time

- Copyright information for:

  - The author/publisher of each song

  - The affiliated performing-rights organization for each song

  - The sound recording

  - The art and photos

  - Cover songs, audio loops, samples, reprinted lyrics, artwork, photos, etc.

- Musicians for each track

- Instruments on each track

- Credits for producers, engineers, artwork design, and photographers

- Thank-you messages

- Mastering and recording studios used

- Band Web site and contact information

- Other albums and merchandise

- Dates recorded

- And don't forget jokes ...

We suggest repeating the copyright, credits, and especially contact information on the back cover as well as in the liner notes. Also, your disc itself should repeat this information.

Get a Proof (Optional)

Many houses charge extra for a full production proof, but they are usually worth the money. As we said above, the last thing that you want to do is repeat a mistake a thousand times.

MERCHANDISING

T-shirts, stickers, posters, and other merchandise can be a major part of an artist's income. In fact, merchandise has only gained in importance thanks to recorded music becoming so easy to copy. Generally, people prefer buying merchandise from the band itself rather than seeking out fakes or pirated versions.

Fortunately, it's also never been so easy to make, distribute, and sell merchandise. Numerous options are available, including print-on-demand services that don't require you to spend money or house inventory. You can make money from the first unit you sell.

YOUR BRAND AND MERCHANDISE

If you've reached this point in the book without going through all of the preparation that we mentioned in the "Your Brand" chapter, you can't put it off any longer. You will need your logo, colors, font, and the rest of your Brand Toolbox to start making merchandise. We'll also be using the terminology that we introduced in that chapter, such as RGB and CMYK colors, rasterized and vectorized images, and flattened and layered formats. Please go back to that chapter if you need a refresher, even if you use graphic artists, because then you will have enough knowledge to at least discuss the issues with them, as well as with your manufacturer.

Many merchandise manufacturers will offer to convert layered, vectorized files into the appropriate formats for their processes. If they want the flattened, rasterized formats instead, carefully size the vector image to the exact dimensions first and use CMYK coloration, which is appropriate for color printing. Resizing a rasterized image can cause serious distortions, so sizing first is particularly important. Also, your use of Pantone colors for your Brand Toolbox images will come in handy and save you time, since most manufacturers work directly with such colors in their printing. If you haven't used Pantone, you may find yourself trying to find the closest matches for your color scheme.

PRINT ON DEMAND VS. KEEPING AN INVENTORY

Previously, to make T-shirts and other merchandise, you would have to print a minimum number to qualify for a volume discount at a manufacturer. Then you would have to keep that inventory on hand or pay for storage, then sell enough items to make back your original investment before actually making a profit. If there's one thing that's difficult for indie bands, it's predicting how many people will want to buy their merchandise.

One positive trend for indie bands has been the rise of print-on-demand services. Typically, there is no initial cost. You upload images and they appear in a virtual storefront where your customers can select the one they want as well as the type of merchandise they'd like the image to appear on. The best print-on-demand services will show your customers what the item will look like with the image printed on it. Once a fan buys an item, the print-on-demand manufacturer makes a single one and ships it directly to the customer.

Your profit depends on the price that you set. The print-on-demand store will charge a base price that builds in their profit, and whatever you charge above this will be your net profit. Shipping is paid by the customer, so your profit per item is set.

Print-on-demand services have a lot of benefits:

- No (or low) up-front costs.

- No inventory required.

- You will profit from the first sale.

- The service will handle ordering and fulfillment.

- You can try as many designs as you want and sell only the successful ones.

- A range of products that use the same image, so you can generate a storefront with clothing, coffee mugs, lunch boxes, calendars, and other merchandise available in just a few clicks.

A few downsides are:

- The profit margin is far lower, so if you can sell a lot of units, volume manufacturing makes more sense.

- If you want to sell the merchandise at your shows, you'll need to buy them in advance and at their cost, which is higher than had you created them at a volume discount.

- Some of the services' financial arrangements are unusual, such as having a minimum required profit before they pay you.

Your volume manufacturers will give you a more consistent-looking product than the print-on-demand services. Fortunately, it's simple to buy a single item from a print-on-demand service to see how it will look.

YOUR MERCHANDISE
T-shirts

A T-shirt with your logo on it not only makes for something unique to sell, it's also great advertising. Of course, to sell a lot of T-shirts, you should have a design that people will think is cool to wear. So getting input from a lot of people can help you decide whether the design looks good and might sell. You can design T-shirts based on songs or your brand. Many musicians include their Web-site address on the T-shirt as well.

Once you have a design, you have a choice: go with a volume T-shirt printing store or use a print-on-demand service such as CafePress (cafe-press.com), Zazzle (zazzle.com), or Spreadshirt (spreadshirt.com). If you decide to go with a volume T-shirt printing store, then you can go with a national chain or use a local one. We highly recommend going local since many of these stores have knowledgeable graphic artists who can help you, and you can actually see a physical proof and make revisions on the spot. You don't want to replicate a mistake hundreds or thousands of times. A local store is more likely to hold your hand through the process, and people who work at T-shirt stores tend to be in or know other bands. They are useful contacts.

One of the downsides of using a volume T-shirt printing store is that you will need to print a range of sizes, colors, and styles, and you might guess wrong about which will sell the most. Plus, once you've made a design decision, it's set in stone, or rather, cotton. Obviously, this is where print-on-demand services excel, since they offer your fans a variety of designs, sizes, styles, and colors.

Stickers

Stickers are more effective than they have ever been in the past because you can put your Web-site address on them. That address can lead users to everything that your band has to offer. Those stickers also reinforce your brand.

The best thing about stickers is that they are cheap enough to give away. They work well as incentives if you want to give someone something for buying an album or signing up for your mailing list. Many services make stickers, such as Sticker guy! (stickerguy.com) and Bandwear (bandwear.com), and a full listing can be found at IndieBandSurvivalGuide.com.

Other Merchandise

Printing shops no longer limit you to the standard items that bands have sold in the past. Today, you can add your images to almost any item. Check the variety of products available at a print-on-demand merchandise service such as CafePress (cafepress.com) or a volume-manufacturing solution such as Bandwear (bandwear.com) or other services aimed at corporate clients such as PRstore (prstore.com) or Branders (branders.com).

One musician who used this branding technique well is Frankendread, a Caribbean musician out of Chicago. He tours the country and plays many outdoor festivals. He decided that one way to make some extra money would be to sell bottled water at his performances, since most festivals occur in the summer and audience members get hot. However, selling bottled water wasn't enough for him. Being creative, and understanding the importance of branding, he found a vendor who would allow him to brand their bottles of water with his logo. The Brobdingnagian Bards did something similar and branded bottles of bubbles. Although they did this on a whim, they discovered that many of their fans saved the bottles for years as prized mementos. So, keep in mind that offering unusual merchandise can help you stand out from the crowd.

SELLING YOUR MERCHANDISE

Selling Online

If you go with a volume manufacturer for your merchandise, you may want to sell it to your fans from your Web site, rather than just at shows. If so, you can always sell it yourself: take orders, ship the items, and handle the entire transaction from your home. If you do this, you can use Web storefronts to take the orders such as Yahoo.com stores (smallbusiness.yahoo.com/ecommerce) or ProStores (prostores.com).

A second option is to use a fulfillment service. For a fee, these services, such as Amazon Fulfillment Services (amazonservices.com/fulfillment), stock your merchandise, take the orders, ship the items, and handle payment. These fulfillment services have created embedded storefronts or widgets that can help sell items on the Web. Nimbit.com offers these applications and allows you flexibility on how to integrate its "online merchandise table" into your Web site and on your Web-presence sites. The only question is whether the money you pay for the services is worth the time that you'll save.

Selling Merchandise at Shows

We talk about selling merchandise at shows in the "Get Booked and Play Live" chapter. It's usually simple to just haul your T-shirts and merchandise to a table and handle sales on the spot. Be aware that the larger venues will take a cut of your merchandise sales, sometimes as much as 40 percent.

Sponsorships

While it may seem that sponsorships are out of your arm's reach, that isn't so. Sponsorships can come from smaller businesses as much as larger ones.

For example, Frankendread got some beach-clothing manufacturers to sponsor him. He had all his band members dress in the manufacturer's clothes and pitched their products from the stage. If you can think of connections that make sense for your brand, you might be able to make the same kind of deals.

LEARNING MORE

To stay up-to-date on all the resources, tools, and sites to help you create and sell your music, albums, and merchandise, head to IndieBandSurvival Guide.com.

CHAPTER 7

YOUR RIGHTS

MUSICIANS, COMPARED to other types of artists, have their rights defined by some of the most convoluted laws ever created. Copyright laws come into play when you write a song, when you cover a song onstage, when you record a song of your own, and even if you hand your song to a filmmaker to use for free. Each of these activities has entirely different legal issues associated with it. Worse, these issues only become more confusing since the laws behind them were originally intended to protect record labels, music publishers, and other middlemen—not indie musicians making music today or using the Web. We're going to give you a step-by-step overview of using the laws to both protect and *promote* your music. You'll soon understand why it's generally safe to play cover songs in bars, but why you owe money if you cover someone else's song on your album. You'll learn how to register copyrights of your own music, how music licensing works, and how to trademark your band name. And we'll do our best to eliminate the legalese and explain it in plain English.

Our goal with this chapter is to introduce you to these topics and give you a basic understanding of the law and the terminology. But many of these topics will spiral beyond the scope of this book. In fact, entire books and law school classes are dedicated to them. But you don't need to be an expert, you simply need to know enough to know *when* to go to an expert, and to be able to understand some of their lingo. Of course, if you have any specific questions, we recommend contacting your attorney or accountant.

YOUR INDIE BAND IS A BUSINESS

Any musician or band making money off music is running a business. And whenever business and money are involved, legal issues tend to follow. This only becomes more complicated when multiple people are in the band. So, to avoid any disputes it's best to agree in advance as to what everyone's individual rights and responsibilities will be.

Many bands do well without any formal legal agreement among themselves, handling issues, business deals, and money case by case. However, an informal approach doesn't protect you from yourselves (a band member suing the band or leaving the group) or others (one of your songs infringes another songwriter's copyright). If you take what you're doing seriously, set up a legal structure such as a partnership, LLC, or corporation for your band. This will solve many of the issues that we'll be talking about throughout this chapter. Such agreements typically solve thorny issues such as:

- Band name, brand ownership, and trademark ownership

- How band decisions are made and who's authorized to enter into agreements on behalf of the band

- How profits, losses, and expenses are handled

- Band-equipment ownership

- Ownership of sound recordings

- How publishing revenue is administered and distributed

- How merchandise and merchandizing rights are handled

- What happens when additional band members join

- What happens when band members leave

- How disputes are handled

This is by no means a complete list.

Creating a legal entity for your specific needs goes beyond the scope of the *Guide*. For an overview, read *Music Law: How to Run Your Band's Business* by Richard W. Stim. Then, when you're ready to take this step for your own band, get an attorney and accountant to assist you.

COPYRIGHT

Copyright protects the authors of original works of music, text, graphics, videos, or other art forms. As an indie band, you will likely be creating all these types of works. While some think of copyright as a single right, it isn't. It's better understood as a collection of many more specific rights—all of which can be divided, sold, retained, or amended as you see fit.

When musicians have copyright questions, they often want clear, black-and-white answers. The truth is, the law is still evolving, and it's often at odds with technology. The law doesn't map well to the needs of a post-Net indie band for a variety of reasons:

- *The law is about getting permission; the Web is about copying and sharing.* The purpose of copyright is to help you control your work, but the purpose of the Web is to easily copy data from one computer to another.

- *The Web is global; the law is not.* While the *Guide* will focus on U.S. law, the instant you put your music and other intellectual property on the Web, it's available to a global audience—with different laws and attitudes toward intellectual property.

- *The law is old and changes slowly; technology changes rapidly.* The law usually evolves by force-fitting old rules onto new situations. Because of this retrofitting, most terms that lawyers use to describe music are out-of-date. For instance, the law calls any recording a *phonorecord*, although most music never makes its way onto a phonograph of any kind.

That said, because copyright affects just about everything a musician does, it's best to understand the basics.

MYTHS ABOUT MUSIC COPYRIGHT

Unfortunately, a lot of misinformation surrounds copyright. We'll go through some of the more basic concepts here.

- **You have to register your music with the U.S. Copyright Office to get a copyright.** Registration doesn't "give" you the copyright—music is automatically copyrighted once recorded in a tangible form. Registering your music with the copyright office does give you some benefits, however, which we discuss later.

- **You can effectively copyright your music cheaply by mailing your CD to yourself.** Mailing a CD to yourself to get a canceled date stamp on the envelope to prove when your song was written doesn't copyright. Registration will do that instead and give you other benefits.

- **You don't need to use the © symbol.** You did before 1979. You no longer need to include a symbol or any notice of copyright to ensure your rights. Of course, providing notice of copyright is always a good idea.

- **You don't need to pay licenses for cover songs, even if you're not making money from it.** Recording someone else's song requires a license. This license is needed even if you're just giving the cover song away for free.

- **"Fair use" is a right and protects you from infringement claims.** Fair use is simply an affirmative defense to infringement. It's not a right. The fair-use defense allows news reporting, commentary, teaching, and criticism (e.g., movie reviews). The courts get to decide what's "fair" based on the facts and a complicated legal test.

- **If you copy just a little bit of someone else's song such as less than four measures or less than ten seconds, you won't be infringing.** No bright-line rule or exception to copyright law clearly explains when "copying" crosses the line into infringement. The rule of thumb is, the more you copy, the more likely you're infringing. It's best to create original songs or to properly license those songs/samples you don't own. ♥

COPYRIGHT LAW BASICS

The underlying principle behind copyright law is that creative works benefit society. Therefore, creators should be rewarded and given protection so that what they create—and any value that comes from it—can be theirs for at least as long as they live. As a result, copyright protects "original works of authorship" whether they be literary, artistic, or musical. In the past, it was necessary to register your original works with the U.S. Copyright Office to receive protection, but this is no longer the case.

Copyright now occurs automatically from the time you:

- **Create and express something original.** Only an original work can be granted copyright protection. Additionally, copyright doesn't protect the ideas underlying your work, just the unique way you expressed them. For instance, with music, the subject underlining the lyrics would not be granted copyright protection. In disputes, however, the courts decide what's original.

- **Capture it in a fixed, tangible format.** With text, this is as easy as writing down your words, but with music, you have more options. You could write it down in notation or record it in some way such as on your computer, with a video camera, or even on your phone's voice mail. Playing a song live, however, would not give you a copyright, unless you record it.

Once those two requirements are met, you instantly hold the copyright in that original work that you've captured, and it's your property. Like any property, you can sell it, rent it, divvy it up, or give it away for free.

As the sole owner, you alone have the right to copy your work. The law grants you the power to use, sell, perform, or display it. It also gives you the right to make modifications, translations, or other such derivative works from the original you've created. If anyone exercises any of the above without your permission, you can enforce your rights and sue for infringement. Most of the time, however, you'll be looking for ways to let others use your work in exchange for money, licensing it to them for specific purposes. The law grants you these broad powers for as long as you own the copyright—currently your entire life plus seventy years after your death, or if you have created a business entity and made it the copyright owner, ninety-five years from publication. This means that, like any property, you'll want to make sure your three-chord wonder is in your will so your children, your children's children, and your children's children's children can continue to license uses for your song and reap any revenues it generates.

TWO FOR ONE: THE SOUND-RECORDING COPYRIGHT AND THE SONG COPYRIGHT

If you write music the old-fashioned way—on sheet music—then your song is copyrighted the moment you write the words and music on paper. Writing down your original song in this way gives you a copyright to the *song*. Most likely though, you'll create your music by recording it onto your computer or some other sound-recording device. If you do, you actually create two copyrights in one: one for the musical performance that was captured (the *sound recording*) and one for the words and music (the *song*). While it's hard to think of the recording as separate from the song, under the law, it is. The Beatles' record company owns the rights to the recording of the Beatles' version of "Yesterday," but it's John Lennon and Paul McCartney who own the song copyright. As owners of the song copyright, they benefit when others record cover versions of their song—not the record company.

The Sound-Recording Copyright

The sound-recording owner can be a person, a group of people, or even a legal entity such as your band. For signed bands, the owner is usually the record label since it needs to have the exclusive rights to these recordings in order to make and sell albums, or to license them to other media to use the recording. As an indie band, you can make money off the sound recording, just as a label would. We'll talk more about this about later.

The Song Copyright

The song copyright ownership is split in two:

- *Author.* This is the songwriter/songwriters who write the words and music to the song and grant permission as to how the song can be used.

- *Publisher.* The publisher works for the author and handles all the business work the song generates, such as copyrighting the song, convincing others to perform it, licensing the song for use in film and television, and collecting the royalties.

The law sees the author and the publisher as a team—two sides of a single coin working together on behalf of the song. Indie musicians usually keep track of who wrote what percentage of each song, but they rarely define who the publisher is. This is a problem since the law states that the two roles split any income a song makes fifty-fifty. To earn all the royalties a song generates, someone has to fill the publishing role. For an indie band, the publisher is usually the author, through an individually owned publishing entity or through a joint venture created with all of the band's members.

Know that you can also sell your publishing rights in a song or a song catalog to an established music publisher that specializes in promoting the use of songs and collecting royalties. Another option is to hire an established music administrator. Just like music publishers, administrators handle all the business issues of licensing and collecting royalties, but won't help actively exploit the songs. We'll talk more about this in a later section.

Dividing the Roles

For an indie band, some of the more common options for dividing up the roles of author and publisher are:

- *Songwriter as author, songwriter as publisher.* Each songwriter creates his or her own publishing company to receive 100 percent of the royalties for a song—50 percent for being the author and 50 percent for being the publisher. If there's more than one songwriter on a song, each songwriter has his or her own publishing company, so the author share of 50 percent is equally divided between the songwriters and the publishing share of 50 percent is equally divided between the publishers.

• *Songwriter as author, band as publisher.* Rather than have the songwriters in the band earn all the licensing royalties, some indie bands have opted to share the publishing rights. The songwriters split the author share according to their author-ownership percentage, while the band's publishing entity receives the full amount of the publishing share. For this method, the band needs to form a publishing entity. This publishing share is then divided among the band members based on their agreement.

• *Band as author, band as publisher.* Some indie bands decide to give the band both the author and publisher shares. To do this, the band needs to form a publishing entity and have an agreement among themselves stating that no matter who writes the songs, the band gets the income from both the author share and the publisher share. This is then split according to the band agreement.

The list above is not exhaustive. You can negotiate any other arrangement you choose. Some indie bands split based on who performed on the song. Whichever method you choose, the point is to get your agreement down in writing. If you want to create your own publishing company, you can find the steps and tools at IndieBandSurvivalGuide.com.

Keeping Track of Copyright Ownership

For each and every sound recording you make—whether it's a studio, acoustic, live, or demo—you will need to keep track of who the author, publisher, and sound-recording owner is since each have legal rights. This is especially challenging when defining the sound-recording owner since recordings may be created over time on multiple band-member computers or at different recording studios. Typically, a band agreement helps define some of these roles. Still, to avoid disputes, we recommend using the "Song and Sound-Recording Split Agreement" to record who's filling these roles for any particular sound recording you make.

SONG AND SOUND-RECORDING SPLIT AGREEMENT

The best way to define the three legal roles for each song you record is to note it in writing. Doing so may help avoid issues in the future. We suggest the following form (which is also posted at IndiebandSurvivalGuide.com):

Song and Sound-Recording Split Agreement

Effective Date of This Agreement:_____

Song Title: _____

Sound-Recording Name:_____

The songwriters and sound-recording owner hereby acknowledge and agree that we are the sole songwriters and sound-recording owner for the above-titled recording of the song and have agreed on the following:

Songwriter	Songwriter %

Publisher	Publisher %

Sound-Recording Owner	Sound Recording %

Notes:

Acknowledged and Agreed:

Name: _____	Name: _____
Signature: _____	Signature: _____
Date: _____	Date: _____
Name: _____	Name: _____
Signature: _____	Signature: _____
Date: _____	Date: _____

Dealing with Multiple Authors on a Song Copyright

Typically, bands and songwriters choose one of two methods to figure out songwriting percentages: they either divide authorship equally among all those in the room at the time of creation, or they work out percentages based on who contributed what part and how much of the song. You can negotiate anything; just have an agreement in place. Having more than one author is known in legal-speak as joint ownership, although this term is often misunderstood to mean something entirely different when musicians talk.

Any one author can grant permission to license a song as long as that license is nonexclusive. It doesn't matter what percentage an author owns. Any of the authors can decide over the objections of the other authors. But any money from the deal is still split according to the ownership percentages. For example, if three people write a song called "Sick of Sandwiches," and one wants to license it to a fast-food burger chain to cover in a commercial, he could do so, even if the other two were vegetarians and objected. All the authors would get paid for this use according to their ownership percentages.

Getting Paid to Write Songs for Others

When someone, such as a company, pays you to create a song for them, they may have you sign a "work-for-hire" provision. This provision makes them the copyright owner in exchange for paying you to create it. As owner, they can publish, record, or license their song in any way that they'd like. For example, if you were hired to write and record "Sick of Sandwiches" by a fast-food burger chain for their commercial campaign, the song would be theirs to do with as they please. If you're ever hired to write a theme for a podcast, commercial, film, or TV show, you'll want to be aware of this provision since it'll affect all the rights you have that we discussed above. Know that whether to sign a work-for-hire agreement is your choice. It's negotiable.

HOW SONGS AND SOUND RECORDINGS CAN BE USED BY OTHERS

When you have the rights to your songs and sound recordings, you can license them for various uses. You can do this for free or charge a fee or royalty. Figuring out whose permission is needed and who gets paid—the author/publisher team and/or the sound-recording owner—depends on what is being used. We'll go over the most popular uses below.

THE SONG

Anytime a song is licensed, it's the author/publisher team that grants it and receives the royalties. The sound-recording owner only comes into play if the user licensing the song also wants to use that specific sound recording. If so, then a separate license will be negotiated with the sound-recording owner (which we'll talk about in the next section). The table, "Rights in the Song," outlines in brief the many uses and rights that we'll discuss below.

The Song Is Released as a Recording

The author/publisher must grant permission whenever their song is released as a recording for the first time. After your song's been published and thus made publicly available, the law allows anyone to record a version. However, you're still entitled to a royalty for each recording copy made, whether physical or digital. This is known as your mechanical right.

Federal law limits how much you can charge for mechanical rights ("statutory royalties"). At the time of the printing of this *Guide*, this rate is locked in at 9.1 cents per copy for songs under five minutes. For songs over five minutes, the rate is 1.75 cents per minute. You always need to

RIGHTS IN THE SONG

(Owned and Controlled by the Author/Publisher Team)

Released as a Recording

Used in an Audio-Visual Work

Played or Performed Publicly

For Broadcast to Public

Your song is incorporated in a video production such as a TV show, film, or video that's broadcasted to the public

Legal Right at Issue:
Your right to allow the user to sync your song to a video image that can be broadcasted to the public

License:
Synchronization License

Who would License:
User of the song such as a TV or film production company, indie and student filmakers, or YouTubers

Who Pays You:
The user of the song

Note: The license fee you can charge is negotiable

For Sale to Public

Your song is incorporated in a video production that is sold to the public on DVD

Legal Right at Issue:
Your right to allow the user to sync your song to a video image that is sold to the public

License:
Videogram License

Who would License:
User of the song such as a TV or film production company, indie and student filmakers

Who Pays You:
The user of the song

Note: The license fee you can charge is negotiable

Physical Copy

Your song is released on CD

Legal Right at Issue:
Your right to allow your song copied to a physical medium

License:
Mechanical License

Who would License:
Users that make your song available on CD such as any band or musician that covers your song (this includes your band)

Note: Historically, the record label would pay this license

Who Pays You:
The user of the song or Harry Fox as intermediary

Note: The license fee you can charge is limited by statute

Digital Download

Your song is released as an MP3 or WAV that's made available for download

Legal Right at Issue:
Your right to allow your song copied for digital download and your right to have your song performed by others

Licenses:
Mechanical License and Digital Phonorecord Delivery License

Who would License:
Users that make your song available for download such as any band or musician that covers your song (this includes your band)

Who Pays You:
1. Mechanical License: the user of the song or Harry Fox as intermediary

2. Performance License: Your PRO (the user of the song pays a license to the PRO which then pays you if such use gets captured in their statistical analysis)

Note: The license fees you can charge are limited by statute

Broadcast and Establishments

Your song is broadcasted on the radio, TV, or played in public at an establishment, such as a restaurant, venue, airport, etc.

Legal Right at Issue:
Your right to have your song performed by others or publicly performed

License:
Performance License

Who would License:
Broadcasters, networks, and establishment owners who make your song publicly available

Who Pays You:
Your PRO (the user of the song pays a license to the PRO which then pays you if such use gets captured in their statistical analysis)

Note: The license fees you can charge are limited by statute

Sampled

Your song (or a portion of it) is used as a sample or made into a loop and incorporated into another song

Legal Right at Issue:
Your right to have your song used as a sample or loop

License:
Sample License

Who would License:
Musicians, bands, or a record label

Who Pays You:
The user of the song

Note: The license fee you can charge is negotiable

Printed

Your song (or lyrics) is printed out in some way such as in sheet music, tablature, book, etc.

Legal Right at Issue:
Your right to have your song or its lyrics put into print

License:
Print License

Who would License:
Anyone who copies your song or lyrics into writing

Who Pays You:
The user who transcribes your song or lyrics

Note: The license fee you can charge is negotiable

Other

Your song is used as a midi file, incorporated in a toy, greeting card, doorbell, video game, etc. or is translated or made into a derivative work

Legal Right at Issue:
Your right to have your song copied for a particular use

License:
You can create a license for any specific use of your sound recording not covered by one of the more established ways outlined in this chart

Who would License:
Phone companies, toy manufacturers, greeting card company, or any other user that would like to use your song for a particular purpose

Who Pays You:
The user of the song

Note: The license fee you can charge is negotiable

Non-Interactive Digital Stream Broadcasters

Your song is streamed over the Web or cable/satellite radio station

Legal Right at Issue:
Your right to have your song digitally streamed

License:
Digital Transmission Right License

Who Would License:
Broadcasters that digitally stream your song to the public

Who Pays You:
Your PRO (the user of the song pays a license to the PRO which then pays you if such use gets captured in their statistical analysis)

Note: The license fee you can charge is limited by statute

Interactive Digital Stream Broadcasters

Your song is made available on a music player that allows users to control the song and song order (pause, rewind, fast forward, etc.)

Legal Rights at Issue:
Your right to have your song performed by others and controlled by the user

Licenses:
Digital Transmission Right License and Mechanical License

Who Would License:
Web sites and broadcasters that provide interactive digital streams of your song to the public

Who Pays You:
1. Performance License: Your PRO (the user of the song pays a license to the PRO which then pays you if such use gets captured in their statistical analysis)

2. Mechanical License: the user of the song or Harry Fox as intermediary

Note: The license fees you can charge are limited by statute round up to the next minute. These rates are adjusted every few years by the Copyright Arbitration Royalty Panel (CARP), so to get the most up-to-date rates see www.copyright.gov/carp. You can always charge less than this rate (including nothing at all), but you can never negotiate anything higher. These royalties are owed to you whether the copies are intended to be sold or given away for free. It doesn't matter if it's for promotional purposes, a charitable cause, or handed out as a gift. As long as a copy is made, you are technically owed these royalties, unless you waive them.

Most songwriters don't realize that when their band duplicates a thousand CDs of the songs they wrote, the authors/publishers are entitled to a royalty for each copy made—to be paid by your band. The law sees your band as covering the songwriter's songs. When you sign an agreement with a CD printing house, that agreement typically has you avow that you have all the necessary permissions for all the songs on the album the house is copying—including permissions from the authors/publishers within your band!

Of course, paying your songwriters $910 for the right to use the songs on your band's album, on top of all the money spent to make the CDs in the first place, may not only break your band's bank, it may even break up the band. But it goes beyond CDs: releasing songs digitally also results in mechanical royalties being owed. This includes uploading MP3 and WAV files to your band's Web site and each subsequent download (whether free or paid). The author/publisher should get a royalty for the upload and the download.

Indie bands often skirt this issue by having the authors/publishers waive their right to these royalties or by working out a deal with them to get paid after the album has recouped the initial outlay of funds. This is yet another reason why a band agreement can help solve these issues at the outset.

Why You Can Record Cover Songs (For a Fee)

The law allows anyone to record a song previously made available to the public. In other words, no one can stop you from recording for your album a cover version of a well-known song. This is called obtaining a compulsory license. Just as we said above, you need to pay a statutory royalty for each copy of the cover song you make. To do so, you need to contact the publisher of the song, although many publishers align themselves with the Harry Fox Agency—an organization that specializes in administering mechanical licenses and royalty distribution. We'll talk in detail in a later section about the convenient role that the Harry Fox Agency plays in helping indie bands track down publishers and pay the requisite fees online.

Dealing with Digital Downloads

Allowing your songs to be downloaded as an MP3 at your Web site triggers an additional songwriter right—the "performance right." This is in addition to the mechanical right. Although your band's songwriters may waive these rights, you will have to obtain this license for cover songs. We'll talk about this additional license in the "Songs Played Publicly" section below.

Songs Used in an Audiovisual Work

The author/publisher can grant permission for their song to be tied to a visual image. The author/publisher can license the use for a royalty. Examples include songs used in:

- Films and film trailers

- Television shows

- Television commercial campaigns

- Documentaries

- Music videos

Using a song in such a way is known as a synchronization right, since the user of the music is syncing the song to the visual image. If the user wants to also sell the audiovisual work to the public in the form of a DVD or digital download, the author/publisher can grant a second license, called a videogram license. Unlike a mechanical right, your synchronization and videogram rights are not limited by statutory royalties. You can negotiate any price or deny the use of your song altogether. It's completely up to you.

Songs Played Publicly

Once an author/publisher publishes a song, the law allows anyone to play it. There are no royalties for private performances of the song, such as when you listen to an artist's album in your car, but when it's publicly performed, that's a different story. A song can be performed publicly at or through:

- Broadcast media such as TV and terrestrial radio

- Public establishments such as restaurants, bars, shopping centers, hotels, theme parks, airports, etc.

- "Noninteractive" digital-stream broadcasters that don't allow listeners to control the music that's being played, such as satellite, cable radio, webcasts or Web-simulcasted radio stations

- "Interactive" digital-stream Web sites that allow listeners to skip, rewind, pause, or control the song or playlist such as the music player on MySpace or on your Web site

Each time the song is played publicly, the author/publisher is entitled to a royalty. This is paid by the broadcast media playing the song and the establishments that allow it to be performed. Performance royalties share the same rates as mechanical royalties. So, once again, the statutory rate is paid to the author/publisher team.

Obviously, knowing when your song was played is one challenge. Trying to get paid for it is another. This is where performance rights organizations (PROs) come in. PROs include organizations such as ASCAP, BMI, SESAC, and SOCAN (Canada). Since copyrighted music is being played all the time, it takes large organizations such as PROs to figure out what's been performed and then to collect and distribute the royalties.

In general, users of music enter into music-reporting and subscription arrangements with PROs to cover themselves for the copyrighted music that they publicly broadcast and perform. For establishments such as a bar, paying a general license fee to a PRO covers whatever bands perform live onstage as well as songs publicly broadcasted throughout the place—including the jukebox, the televisions, music on hold, and whatever the sound guy plays before and after the band.

But just because your song's played doesn't mean you'll get paid. There's too much music for even the PROs to keep track of. Where economically sensible, PROs conduct surveys for a complete count of what exactly has been played, for instance by gathering playlists from radio stations. Otherwise, they conduct sample surveys to give an approximation of what songs have been played and how frequently.

Unfortunately, such methodology does not bode well for indie bands. The more plays, the greater the chance of being represented in these statistics. However, as we will discuss in the "Get Played and Heard" chapter, most of the media that PROs monitor are gated off or extremely difficult for indie bands to get played on. It comes down to luck as to whether any of your performances get caught in one of their surveys. If you're lucky enough to have that occur, however, the check can be quite sizable—anywhere from hundreds of dollars to thousands. More likely, however, you'll only get a letter at the end of the year stating that their sampling showed that none of your songs were performed during the last twelve months.

So, for us indies, receiving performance royalties is rare—even if you can point to exact instances where your music was performed in public (although some PROs have set aside royalties for members who get played in media and venues that are not included in their surveys). Ironically, when you perform your own songs live, you should get compensated for the performance of these copyrighted works. Unfortunately, PROs in the United States do not survey venues where indie bands typically perform. Instead, they put money from these venues into a general license fund that is then distributed to PRO members based on featured performances on radio and television—where most indies never get played.

Still, the relative cost of joining these PROs as authors and publishers is minimal. If you expect to have your songs performed by others beyond your own band, then it's worth joining and registering your published songs with one of them. While it's possible you won't receive any royalties, not registering guarantees that you won't. We'll discuss registering as an author and a publisher in a later section.

Digital Downloads and Interactive Digital-Stream Web Sites

Two digital distribution methods that generate public performances of music include Web sites that offer digital downloads and Web-based music players that allow the user to control the music delivery, such as by allowing the listener to pick the next song in a playlist, which is the case with MySpace's music player.

PROs generally offer Web sites like this blanket licenses. Just as your band's author/publisher is owed mechanical royalties for any CDs you press, so, too, is the author/publisher owed performance royalties for any digital downloads made from your Web site or songs played from an interactive music player. The same advice we gave above in dealing with this situation applies here as well: you will need to handle or waive the performance royalties technically owed to the songwriters.

Sampled

The sampling right to a song is not as straightforward as the other rights we've discussed above. In general, when a sample of a song is incorporated into another's work, it's the sound-recording owner who gives permission and gets a royalty, since it's the recording that's being used as an instrument.

However, depending on the length and use of the sample, the author/publisher may also be asked for permission as well. Typically, to avoid any legal issues, artists and labels that use samples in their music err on the side of caution and get a license from both the author/publisher and the sound-recording owner.

Printed

The author/publisher must be asked permission whenever the music or lyrics of their song are printed. The author/publisher can license such use for a royalty. The music and lyrics can appear in magazines, books, on Web sites, and even in greeting cards.

Although anyone can perform or record a published song as long as the the statutory royalties are paid, the printing rights are different and not subject to the same limits. If you print the lyrics of your songs in the CD booklet or on your Web site, your band's author/publisher are owed a royalty. The same is true for cover songs. Even if you've gotten a mechanical license to record the song, you'll still need to negotiate a separate license for the right to print the lyrics.

THE SOUND RECORDING

Anytime someone wants to use a sound recording, he or she must ask the sound-recording owner for permission. The author/publisher team is always excluded in sound-recording license analyses (to the extent they aren't the sound-recording owner!). However, as outlined in the above section, any licensed use of the sound recording usually results in a separate license being needed for the song since, by definition, using the sound recording is using the song. The table, "Rights in the Sound Recording," outlines in brief the many uses and rights that we'll discuss below.

Sound Recording Is Released

The sound-recording owner must approve any release of the sound recording and is entitled to a royalty for each copy made. This includes the use of the sound recording by others such as on compilation CDs or sound tracks. It also includes any digital downloads whether at your Web site or in someone else's podcast. This is called the master use right.

The master use right is similar to a mechanical right with one important exception: no compulsory license option forces the use of the sound recording. Unlike a published song, which can be played by other musicians, the use of a sound recording depends solely on the permission of the sound-recording owner. And unlike with a mechanical royalty, no statutory rate is imposed on how much the owner can charge.

RIGHTS IN THE SOUND RECORDING

(Owned and Controlled by the Sound Recording Owner)

Released as a Recording

Used in an Audio-Visual Work

Played or Performed Publicly

For Broadcast to Public

Your sound recording is incorporated in a video production such as a TV show, film, or video that's broadcasted to the public

Legal Right at Issue:
Your right to allow the user to sync your song to a video image that can be broadcasted to the public

License:
Master Use License

Who would License:
User of the song such as a TV or film production company, indie and student filmakers, or YouTubers

Who Pays You:
The user of the song

Note: The license fee you can charge is negotiable

For Sale to Public

Your sound recording is incorporated in a video production that is sold to the public on DVD

Legal Right at Issue:
Your right to allow your sound recording to be used in the video production that is sold to the public

License:
Videogram License

Who would License:
User of the song such as a TV or film production company, indie and student filmakers

Who Pays You:
The user of the song

Note: The license fee you can charge is negotiable

Physical Copy

Your sound recording is released on CD

Legal Right at Issue:
Your right to allow your sound recording copied to a physical medium

License:
Master Use License

Who would License:
Users that make your sound recording available on CD including CD compilations or soundtrack albums

Note: Historically, the record label would own the Master Use License

Who Pays You:
The user of the song

Note: The license fee you can charge is negotiable

Digital Download

Your sound recording is released as an MP3 or WAV that's made available for download

Legal Right at Issue:
Your right to allow your sound recording copied for digital download

License:
Master Use License

Who would License:
Users that make your sound recording available for download

Who Pays You:
The user of the song

Note: The license fee you can charge is negotiable

Broadcast and Establishments

Your sound recording is broadcasted on the radio, TV, or played in public at an establishment, such as a restaurant, venue, airport, etc.

Legal Right at Issue:
None

Note: Historically, this media has not had to pay for sound recording rights

License:
None

Who would License:
No one

Who Pays You:
No one

Sampled

Your sound recording (or a portion of it) is used as a sample or made into a loop and incorporated into another song

Legal Rights at Issue:
Your right to have your sound recording used as a sample or loop

License:
Master Use License

Who would License:
Musicians, bands, or a record label

Who Pays You:
The user of the song

Note: The license fee you can charge is negotiable

Printed

Your song (or lyrics) is printed out in some way such as in sheet music, tablature, book, etc.

Legal Right at Issue:
None

License:
None

Who would License:
No one

Who Pays You:
No one

Other

Your sound recording is used as a ringtone, incorporated in a toy, greeting card, doorbell, video game, etc. or is translated or made into a derivative work

Legal Right at Issue:
Your right to have your song copied for a particular use

License:
You can create a license for any specific use of your sound recording not covered by one of the more established ways outlined in this chart

Who would License:
Phone companies, toy manufacturers, greeting card company, or any other user that would like to use your song for a particular purpose

Who Pays You:
The user of the song

Note: The license fee you can charge is negotiable

Non-Interactive Digital Stream Broadcasters

Your sound recording is streamed over the Web or cable/satellite radio station

Legal Right at Issue:
Your right to have your song digitally streamed

License:
Digital Performance Right License

Who would License:
Broadcasters that digitally stream your song to the public (including radiostations that simulcast over the Web)

Who Pays You:
A PRO such as SoundExchange (the user of the song pays a license to the PRO which then pays you)

Note: The license fee may be limited by statute

Interactive Digital Stream Broadcasters

Your sound recording is made available on a music player that allows users to control the song and song order (pause, rewind, fast forward, etc.)

Legal Right at Issue:
Your right to have your song publicly performed by others and controlled by the user similar to a digital download

License:
Master Use License

Who would License:
Web sites and broadcasters that provide interactive digital streams of your song to the public

Who Pays You:
The user of the song

Note: The license fee you can charge is negotiable

Sound Recordings Used in an Audiovisual Work

Sound-recording owners can license their master to be used with a visual image such as in a film, documentary, music video, television show, or commercial. Similar to the above, this licensing is not compulsory, and the rate is negotiable.

Sound Recordings Played Publicly

In the pre-Net era, there were no performance rights in a sound recording. When terrestrial radio started, the powers that be negotiated and decided that radio would not need to pay any license fee for the use of the sound recording over its airwaves. They reasoned that radio was a promotional arm for the record labels; record labels wanted to sell records, cassettes, and CDs, and radio was one "safe" way to have the public sample the music that was available for sale without giving the public control over the sound recordings.

Unfortunately, this is not true for the Web and other new broadcast mediums such as satellite and cable radio. Sound-recording owners—which are mostly record labels—lobbied Congress to create a performance right for the sound recording. Their efforts have been successful, but in a limited way: only "noninteractive" digital-stream broadcasters must get permission. "Noninteractive" is a legal category that simply means any technology that mimics terrestrial radio. If the listener can interact, the law doesn't see this as a sound-recording performance since it's the equivalent to a track on a CD. Any service that meets the noninteractive definition must license the use of the sound recordings they play. Basically, this boils down to satellite radio, cable radio, and people streaming audio on their Web site. It also covers any terrestrial radio station that chooses to simulcast its signal over the Web.

Once again, knowing where and when your sound recording was played is a challenge. Therefore, the U.S. Copyright Office designated a new PRO, SoundExchange, to help sound-recording owners collect and distribute royalties. We'll discuss how to register your sound recordings with SoundExchange in a later section below.

Sampled Sound Recordings

Sound-recording owners must be asked permission whenever their sound recordings are sampled or otherwise used as a loop, groove, or instrument.

Once again, the sound-recording owner can deny use or license the master use rights for a royalty. As with all sound-recording owner rights, there is no standard fee or process to obtain permission.

OTHER USES AND RIGHTS

The rights we listed above for the song and sound recording are the more common ones you'll run into. But those aren't the only ways your song might be licensed. Other uses for music include ringtones, musical greeting cards, musical toys, or even the creation of that singing plastic fish on the wall of your dad's den. You can license your song or sound recording for any of these uses, and new uses for music seem to be invented every day.

Your licenses for novel uses of your music (or any use that's not limited by statutory rates, such as sync and videogram licenses) should be:

- *Nonexclusive.* This way you can continue to license the song to others at any time. Exclusivity should come at a higher royalty rate.

- *Limited for a specific use.* Don't grant more rights or uses than the user wants at that moment. That way, the users have to come back for additional licenses should they ever need to use the song in different ways in the future.

- *Limited by territory.* Worldwide rights should earn higher royalty rates than rights in one territory.

- *Limited in duration.* Never grant rights "in perpetuity," which would allow the licensee to use your song forever.

Taking these factors into account can help you reserve the rights you have in your song so that, if a new technology comes along, the licensee will need to come back to you to make a new deal.

USING YOUR RIGHTS TO GET YOUR MUSIC OUT THERE

As an indie band, you need to do anything you can to get your music out there. This includes creative licensing, which we'll talk about below.

License Your Songs and Sound Recordings Under
Creative Commons

To paraphrase Tim O'Reilly, a publisher and Internet luminary, "Obscurity is a far greater threat to authors and creative artists than piracy." Uploading music to your Web site and shackling its use does not encourage people to discover it. That's why we strongly encourage everyone to "download, play, and share" our songs at TheSongOfTheDay.com. The best way for people to discover what we're all about is to hear our songs.

Unfortunately, the default setting of copyright is "You can't copy without permission." So unless you state otherwise on your albums or at your Web site, fans who share your music with friends are infringing on your rights. One way to encourage people to share your music is to issue it under a Creative Commons license. That way they can share it freely.

Creative Commons (creativecommons.org) is a nonprofit organization that provides free tools to help authors, musicians, and other artists create simple licenses that change their copyright terms from "All Rights Reserved" to "Some Rights Reserved." The organization has drafted a number of premade and linkable licenses that are free to use and customize depending on your needs. These Creative Commons licenses tell the world which rights you're willing to grant and which rights you wish to retain—whether for your music, Web site, photos, artwork, or other rights. If a user wants to use your music for a purpose not expressly given by your Creative Commons license, then the user needs to contact the author/publisher and sound-recording owner as outlined above.

The license we recommend using is their music-sharing license, also known as the Attribution-NonCommercial-NoDerivativeWork. Licensing your music this way allows anyone to use and copy your songs as long as they attribute them to your band, don't modify them, and don't use them for commercial purposes. Any person who wants to use your song or sound recording for a commercial reason (e.g., TV show, film, Web site with advertising) must license it from you as outlined in the previous section. Other licenses include one that allows users to sample, mashup, remix, loop, or otherwise transform your songs. We use this license for our music to encourage our fans to get creative with our songs.

When you issue such a license, you need the permission of both the author/publisher and the sound-recording owner. They all have to be on board with this decision, otherwise you don't have the necessary rights to issue the license. And they should be aware that the license is granted in perpetuity—you can't revoke it once you've released your songs under this license. We suggest that you read it carefully and be comfortable with the terms before using it. However, if you license your music this way, it helps to promote your music and could lead to opportunities.

For instance, Jonathan Coulton released "Code Monkey" during his "Thing a Week" project under a Creative Commons license that restricted commercial use. When a television production company wanted to use the song for their television show of the same name, they still had to obtain the necessary rights from Coulton. In fact, the company will need additional licenses if the show makes it to DVD. Also, since the show airs on the G4 network, its airplay is monitored by Coulton's PRO. If the song is detected in its survey, Coulton will have a sizable check coming to him.

Sublicense Your Publishing Rights with External Music Publishers
Another way to get your music out there is to negotiate a deal with a professional music publisher who will actively lobby television production companies and other commercial music users to license your music. These publishers are essentially agents for your songs. They spend their entire day promoting, marketing, and pitching the songs in their catalog to others in the hopes of getting someone to license them.

Music publishers get a cut of your publisher share in order to earn royalties on the songs they promote. Sometimes, they will pay you an advance against the royalties they expect the song or catalog to earn. Music publishers include major companies such as BMG, Sony, and Warner/Chappell, as well as midsize and independent publishing houses. Typically, music publishers work song by song, although some may want to publish your entire music catalog. Whether you can get an external music publisher interested in your music depends on whether they believe they can get your music licensed. Since their job is to match existing music to the needs of their customers—the music users—a lot depends on your style, genre, lyrics, the quality of the sound recording, and, of course, luck.

Alternatively, you can negotiate a deal with a music administrator. Unlike a music publisher, music administrators do not actively try to get a song licensed. They simply handle the business side of things should you make a licensing deal happen on your own. In exchange for handling this work, you pay them a recurring fee.

Other music services are stepping into the music-publishing arena. For instance, although they do not actively promote your songs the way a music publisher would, CD Baby offers its musician clients the option of giving CD Baby a percentage of any synchronization license royalties in exchange for CD Baby's listing the musician's songs in its catalog to television producers and filmmakers of what is available for licensing. The virtual record label Magnatune (magnatune.com) does something similar with the artists on its roster. Since synchronization fees are not limited by statute, these licensing deals can be substantial. To the extent you make the deal happen (or it comes to you), you're now obligated to pay these third parties a share of the revenue. When it comes to your rights, you always want to weigh the pros and cons.

Acting as Your Own Publisher

Of course, you don't need a publisher to license your music. Given your well-branded Web site, a music user who wants to license your music can come directly to you. For instance, ABC Family/Disney contacted us at our Web site to license our song "Get Out!" from *The Cheapass Album*. They decided that the song, about "living life in my parents' basement," was perfect for a television commercial campaign promoting their new reality TV series about twentysomethings who were forced to leave their parents' house to get an apartment, a job, and a life.

Given that they specifically wanted to use the sound recording from our album, we negotiated both a nonexclusive synchronization license (for the song) and a master use license (for the sound recording). Because they needed the song for thirty-second spots, both licenses gave them the right to make a derivative work so they could chop up the song and have a narrator talk over it. Lastly, although both licenses gave them the right to use the song and sound-recording worldwide (since they're a cable network), we limited their use to the length of the commercial campaign (nine weeks). Because we had all the rights in the song and sound recording, we negotiated and finalized the deal within a week, and the author/publisher and sound-recording owner received all the money negotiated.

We predict there will be more direct licensing deals with indie bands in the future now that many production companies simply surf iTunes looking for a song title or style that fits their needs. Brad Turcotte of Brad Sucks believes this is exactly what happened when VH-1 licensed his song "Sick as a Dog" for a scene in a television show that showed someone puking. Often, companies don't care if you're a "known artist." They just want a song that fits their needs. It's only a bonus that indie songs are less expensive than those encumbered by middlemen.

If you're interested in music publishing and want to know more about what publishers do, we recommend *Making Music Make Money: An Insider's Guide to Becoming Your Own Music Publisher* by Eric Beall.

Requests for Music: License Your Songs Through Music Aggregators

Sometimes production and advertising companies rely on music aggregators to find music. There are two types: a "go-between" music aggregator that connects musicians with production and advertising companies, and music production libraries.

A go-between music aggregator gathers music requests from production companies and publishes these requests on its Web site. Musicians who subscribe to the aggregator's Web site can upload their music (or even create new material) for consideration, usually for a fee. The aggregator then filters the submissions, passing along the closest matches to the production company for consideration.

This is how Taxi (taxi.com) works. They make "wanted" listings available to their members for a yearly fee of approximately $300. Submitting a song for consideration costs a small fee (to encourage musicians to discriminate rather than upload their entire catalog for each listing). Taxi's staff reviews each submitted song and decides which ones to send on.

They'll even critique the song and the recording for the musician. If the music user chooses your song, Taxi puts them in touch with you to work out a licensing deal.

Production companies can also license music from companies that create music libraries. These music aggregators hire songwriters and musicians to create original music in a variety of styles, which they in turn sell or license to music users for use in their productions. Because their clients are often in radio, television, and film, they create a variety of versions of each song, chopping them into fifteen- and thirty-second clips and making instrumental versions. Depending on the music aggregator, the music is either licensed per use, covered by a yearly subscription arrangement, or sold royalty-free.

These music aggregators often negotiate a work-for-hire arrangement with musicians, paying in advance in exchange for the song and sound recording. Others work out deals that allow the songwriter to retain some of the rights and receive additional royalties when a song is licensed. Typically, performance rights for the author/publisher are not affected, but the music aggregator may want part of the publishing rights. Songs are licensed to these catalogs exclusively, as the music aggregators need to ensure that the song and sound recording are only available through their library.

Musician Brett Ratner, of the indie band Socialite Fiasco, writes and records music for the music aggregator WildWhirled (wildwhirled.com). WildWhirled has paid agreements with nearly a hundred songwriters like Ratner, who specialize in writing and recording different genres of music. The company's music has been used in countless television shows, films, and advertising campaigns. For instance, many of Brett's original alternative-country songs have been used on the television show *My Name Is Earl.*

Some music aggregators such as WildWhirled do not take unsolicited submissions of recordings. Instead, they assign musicians in their roster to write songs to match what they're looking for. Others, such as NOMA Music (nomamusic.com), do accept submissions. If you wish to use a music aggregator, you should carefully look at their licensing options and requirements.

Get Commissioned and Write Songs for Others

Rather than exploit your existing songs, you can always exploit your talent at writing songs. Music made to order for television shows, films, commercials, the theater, and video games is big business. Professional songwriters usually create under work-for-hire agreements. While writing themes for television shows and films may seem out of your arm's reach, you can still write music for podcasters, YouTubers, indie and student filmmakers, or other Web-site owners. Often, these music users just use whatever music is handy, infringing on copyrights simply because they don't know where to find the right music to fit their needs. As an indie band, you can not only help improve their production values, but also keep them out of legal trouble. At the same time, you'll be getting your music heard while promoting your band.

We've been writing songs, themes, and other incidental music for years under Beatnik Turtle's "Songs-On-Demand" service, offering to write themes, beds, and bumpers for anyone for money, barter, or sometimes for free. We generally keep the rights to the music and grant a nonexclusive license solely for the intended purpose, making that clear in an e-mail to the requester. We also ask for attribution (and a link back) and allow derivative works so users can cut, speed up, talk over, and otherwise incorporate the song into their work. Then we expressly state that all other rights not discussed are reserved. That way, if they have a new use, such as putting their work on a CD or DVD to sell, they need to come back to us for permission.

When we write music for a fee, we enter into a more detailed agreement to clarify which rights the music user is getting and which we retain. This, too, typically occurs over e-mail. However, if we're hired to write music for a commercial endeavor, such as a theme for a television show, a contract is always drafted, and if it's not a work-for-hire relationship, we typically license many of the rights to the song and sound recording (including derivative rights) so the music user has some flexibility.

Get every commissioned work arrangement—whether free, for barter, or for pay—in writing. For expediency, we usually rely on e-mail to work out the license details, but that's not without its risks. Any good lawyer would tell you that, given that you can never know exactly how a song or sound recording might be exploited and used in the future, it's always best to be as explicit as possible. If you decide to travel down this road, know what you're risking or, better still, mitigate this risk by enlisting an attorney to help draft the license.

COPYRIGHT PRACTICALITIES

Now that you have the basics down about copyright and licensing, let's address some practical issues that indies face.

REGISTERING YOUR SONGS AND SOUND RECORDINGS
Registering Your Songs and Sound Recordings with the Copyright Office

Registering your songs and sound recordings with the U.S. Copyright Office makes a public record of your copyright claim. It's a way to declare to the world that you've created a specific song or recording and confirms the date of creation by a recognized authority. This is extremely useful if there's ever an infringement claim, clarifying who wrote what and when.

Registering amounts to filling out the proper paperwork and providing a copy of the work—usually on CD. It's important to note that the Copyright Office doesn't listen to what you send in or compare it to other works in their system. All it does is create a file in its database outlining the details of your claim. Then, it puts the physical submission in that huge warehouse from the ending of *Raiders of the Lost Ark*. It's only later, if you run into a copyright dispute, end up in court, and need to prove when you wrote the song, that they retrieve the file. Given that it's the U.S. Copyright Office providing the evidence, the court will give a lot of weight to what was registered.

The registration process is rather time-consuming and there's a fee. Unfortunately, this is rather steep, currently $35 for online submissions and $45 for hard-copy submissions. But registration provides some important benefits, such as:

- Registering is necessary before you can file an infringement suit against someone.

- Registration prior to infringement of the work can result in additional money awarded should you win—possibly including attorney's fees.

Both the U.S. Copyright Office (copyright.gov) and the Canadian Intellectual Property Office (cipo.gc.ca) provide instructions on how to register your songs and sound recordings. For a no-nonsense, real-world guide to registering, head to IndieBandSurvivalGuide.com.

Registering with a PRO for Song Performance Royalties

As stated above, when your songs are performed, it can result in performance royalties. To ensure you get any money that might be owed to you, you'll want to join a PRO. Becoming a member allows you to register information about your songs (usually online) so the PRO knows which songs to track in their surveys. Typically, once you've made your music available to the public, such as by releasing an album for sale, you can register as an author and publisher with one of these PROs. For simplicity, PROs encourage, and often require, membership in only one organization. Each PRO calculates royalties differently. Some also offer perks such as discounts for music equipment at music chain stores, career assistance, and health insurance benefits, so you'll want to choose the best one for your needs. Two of the most well-known PROs are ASCAP and BMI; however, there are PROs in different countries as well as ones for specific genres of music.

Once you've picked your PRO, remember that it only pays author royalties to authors and publisher royalties to publishers. As stated above, if you're both the author and publisher of a song and neglect to sign up as a publisher, you will lose out on the publisher royalties they collect. Each PRO has its own registration method and (nominal) application fees, so you'll need to visit their Web sites and contact them to register.

PERFORMANCE AND MECHANICAL RIGHTS ORGANIZATIONS

Performance Rights

Performance royalties for songs:

- ASCAP (ascap.com)

- BMI (bmi.com)

- SESAC (sesac.com) (Note: To become a member of SESAC you must be invited.)

- CCLI (www.ccli.co.uk) (Note: CCLI licenses performance rights specifically for Christian music.)

- SOCAN (socan.ca) (Canada)

Performance royalties for sound recordings:
- SoundExchange (soundexchange.com)

Mechanical Rights
- Harry Fox Agency (harryfox.com) ♥

Registering with SoundExchange to Get Sound-Recording Performance Royalties

You should also register your sound recordings with SoundExchange (sound exchange.com), the PRO that obtains performance royalties for sound recordings. Since sound-recording rights are different from the song rights, you can join this PRO in addition to one of the song-performance PROs.

This type of royalty is rather new and the subject of much discussion and negotiation. Sign up as a "sound-recording copyright owner" and designate the "featured artist" for the sound recording—your band—since royalties are split between the two. If you don't register both, it will result in lost royalties. SoundExchange will adjust these splits if there is more than one featured artist, or if you wish to provide a cut to your producer or another band member. For more information on these issues and to learn more about registering your sound recordings, see the SoundExchange Web site.

GETTING PERMISSION TO RECORD AND PLAY OTHER PEOPLE'S MUSIC

Playing Cover Songs Live

In general, when playing live, whether onstage or for a radio station in-studio, you can perform any published song you want—even "Free

Bird." Copyright law grants you the right to perform any published song, and the author/publisher doesn't get a say in the matter. Lynyrd Skynyrd can't stop you from playing "Free Bird" even though they, and everyone else in the room, may want to. The owner needs only to be paid the statutory rate. Chances are, however, that you've never paid a cent to the owners of "Free Bird." Are you in trouble?

Yes.

And no. Recall that PROs work out deals with establishments and venues for the right to have music performed publicly. This is likely to include the very place you're playing at since music no doubt makes up a lot of its business—check the front window for a PRO license sticker. So when you wind up your original songs and launch into "Free Bird," it's the venue that's paying for your performance—not you.

Technically, however, if the venue doesn't have license with a PRO to cover your performance, you're actually liable and need to pay for the performance right. Now, being liable and actually being sued are entirely different things. It's most likely that the song owners won't come after you and all the other bands that have performed copyrighted music at the venue, since it's the venue itself that should have known better than to operate without a PRO license. Most important, the PROs know exactly where the venue is. If you discover that a particular venue isn't paying a licensing fee, then PROs probably want to know. Be sure to leave the tip anonymously, though, since you'll still want to play the venue.

Recording Cover Songs

When you record a cover song, you need to obtain a mechanical license from the author/publisher and pay the requisite fees (usually the statutory rate). As outlined above, it doesn't matter if the song is given away for free or used as a promo, a copy is a copy, and to avoid an infringement claim, you're supposed to obtain a license. If you plan on having your recorded version on CD as well as making it available as a digital download, you need to obtain two mechanical licenses.

Although a mechanical license allows you to record a cover, it does not allow you to make a derivative version of the song. What constitutes a derivative version as opposed to a cover version is up in the air, but in general, it means you can change the style and genre to make it your own, but can't change the basic melody or a substantial part of the lyrics. Also, obtaining a mechanical license does not allow you to do anything with the original sound recording of the song. That's a different license, obtained from the sound-recording owner.

There are two ways to get a mechanical license. First, you can always contact the author/publisher of the song directly and work out a deal. You can find the publisher's contact information by checking the ASCAP, BMI, or Harry Fox online databases (discussed below), checking the U.S. Copyright Office online database, searching the Internet, or checking the CD booklet.

A much more convenient method is the Harry Fox Agency's online database, Songfile (harryfox.com). In many cases a publisher has affiliated itself with Harry Fox to administer the mechanical licensing and collect royalties on its behalf. Checking with the Harry Fox Agency first is always the best way to go. You simply type in the name of the song, and if they have the rights, they'll issue you a compulsory license. Songfile will ask you to answer a few questions about how many copies you intend to make, whether they will be available physically or digitally, and will gather your contact information.

There are some limits to the number of copies Songfile can license in this manner. For physical copies, the minimum is 250 and the maximum is 2,500. For downloads, the minimum is 150 and the maximum is 2,500. Although you'll know how many CDs you intend to press, with digital downloads, you'll need to estimate. If you are making anything less or anything more than these limits, you'll need to go to the publisher directly to negotiate.

Once you've answered all the necessary questions, a fee is calculated based on the number of copies, the statutory rate, and a small percentage to cover Harry Fox's administrative costs. Once paid, Harry Fox will e-mail you the license. Read it carefully so you know how to properly attribute the author/publisher.

The license for physical copies is a onetime fee. Digital downloads, however, require you to renew every year you continue to make the song available for download. Unfortunately, you can't roll over copies you haven't distributed within the year. If you buy a 1,000-download license but sell only 3 within the year, the remaining 997 won't carry over to the next year. So estimate carefully.

Also, failing to renew the license at the end of the year while allowing it, for instance, to stay up at iTunes is an infringement. Once you make this commitment, be sure to remind yourself each year to renew. Additionally, if you end up distributing more than the number of copies you initially paid for, you are required to purchase an additional license.

We used SongFile when we recorded a version of "Older" by They Might Be Giants for our live album *Thanks for Coming Out: Beatnik Turtle Live!* We only wanted to release the album digitally, so we purchased a mechanical license for digital distribution. If at some point we decide to release the album on CD, we'll need to obtain a mechanical license for pressing physical copies. And the CD printing house will require proof of this license.

Recording Works in the Public Domain

Of course, if the song you're recording is in the public domain, as is the case with traditional folk music, you don't need anyone's permission. We did this when we recorded a series of traditional Irish pub songs for our album *Sham Rock* such as "Tell Me Ma," "Beer, Beer, Beer," and "Whiskey, Yer the Devil." Since these songs have been passed down through the generations and are safely within the public domain, we didn't need to license any rights. Of course, our versions of the song and the parts we added—our unique guitar, horn, and lyrical arrangements—are copyrighted by us, as are the sound recordings. If another band wanted to do a cover of our cover using our arrangements and the parts we added, they would need our permission.

Using Other People's Samples and Audio Loops

Whenever you incorporate any samples and audio loops in your music, you need permission from the sound-recording owner. Whether the owner allows you to use the sample in your song is entirely up to them, and if permission isn't granted, you're out of luck. If the owner does grant you permission, however, be prepared to pay large fees, since there's no limit to the amount the owner can charge for a sample clearance license. The clearance may cost you anywhere from a few hundred to a few thousand dollars. Additionally, the owner may ask for a percentage of the income derived from your song and a bonus payment when a certain threshold of copies are sold. Depending on the type and extent of the sample or loop, you might need to get permission from the author/publisher as well. This, too, will result in fees.

Solutions to this financial nightmare include:

- *Recording a cover version of the sample or audio loop.* You can always record a cover version of the sample or audio loop you wish to use. If you do so, you'll need permission from the author/publisher as outlined above.

- *Using precleared samples and audio loops.* Some companies produce royalty-free loops, available on CD, DVD, and online. See the "Your Albums and Merchandise" chapter for a list of such sites. Always verify the license restrictions to confirm that they allow derivative works.

- *Use samples and audio loops issued under Creative Commons licenses.* A large number of musicians believe in sharing their loops royalty-free and release them under a Creative Commons license. Of course, some of these samples and loops are not licensed for commercial purposes, so if you decide to sell a song incorporating such samples, you'll need to clear it with the sound-recording owner.

- *Record your own samples and audio loops.* You can always create your own loops and license them to yourself—if you're feeling generous that day.

COPYRIGHT BEYOND MUSIC: TEXT, PHOTOS, GRAPHICS, AND VIDEO

So far we've focused on your rights as they apply to music. As an indie band, however, you're probably doing it all—creating text, photos, graphics, and video for your brand, Web site, albums, merchandise, and more. All these intellectual properties are copyrighted, too. Often a band agreement will outline who owns the copyrighted works you'll be creating as a band.

It's on the flip side of this copyright issue that most indie bands get in trouble. Often, they'll incorporate other people's copyrighted works into their own materials. Many indies use copyrighted images on their Web site, sync their music to copyrighted video footage on YouTube, or use copyrighted band photos on their albums and posters. Just as you need to get permission to use and cover other people's music, so, too, do you need permission for the use of other nonoriginal works.

Although we suggest sources for royalty-free text, photos, graphics, and video throughout the *Guide*, the intricacies of getting permission from copyright owners for this material is outside our scope. Instead, we recommend a detailed book on the subject, *Getting Permission: How to License & Clear Copyrighted Materials Online & Off* by Richard Stim.

Working with Photographers

If you get a photographer to take pictures of your band, know that the photographer owns the copyright to the photos of your band—not you. This is the case even if you pay the photographer to take the photos. Each use you want to make of the photos must be cleared and licensed with the photographer. So, just because your photographer gives you permission to use one photo for use on your Web site doesn't mean you can necessarily use it for promotional materials or an album cover.

Make sure that you are clear what rights you are getting from the photographer. And, of course, get it in writing. If you can, you want a photographer who will work for hire so that you own the photos. Some might charge you more for this option.

MORE ABOUT COPYRIGHT

If you are interested in learning more about copyright, including its history and how the Internet is changing the law, we recommend *Free Culture: How Big Media Uses Technology and the Law to Lock Down Culture and Control Creativity* by Lawrence Lessig, professor of law at Stanford Law School and founder of the Creative Commons organization.

The book is freely available under a Creative Commons license at free-culture.cc.

MERCHANDISING RIGHTS

As mentioned in the "Your Albums and Merchandise" chapter, merchandising—the business of using your brand iconography to sell products—can be a major part of your income. Merchandising involves:

- The owner of your copyrighted brand images and text

- The merchandising-rights owner, who has the contractual right to sell products with your copyrighted brand images and text

Your band agreement should outline who or what owns your band name, brand, and merchandising rights, although, to the extent that your products have lyrics from your songs printed on them, such use actually falls under the author/publisher's printing rights. Permission must be obtained or worked out beforehand before using any lyrics. Song titles, on the other hand, can't be copyrighted and are fair game.

Record labels often try to take a cut of merchandising rights. Bands that hold on to these rights typically sell them for an advance (and possible royalties) to a merchandise company that handles everything from design to order fulfillment. However, these one-stop shops only purchase the merchandising rights from national or major-label acts.

As an indie band, these rights are yours, and doing the merchandise yourselves means that all the profits will be yours as well. One notable exception: often, venues want a cut of any merchandising revenues earned in their establishment. Any such cut should be negotiated ahead of time, with an agreement in writing.

TRADEMARKS

Since indie bands now reach a global audience, protecting your band name and brand is more of an issue than ever. The law protecting your band name and brand is known as trademark law. Trademark law is an entirely different body of law from copyright law, with different principles and procedures to learn.

TRADEMARK LAW BASICS

A trade or service mark (for simplification, we'll stick with the word *trademark* since both are essentially the same) is a distinctive word, phrase, or symbol that uniquely identifies your product or service to the world and separates you in the mind of the public from competing products or services. For an indie band, trademarks include your band name, logo, tagline, or mascot. The value of these marks grow over time as you repeatedly and consistently use them to represent your band and music to the public. This value can be protected under trademark law. In fact, the more you use your marks and the longer you use them, the stronger your trademark rights become.

Under the law, the first person to publicly use a mark for a specific product or service in commerce automatically owns it. So, if you were the first indie band in the world to use your name, logo, tagline, or mascot online in some public manner such as your Web site, a newspaper ad announcing a show, or a poster, you likely are the trademark owner. This doesn't mean a person or company can't use the same marks with a different product or service, however. In general, you only have the rights to those marks for music purposes.

Of course, to the extent that your mark is at all similar to another famous mark outside of music, you'll likely be infringing and may be contacted to stop using it. For instance, in the "Your Brand" chapter we said you would not want to name your band *Google* even if no other band exists under that name. Given trademark law, it's likely that Google would successfully prevent you from operating under this name even though you're a band, not a search engine.

Why? Unlike copyright law, which protects your copyright for your life plus an additional seventy years before your work falls into the public domain, trademarks—even famous ones—can fall into the public domain if not diligently protected. After all, if you're taking a word or symbol out of the public domain but aren't actively using and protecting it to ensure that it identifies your product or service, then someone else should be able to use it. This is why famous brands such as Coca-Cola, Budweiser, and McDonald's have to aggressively protect their trademarks from any use that might confuse and "dilute" the value they've built in their marks with the public. Only through active maintenance of their marks does the law allow companies to keep them.

Additionally, the law gives trademark owners some commonsense rights. For instance, if you name your band a variation of the word *Google* such as *The Google, G00gle, Gooooogle,* or even *Gue Gull,* the company would have a strong case against your band as well. Courts make these fact-based decisions, and there are always exceptions for attorneys to argue over, but our general advice is to avoid any name or mark similar to ones already in use. If you're still stumped about what name or mark would be considered fair game, consult your attorney.

Once you own a trademark, on the other hand, you will need to protect it from dilution and confusion in the marketplace just as aggressively. If another band starts using your name or any other marks of yours, you have the right and obligation to prevent them from doing so. This is true even if the other band plays different music from yours. The public—and your fans—may become confused about which band is which when it comes to shows, albums, and merchandise, and the longer you let the other band's use of the mark stand, the more strength they will have to defend it in a court of law.

Unfortunately, enforcing your rights usually costs money. You'll want to hire an attorney to send a cease-and-desist letter to any infringing party and either negotiate a compromise such as allowing them to choose a different name retaining some element of their former name or to prevent them from engaging as a band under that name.

You'll need to determine who in your band is the trademark owner. Typically, band agreements turn the band name, brand, and trademark over to the band as an entity.

DO YOU NEED TO REGISTER YOUR NAME?

Like a copyright, a trademark is automatically generated as long as you meet the requirements outlined above. However, registration with the U.S. Patent and Trademark Office (uspto.gov) or the Canadian Intellectual Property Office (cipo.gc.ca) will give you additional rights, a public record that you spent the time and money to protect the rights you have in your band name and brand, and act as a deterrent to other bands searching for a name of their own. Whether you choose to register your mark is typically a matter of cost. Unlike copyright law, registering a mark is expensive.

As an indie band you do it all: you sell products (which are covered under trademark) and perform music (which is covered under a service mark). Every product and service is designated into a particular class of goods and services. You should consider registering your marks under the following classes:

- *Class 9.* The sale of digital media (CDs, downloadable audio files, etc.) under your band name

- *Class 16.* The use of your band name in posters, pamphlets, newsletters, and other promotional materials

- *Class 25.* The use of your marks on T-shirts and other merchandise

- *Class 41.* Entertainment services including the use of your name in conjunction with performing as a band

Keep in mind that each trademark you register (name, logo, tagline, mascot) and each class you register it in costs money. Registering under each class can cost around $300 for the application alone. This does not include attorney costs. If you have to choose just one, we recommend trademarking your band name in class 41.

REGISTERING YOUR TRADEMARKS WITH THE TRADEMARK OFFICE

Trademark registration is more complicated than copyright registration, but both the U.S. Patent and Trademark Office (USPTO) and the Canadian Intellectual Property Office have detailed online registration systems that walk you through the process. You can register on your own, but we recommend using an attorney. Unlike the U.S. Copyright Office, the USPTO employs examiners to review your application, perform their own trademark search, and send you an "action letter" asking for additional information if they find an issue with your application. Once your registration is approved, you can use the registration symbol, ®. Until then, it's against the law.

OTHER ISSUES: TAXES, INSURANCE, CONTRACTS, AND MORE

Many legal and business issues go beyond the scope of the *Guide*. Links to government, legal, and business resources are posted at IndieBand SurvivalGuide.com. We once again suggest reading *Music Law: How to Run Your Band's Business* by Richard W. Stim for more information, as well as consulting your attorney and accountant.

PART II
GET FANS

CHAPTER 8

GET NOTICED

GETTING NOTICED is no longer about trying to get the attention of the "music industry" and getting signed; it's about getting people interested in your music. Fortunately, this doesn't have to cost you money. You simply need to be smart about making your music and your message stand out from the crowd.

In this chapter we will detail powerful strategies for winning over new fans.

THE LONG TAIL (REPRISE)

We mentioned the main concept in Chris Anderson's book *The Long Tail*, in chapter 1, but in this chapter, we'll talk about how to apply the Long Tail to gain traction. We live in a world of niches. Each niche has its unique interests, and each niche can have its own sound track as well.

Getting played on television or commercial radio is daunting. But getting your song about the beauty of riding a chopper down the highway featured on a motorcycle Web site doesn't seem all that difficult. If you've written a song about motorcycles, motorcycle enthusiasts will listen to it whether or not they know who you are.

The top-down approach made sense in the old days, when most media were mainstream media. Now, the world is filled with what we like to call niche media. The Internet isn't just a broadcast medium, it's a two-way (or more) street with an endless number of channels. Because of this, you can find a forum on most any topic imaginable and participate through your music or just about anything else you can create.

Once you can see the world as a universe of niches, each one seems a lot easier to break into. Seven effective strategies exist for getting your band and music noticed. But before you reach out to them, you need to know who your audience is.

KNOW YOUR AUDIENCE

In the pre-Net era, you focused on getting noticed locally. Today, focus on getting noticed globally. The Internet allows you to win over more fans than you can imagine. But that wonderful planetary reach makes it much harder to know who's actually listening. Instead of seeing the faces of your fans, many of them will look like nothing more than cold, hard Web statistics. Still, you need to get to know them so you can put your music where they'll find it. Who are your fans, and what do they like?

Our band straddled both the pre-Net and post-Net era, and we found transitioning from one to the other to be enlightening. Our pre-Net fans loved our live show. They had a good time listening to our music, and they loved our horn-powered energy. As the post-Net era arrived, the most popular elements of our live show didn't translate to the Internet. We had to rely on different strategies to win over global fans. These included projects targeting niches beyond our locale such as creating *The Cheapass Album*, which we'll discuss below.

If your music means something to you, then it will probably resonate with the people who share your interests, no matter where in the world they are. So who are your fans? Are they teenagers? Baby boomers? Kids? Thirty-somethings? Geeks? Truckers? Knitting fanatics? The more you know about your fans, the easier it will be to target them in new and compelling ways.

SEVEN EFFECTIVE STRATEGIES FOR GETTING NOTICED

THE STANDING-OUT STRATEGY

More than two hundred thousand indie artists are at CD Baby. The bestsellers all have stories to tell, but one of the most surprising ones is about an artist who wrote an entire album about sailing. While that topic alone isn't enough to get an album to the top sellers' list, the musician got her album reviewed in a popular sailing magazine, which got her tons of sales. A review of a sailing album in a *music* magazine would probably have gotten little notice. But because the review appeared in a *sailing* magazine, people read the article and bought the CD.

Dedicated music publications and sites review stacks of CDs and songs. Even if your band gets its album reviewed—and even if it's a good one— it just doesn't stand out. It's just one of many in a sea of other music reviews. Sailing magazines, on the other hand, don't get many albums to review, they're focused on sailing. So when a review of an album is actually published, it stands out. This goes for *any* nonmusic specialty magazine, blog, or Web site. By targeting her niche, the woman's CD sales skyrocketed.

We call this the standing-out strategy. The great thing about it is, there's room for everyone. While your music probably occupies a musical niche depending on the type of music you play, this represents only one, highly competitive channel for your music. By using nonmusic channels where your music will be the only music to choose from, you'll get noticed.

This is a major shift in thinking that takes some getting used to. It's no longer necessary to stick to places where people listen to music. Forget radio—music can be played on any Web site. There are forums, podcasts, online zines, publications, and sites dedicated to activities where an existing audience might appreciate your music.

Our example of this started out accidentally, after we found inspiration in an usual place: an off-the-wall board game designed by Cheapass Games, called Deadwood. A card in the game led us to write a song called "Were All These Beer Cans Here Last Night?" Only a few weeks later, we hit on the idea to e-mail Cheapass Games and share the song that they had unwittingly inspired. We sent them the song, and surprisingly, they wrote back the next day and asked if they could put it up on their Web site. Within a few months of its being posted, the demo was downloaded well over five thousand times since they had a large audience. Soon, it took on a life of its own, winding up on blogs, message boards, and Internet radio stations, all without our help. Their Web site was so popular that when we searched on *beer cans* on Google at that point, our demo song was on the first page of links. This was great exposure, but it didn't end there. We applied the standing-out strategy and took this idea a step further. We teamed up with Cheapass Games to create an entire album of songs based on their games, *The Cheapass Album*. Best of all, they agreed to give it worldwide distribution along with their games.

Carla Ulbrich (carlau.com), who makes her living as a folksinger, summed it up best: "Go to where you're a novelty." Ulbrich did this by using her wit and off-center perspective to turn an unfortunate series of medical illnesses into inspiration for new music. After releasing albums on these topics, she found new audiences and not only gets traditional gigs, but also plays lucrative gigs at medical conventions, where any music stands out.

THE PIGGYBACKING STRATEGY

Piggybacking can broaden your exposure by your taking something people already know well and leveraging it for yourself. There are three different ways to apply this strategy.

Ride Coattails

As we said in the "Your Brand" chapter, one of the simplest ways to piggyback is to mention the bands that you actually sound like on your Web site. People who know those bands and search on them will find your site and are likely to give your music a chance. In fact, this is exactly how Web-presence services such as Last.fm work. The ultimate way to piggyback is to cover a well-known song by a famous artist. These cover songs are usually an indie artist's best initial sellers. They act as a great gateway for people to discover the artist's original music.

But music is not the only thing that you should piggyback on. Consider all the niches in the world and see if there's a place for your music inside one. And niches don't have to be small. We know of one band that wrote a song about the Indianapolis Colts football team before they went to the Super Bowl. While Colts fans are a niche, it's a large one. The band got a ton of airplay and articles, and a lot of fans bought their music because it successfully piggybacked on the Colts at a time when people were paying a lot of attention to them.

There is more than one way to piggyback on a niche. For example, Pete Shukoff, of the group Nice Peter, wrote a song called "50 Cent Is a Pussy." The forums on his Web sites were buzzing after he released it, and he got a lot of angry comments but an equal number of supporters and new fans. He successfully piggybacked on the same guy he was dissing in his song.

Even album art can provide you an opportunity for piggybacking. The art for Beatnik Turtle's *The Cheapass Album* was drawn by the renowned comic-book and game illustrator Phil Foglio (studiofoglio.com). Foglio has millions of fans, and when we released the album, some people bought it just because they collect his artwork. Our album got listed on a Web site that tracks everything that Phil Foglio illustrates, and he even sells the album from his site.

Again, the place to start is not the traditional music mediums. Instead, brainstorm about concepts, ideas, or even events that can take you further than you would be able to go on your own. For example, when the *Star Wars* thirtieth anniversary came up, we leveraged a song that we had written for the Song of the Day called "Star Wars (A Movie Like No Other)." We summarized the entire original *Star Wars* trilogy in a single song. Later we made a video using a video mashup feature at StarWars.com. It ended up getting played over fifteen thousand times thanks to the active community at that site.

Ride a Tradition

Another way to piggyback is to make an album or a song about a holiday, festival, or other tradition that people know well. When people search on *St. Patrick's Day,* for example, your band might come up if you do an album for it.

We did an album for Christmas called *Santa Doesn't Like You,* and like clockwork that album gets a slew of new sales every December. We come up in searches for terms such as *Santa, Christmas,* and *holiday.* The titles of songs, such as "Coed Naked Drunk Xmas Shopping" and "Smokin' the Mistletoe," get people to sample our music online out of sheer curiosity.

Ride Trends

Current events and popular culture provide opportunities for piggybacking as well. When a topic is hot, a large number of people is guaranteed to be searching for information about it.

The Brobdingnagian Bards are always looking for trends to ride, so when the Monty Python musical *Spamalot* got popular, they posted a blog entry about *Spamalot* and also mentioned that they covered a Monty Python song previously. The post got a ton of hits, got them noticed by new fans, and resulted in sales.

Piggybacking can also be a tool for good, not just good publicity. Grant Baciocco of Throwing Toasters put together two compilation charity albums called *Laughter Is a Powerful Weapon*, with music donated by himself and many other well-known comedy artists. The money from one went to the Twin Towers orphans fund and the other went to the Red Cross for Katrina victims.

THE AGENT STRATEGY

Most bands start out promoting and representing themselves because they start out small. But, when possible, it's a powerful advantage to have a person outside the band represent you. People tend to pay attention when someone who is not directly part of the band talks it up. There's an air of objectivity, even if it's promotional.

Agents are distant enough from the music that they can come up with promotional angles, strategies, and ideas that you might never have thought of. They can claim that you're the best band ever. And if they do something that's a little too outrageous, well, they're just an agent, it doesn't reflect directly on the band. It's also why agents are most useful during negotiations, because they can be mercenary. If you negotiate for yourself, and you give the other side a particularly hard time, they'll start to dislike *you*, rather than your agent.

Also, people tend to assume that you've reached a certain threshold of popularity simply because you can afford to have someone act on your behalf. Before she got an agent of her own, Carla Ulbrich would often pretend to be her own agent over the phone, employing a thick New York accent. When people asked to have lunch with the agent, she'd always be too busy, but they were always in luck because Ulbrich herself could make it.

THE MULTITASKING STRATEGY

None of the musicians we interviewed for the *Guide* rely on one project for their income. Most of them were working on *many* different projects beyond playing live, selling albums, and selling merchandise. For instance, Jonathan Coulton participates in the *Popular Science* magazine podcast at popsci.com and licenses his music. Brad Turcotte of Brad Sucks maintains multiple Web sites including stripcreator.com and also licenses his music. Grant Baciocco of Throwing Toasters writes and produces the multiple-award-winning podcast *The Radio Adventures of Dr. Floyd,* does voice-over and acting work, and produces a podcast for the Jim Henson Company, among other projects. George Hrab is a drummer in a popular cover band that plays at weddings and corporate events, writes and produces his *Geologic Podcast,* and has written a book. The Brobdingnagian Bards produce a popular Celtic-music podcast called *Celtic MP3s Music Magazine* (in addition to four other podcasts and multiple newsletters), maintain multiple Celtic-music Web sites, and even have a comic book.

The notable thing is not that these musicians do so many projects, but that they use each one to promote the other. The Brobdingnagian Bards' Celtic podcasts originally featured their own music, but eventually they got so many submissions from other Celtic bands that they began to highlight the music of others. This not only grew their Celtic-musician network, it also drew in new Celtic-music audiences, broadening their fan network. And once a fan discovered one of these projects, he or she would find the others because the Bards had cobranded everything.

THE LONG-HAUL STRATEGY (THE DEATH OF THE BIG SPLASH)

For some reason, indie musicians have internalized the big-splash strategy that major labels were forced to use because of their business model. The major labels are rarely focused on long-term artist development, instead relying on the power of newness and huge initial sales. Their back catalogs are just gravy, more fuel to pay for new artists rather than for developing established ones.

As an indie band, it's unlikely you'll have the money for a huge initial marketing push with billboards, paid-for radio play, and expensive publicists. Instead, indies must allow development to occur naturally and gain audience and momentum over time.

For instance, Brad Turcotte created his own development cycle to maximize his exposure. In 2001, he released his album online in the form of MP3s, garnering some initial interest and some donations. This money allowed him to make a CD, and when he released this, he gained another surge of new fans. A little later, he released the source tracks to his music, this time making new fans among people who enjoy remixing songs. When he packaged the best remixes into another CD, another surge of new fans loved both the remixes and the original material. Finally, when he released his second album, it generated interest in his previous albums. This album cycle should continue as he releases additional albums and new material. As you can see, Turcotte's original material has generated exposure and income for him over the years.

Just as the album cycle takes time to gather momentum, getting noticed within a niche also takes time. Carla Ulbrich noticed that live festivals and conventions also have a cycle. Effectively breaking into each live festival and convention took about three years. Ulbrich needed that time to make the necessary connections and establish her reputation so that she could consistently get booked at events.

Most of the artists we've interviewed have agreed that it takes time to get noticed, develop a following, and acquire a steady income stream. Jonathan Coulton noticed, during his "Thing a Week" project, bursts of traffic for particular song releases: visitors to his site showed up in huge groups and quickly left. But with each surge, some stuck around, and his regular visitors steadily increased. This will happen for you as well. So whatever you do to get noticed, keep your mind on long-haul strategies.

DRAW THEM A MAP

Your fans have the most power to spread the word about your music, but they don't necessarily know how to do it best or even know if they should. You will have to tell them. For instance, the Brobdingnagian Bards noticed that their mailing list had fewer entries than they had podcast listeners. So, they decided to ask people to sign up. When they announced it on their podcast, they got three hundred new members. All their fans needed was a push. They decided to take this further and told their fans exactly how to promote and book them, which we discuss in the "Get Publicized" chapter.

THE STAY-TUNED STRATEGY

When radio DJs are about to play commercials, they never go directly into the ads. Instead, they announce what they're going to play after the break, to keep people tuned in. You should adopt this same technique. Always talk about your next project when you talk about your band, whether you're talking to the press, your fans, or other musicians. Here's why:

- Your fans will be motivated to keep tabs on you until that next project is released.

- It entices the press to ask questions about your upcoming projects and write future stories.

- It encourages people to get involved and help out. If you don't announce what you have planned, no one will know that he or she can help.

- It will also keep your own band members motivated and working toward the same goals.

So always have a sound bite on the tip of your tongue about what you're doing next. Movies have trailers, and a band should have announcements of what's to come.

THE ARM'S-REACH LESSON

The arm's-reach strategy, which we first introduced in the "Your Network" chapter, should be a key part of everything you do. No one expects you to get your music into a major motion picture immediately, or to play a stadium. You have to focus on strategies within your reach. But once you succeed at a few projects here and there, you'll find that your reach has expanded. You'll have new people in your networks and new opportunities available. Once you become established, opportunities will come to you.

This isn't to say that you can't dream of playing a stadium, but it doesn't pay to focus on things that are not currently within your reach. Don't aim low, but focus on what you can imagine yourself doing right now. In fact, that's what this second section of the *Guide* is all about: getting you opportunities that are well within your reach today.

ALWAYS BE PREPARED

You might start out in smaller niches, but you never know where those opportunities might lead. You should prepare to take advantage of those opportunities when they come your way.

The Cheapass Album is a good example of this. It got us a licensing deal with ABC Family/Disney for a commercial campaign. It also got us in touch with podcaster and author Mur Lafferty, who requested our music out of the blue because she was a fan of Cheapass Games. She discovered us through that niche, liked our music, and asked us if she could play "Were All These Beer Cans Here Last Night?" on her podcast, *Geek Fu Action Grip*. Little did we know that this chance acquaintance would eventually lead to creative collaborations and an introduction to her network of podcasters. This resulted in many podcasters using our music, and tens of thousands of song plays, and many new fans. Lafferty also ended up using our music videos in a business project for Lulu.tv that got our videos displayed round the clock in a convention with over thirty thousand attendees.

SEE WHAT STICKS

As you can see, many different strategies are available to help you get noticed. There are no rules to this new music business, so we suggest experimenting with many projects and ideas to see what works best for you. Just keep what sticks, and move on from what doesn't.

CHAPTER 9

GET BOOKED AND PLAY LIVE

WE ASKED both Jim DeRogatis, music editor for the *Chicago Sun-Times* and cohost of NPR's *Sound Opinions,* and Todd Martens, a music writer who has written for *Billboard* magazine and the *Los Angeles Times,* how they find out about new bands. Their answer: live shows. And if they hear buzz about a band, they look at the listings to see where they're playing. This makes sense. After all, the larger clubs and venues need a minimum audience to make it worthwhile to book a band; they don't take chances. By the time a major venue books a band, it's safe to say that band has a following.

Getting to those venues takes time, but we can summarize the essence of how to put on a great show in one sentence: You are there for the audience.

We've seen bands go onstage thinking that the audience is there for them. That's the wrong focus. Many musicians forget that music is entertainment. The audience is there to have a good time, and you are there to make sure that it does. A gig is more than just music; it's a show.

In this chapter, we'll cover all aspects of playing live, from practicing to publicity to packing up afterward.

BOOKING

Booking gigs is another of those art forms that could fill a book by itself. We can't cover everything here, but as in the rest of the *Guide* we will give you an overview and all the gotchas.

As George Hrab told us, "Talent won't get you the gig, but it will let you keep the ones you get." So we'll make you a deal: you bring the talent, and we'll tell you how to get the gigs.

DESIGNATE A BOOKER

We suggest designating a single person in the band to handle bookings. If you use an agency, you should still have just one contact. You don't want any embarrassing collisions when multiple gigs are booked for the same date. Nor do you want any confusion among the venue bookers over whom they should talk to.

The person doing booking should be a "people person." Booking is about relationships. It's about having a beer with the people who book bands at the bars, and also about having a thick skin to deal with rejection. Your booker should be persistent and have a cell phone. It also helps if your booker researches the bands that are most similar to your own that book in your area. The phrase "I see you've booked so-and-so, we're very similar to them" can get you into a lot of doors.

SCHEDULING

Bookers struggle with scheduling more than any other obstacle. Most bands need every single member to be available to put on a gig. We recommend creating an online band calendar marked with all of the dates that band members *can't* make. Google and Yahoo! both offer nice shareable online calendars for this purpose, although there are lots of options. We prefer the Web-based ones, though, because they allow the band members to add dates to the calendar as they learn of activities or dead dates wherever they are, and this lets the booker check the calendar from any Internet connection.

Of course, you'll also want to add all solid show dates to the calendar after they're booked, so the band members know not to book new events on those nights.

BOOKING KIT

Dealing with bookers is one of the few times as an indie musician that you'll still need printed materials. You're going to be handing them a CD, and you also need to hand them basic bios and contact information. You should have all the source documents for your booking kit online so that you can print them at a moment's notice, and so that bookers can download them if they find your Web site.

A booking kit should have:

- *A CD.* Include a CD of your latest album, and perhaps even more than one if you think it'll help you get booked. (And keep *all* of your contact information on the CD itself, in case it gets separated from the rest of it.)

- *A cover page.* Include your contact information, your Web site, and some basic details about booking such as where to find your sound setup and other show needs. You need a page on your Web site (see the "Your Web Site" chapter) that has booking and show information. Note that you should have contact information and your Web site address on every page that you give bookers, in case they lose one.

- *Your band bio.* See the "Get Publicized" chapter for information on how to create a band bio. You will include this one-page document here.

- *Press clippings.* Nothing sells a band to a venue better than a press-clippings page, or a page of review quotes if you're fortunate enough to have them. Sometimes, it helps to have a list of prior show dates to convince a new venue that you're an experienced band.

- *An eight-by-ten photo.* The eight-by-ten-inch band photo is the size most often used by venues, so you should have one available on your Web site. Most venues don't ask for glossy photos anymore because they have an easier time getting copies off your site, but some might. You need to find out ahead of time what their expectations are.

- *A live DVD.* Possibly the most effective part of your press kit would be a DVD of your band in action, especially if you're trying to book a wedding or corporate show. Video will prove better than anything else that your band can perform.

- *Testimonials.* Providing testimonials can propel someone who is on the verge of buying an act to make the commitment. Include them if you can.

GETTING YOUR FIRST SHOW

Most venues hate taking a chance on new bands, so first shows are some of the most difficult ones to get. It's the famous saying "How do I get an audience if no one will give me a gig?"

You might have to do some footwork to get that first show. Ask around at local venues to see how they handle new bands. Many require you to perform at an open mic. Others will give you an off-night, a Monday or Sunday, to prove yourself.

One of the easiest ways to get that first show is to open for an established band. As we explained earlier, it's a good idea to build relationships with other bands in your area because they can leverage you into venues where you haven't played before. But be ready to play for the exposure and the experience—i.e., for free—rather than for a cut of the door.

No matter how you get your first show, you need to impress the venue enough to get asked back, hopefully to headline on a weekend. And what impresses a venue isn't usually the music. They don't make money on that. The door funds also don't make them money, as that money usually goes to the bands and the sound guy. Smaller venues exist to do one thing: sell alcohol. That means they want you to pack the place with as many warm bodies as possible.

So how do you pack a place for your first show? Here's a simple recipe that has worked for many bands, including ourselves: buy a keg. Invite all of your friends, and all of their friends, to see your band debut and then to a keg party right afterward. You want to pack the venue when you play and have them all leave when you're done to go to the party.

This should get a lot of people to come see your band (with, admittedly, a bribe of beer, but if you split that among the band members, it's not that expensive). It also makes a big party out of your first show. (And if you're not old enough to get beer, just throw a party.)

We did this when we debuted (after a few tentative open-mic nights in dive bars to get us used to playing) at the U.S. Beer Company in Chicago. We jammed people into the place when we played, and we emptied it when we left. We also played a great show musically. The management not only asked us back, they had us headlining at our second show.

GETTING MORE VENUES AFTER STARTING OUT

Once you're an established player, it might still be difficult to book new venues. In Chicago, where we operate, until you become well-known, getting into one venue doesn't help you get into any others. You need to prove yourselves anew for each one. This is why your press clippings and previous show calendar can be helpful.

Your most important tools in booking venues are personal relationships and persistence. Every venue has an in-house booker, so the key is to know who it is, to present your materials, then to follow up. It takes a special knack to know the difference between being persistent and being annoying. Make sure your band's booker possesses that knack before setting him or her loose on the venues. Most bands that we've interviewed agree that persistence gets them their shows, but you don't want any restraining orders either.

The simplest way to grow your bookings, besides using a professional booker, is research. Which bands are similar to yours, and where do they play? It's much easier to convince a venue to book your band if the venue books similar ones. This is where your press kit can work for you, especially if you give venues a good clippings page and a live DVD.

Another technique is to form a cartel of bands and alternate opening for each other. Often, venues want an entire night of entertainment. A group of bands can work together to provide this.

And as we've said, it's especially effective to network with bands elsewhere. If you can get in touch with a band in a town you're heading toward, you can share the bill with them to get access to their audience.

Once you do book a gig, do not *ever* cancel. Ever. Venues will often ban you if you cancel, especially if it's on short notice. Our drummer once canceled on us a few weeks before a gig, and we ended up playing the show without him! We called it the Beatnik Turtle "acoustic night." Although it was a difficult gig, the bar was grateful, and we kept the relationship. We've played there many times since. Another option is to find another band to play in your place. It's always useful to have subs available.

BOOKING AGENCIES

If your band gets really busy, it's often a good idea to use a booking agency, which has established connections with bookers and venues. If they are a reputable company, they will audition you first to make sure you have a quality group. Venues will put more trust in bookers that are picky about which bands they represent.

Generally, you might form one of two types of relationships with a booking agency. In an exclusive booking arrangement, all of your bookings go through the agency. The booker will be listed as your main contact, and anyone looking to book your band will have to call the booker. In a nonexclusive agreement, you can still find bookings through others. Usually, a booker will book their exclusive clients for gigs before their nonexclusives.

No matter which way you go, make sure that your relationship with the booking agency is good and that you understand the business relationship before agreeing to it. Often, the booker will take a cut of the door, and the venue will pay them, not you. Your cut then comes from the booking agency.

Booking agencies don't want to deal with multiple people in a band. They aren't there to drag the drummer off the couch before the gig if he's got a hangover. They prefer to deal with the band manager. If you're managing yourselves, designate a single contact to deal with them.

HOUSE CONCERTS

Thanks to the Internet, house concerts—small shows hosted at people's residences—have continued to grow in popularity. Although these types of concerts are better known in the folk-music community, where the intimate setting is appropriate, some bands have added these small shows to coincide with and supplement a standard tour. If you do decide to perform house concerts, ask your hosts to guarantee a minimum payment. You might want to suggest the cover amount and the minimum number of people paying that cover—with the difference to be covered by the hosts, if necessary. This way, they share in the risk and have an incentive to bring in enough people.

Some legal issues are associated with house concerts due to zoning laws, so keep in mind that your show might get shut down. For more information about house concerts, we recommend the book *Host Your Own Concerts* by Joe Taylor as well as some online resources such as House-Concerts (houseconcerts.com).

TOURING

If you're serious about your live shows, playing on the road is a necessity. According to Fletcher Lee of Lee Productions, (leeproductionsinc.com) an agency that's been booking for decades, touring is a critical component in developing a live band. You need to play live often to grow your audience, but there's only so much you can do in one area over time. At some point, the local audience needs a break from your sound, and you must spread your wings a bit. Shows on the road win over entirely new networks of fans and are worth the extra time developing the necessary out-of-town relationships.

Marc Gunn and Andrew McKee of the Brobdingnagian Bards spend much of their time touring and always perform along the way to each destination. For example, if they play a convention, they will plan house concerts going in both directions, often getting themselves a place to stay as well as travel money. If you are too loud or your band just won't work in a house setting, there are always smaller venues in towns on the way to destinations. The Bards also recommend taking a break in between each tour to avoid burnout.

SETTING A PRICE AND GETTING PAID

When setting prices, consider how much you *need* to do the show, rather than how much you're *worth*. This will give you a solid basis for your price quote. You'll also have a better idea of how far you can bend on the prices that you set.

To do this, take stock of all of the expenses for doing the show, especially if you have to travel. Also factor in your time, and the lost opportunity to do other shows or projects during those dates. Once you determine this number, you'll feel more confident when it comes time to negotiate.

Make sure that you are clear on any cuts of your CD and merchandise sales that the venue demands. The larger venues will ask for as much as 20 percent of your take. If there's a contract, read it carefully. Some venues, such as colleges, won't let you sell merchandise at all. All of these factors need to be figured into your costs.

Carla Ulbrich warns that musicians often think they're making more than they actually do because they get paid in cash. If you've got a fat wad of cash in your wallet from the CD and T-shirt sales, it can feel as if you've hit the jackpot, even though some of it has to be shared with your silent partner—the government—in the form of income tax.

CONVENTIONS

Many successful independent bands have found that conventions can be a fantastic source of paid gigs that also expose their music to large numbers of new people.

The conventions that you can play depend on your style of music, and the contacts you manage to make. While it might seem obvious to seek out music conventions, most bands actually do other kinds of conventions because there is less competition and more opportunity to stand out. For example, Ulbrich makes a good living playing conventions, especially medical conventions, because some of her music is based on her experiences as a patient. The Brobdingnagian Bards, being a Celtic band, are partial to Renaissance fairs and similar events.

As we've said, it usually takes a few years to really insinuate yourself with a convention and get regular bookings with them. Many will ask for your credentials, which need to be in great shape to be considered. The key to conventions is the convention committee. Find out who are on the committee and focus your marketing efforts on them.

WORKING WITH FANS TO HELP YOU BOOK

Some bands have had luck letting their fans help them book gigs. The advantages are that your fans know the venues in their local area and can actually do the footwork for you. By the time you get contacted by the venue booker, a lot of the difficult initial steps have been handled, and you can just deal with the details. Another advantage of fan booking is that fans don't usually ask for a booking cut. They just want you to play in their area and are happy to convince you to come to their town.

As we mentioned before, Jonathan Coulton had luck with fans helping him book. The Brobdingnagian Bards have gone a step beyond and requested that their fans make the arrangements for them. This worked out so well that they eventually put together a list of steps for their fans to take to help book them.

ONLINE TOURING AND GIG TOOLS

Playing live is a huge part of a musician's life, so it shouldn't be surprising that online tools now help to connect performers with venues.

Message Boards

Many message boards help musicians get each other shows in different cities. You don't even need to know someone in a city to try to get gigs there. It can be as simple as posting that you'll be on tour in that area, and asking for suggested venues to call. Some bands will offer to let you open for them, which is ideal because you don't need to arrange anything on the ground in that city, leaving logistics to the local band.

Naturally, you should also watch these boards to see if there's anyone you can help book in your own city. Some of the message boards we recommend are Just Plain Folks (jpfolks.com), Velvet Rope (velvetrope.com), and IndieBandSurvivalGuide.com.

Gig Demand Sites

Gig demand sites such as Eventful (eventful.com) provide a widget for your Web site to let fans request a performance in their area. Each visitor who votes using the widget raises the count higher for his or her area, giving you a clear idea of how your fanbase is divided geographically. This is important information when assembling a live-show schedule, particularly if you are gaining popularity through the Internet. Your fans could be all over the world, and you need to know where they are so you can go play for them.

Because the people on these gig demand sites are hoping that you'll come to their city to play live, all of the ones who asked become an instant resource to do footwork for you and can help you book. Remember that these sites often undercount the number of people who would come to your shows. Not everyone wants to sign up to be counted. Jonathan Coulton said, "I've found that if there were forty people signed up, probably there'll be eighty people that will come to the show. They'll bring their friends, there are other people that will hear about it, and fans who aren't signed up."

Eventful offers musicians a series of free booking and Web tools. If you tour—or have any plans to in the future—check out Eventful.

Online Booking Agencies

Naturally, the Web now also gets people in touch with bands for bookings. We're going to cover just two examples of this, both with a different focus.

Sonicbids (sonicbids.com) allows you to create an Electronic Press Kit (a term they've trademarked) so that you can make yourself available to book shows, connect with talent buyers, and perform other show-management tasks. Bands can use it to connect with venues, and to host their Electronic Press Kits for the general public as well. Setting up a presence on Sonicbids won't guarantee you gigs, but it may help open up some opportunities. Some festivals and venues use it as their exclusive way to handle submissions. Note that Sonicbids has a monthly fee.

Gigmasters (gigmasters.com) aims itself more directly at people booking such events as weddings, parties, and corporate events. If you are on a social committee of an organization and just want to "book an act," Gigmasters can find you a band based on style, size, or any other needs. Gigmasters also has a monthly fee, but Carla Ulbrich, whom we mentioned earlier, said that she booked many gigs using this tool.

GIG OPPORTUNITIES

The average number of fans you bring to any particular show is called your draw. It's your draw the venues are interested in, not you! You might have three hundred people on your mailing list, with only thirty coming out to see you on a show night. Only a fraction of your fans will ever attend any one of your shows. To get as large a draw as possible, you should always be trying to get new fans.

To do so, you need to play many different types of shows, not just at regular venues. If you get more established, of course, you can play larger shows. But by then, it's likely that you've already got a publicity machine large enough to advertise and bring people in.

These techniques will help a band get established and large enough to be a draw on their own.

Opening for Other Bands

One of the easiest ways to get new fans is to open for another band, especially if your group is similar. You should only open for bands that have a bigger fanbase than your own. While this might seem obvious, we've ended up playing for many "headliners" that didn't have close to the draw that we did.

Many people show up quite late for shows because they know that there's an opening band, so remember that the other band's draw will probably only see the end of your set. Also, the opening band will get less money than the headliner, or no money at all.

We suggest that you also be open to sharing your own audience with others by letting bands open for you. Some bands are possessive about their draw, which makes little sense. Everyone's fans are people who like to see live music. The more people who go out to see music, the better it is for everyone.

Another common misconception is that one band's fans only like the kind of music that they play. People who enjoy live music tend to have broad musical tastes. Don't assume that people who like folk music won't like heavy metal. In the end, it's all live music, and audiences often enjoy more diverse entertainments than they are given credit for.

Playing Charity Events

Charity events deliver a lot of benefits to bands that play them. Usually, all proceeds are donated to the charity, but the events usually have their own press releases, which often get mentions by the press. The resulting articles invariably list the participating bands. You can also do a press release of your own about the show and the cause that you're supporting. Those press releases often get more attention because of the human-interest element.

Playing a charity event is a great way to piggyback, as well as network with other bands and even other community artists—sometimes charity events are more than just music shows. It's a good value for fans, too, because they can sample a variety of bands for the price of admission.

Playing Music Festivals

Because festivals are such good opportunities to play for new audiences, getting booked can sometimes be a challenge. There can be a lot of competition. Your best bet is to get to know the organizers of the event or, if that isn't possible, at least connect with someone who knows them. The "cold handoff" almost never works. Always try to forge a personal connection to the organizers in any way you can. Your booking kit needs to be especially good to book a festival, and this is where your press clippings can really help you stand out.

If you manage to get in a festival, get the most out of it by doing the following:

- **Reinforce the brand.** Announce your band name often as the audience will probably not know you. Ideally, bring a sign or banner onstage.

- **Build your list.** Make sure that you bring your mailing list and ask people to sign up.

- **Sell merchandise.** Get a friend to run a store with your CDs and merchandise. Keep your mailing list at the table, too.

- **Call to action.** Announce your next shows and upcoming projects to draw people in. If you have a poster for your next show, place it around the festival.

Some cities have an events committee to evaluate bands for city-sponsored festivals. Chicago, our hometown, has a committee to book bands for the city's frequent street festivals. Getting onto their roster of bands is, of course, rather difficult, but if you can manage it, you have access to a lot of shows.

There's a good listing of festivals at Festivals.com as well as Indie BandSurvivalGuide.com to get you started.

Conferences and Showcasing

Showcases give you an opportunity to play for a conference or event that is attended by people within the music industry. Examples are booking conferences, college conferences, or a meeting for the performance rights organizations such as ASCAP or BMI.

Some showcases let you just pay to get your chance to play for the people at the conference, and others are juried, which means that you'll have to send in a demo and prove yourselves to a panel (although they may *still* charge you after asking you to come in and play). Either way, you'll have to decide if the showcase is worth the cost of attending.

Besides the college booking conferences, which we talk about below, some of the more well-known conferences or organizations that have showcases are South by Southwest Conferences (sxsw.com), the National Association of Music Merchants (namm.org), and the College Media Journal (cmj.com).

College Gig Bookings

The best way to break into the college tour market is to work with the Association for the Promotion of Campus Activities (apca.com) or the National Association for Campus Activities (naca.org). Both of these associations hold once-a-year conventions to showcase bands that draw in talent buyers from colleges across the country. Both of these conventions charge the bands to play. We've been told by other musicians that by the third college gig you book out of these conferences, you will probably have recouped your convention fee.

Also, an entire world of college gigs is waiting for you in venues that are simply near or on campus. Venues near colleges are always looking for bands to play, and their audiences are always looking for new music.

Playing Weddings

Many bands play weddings to supplement their income. It's an area with its own pitfalls, but those who can successfully navigate it can secure a dependable source of gigs. George Hrab buttresses his indie music income with steady work playing with a wedding band, the Philadelphia Funk Authority.

One of Chicago's top wedding bands is the High Society Orchestra (highsocietyorch.com), run by Allan Heiman, who has been in the booking business for decades. His number one piece of advice is to treat a wedding band as a business. The professional expectations for a wedding are very different from those at regular venues. Your marketing materials need to be flawless, your band's presentation has to be polished, and your dealings with customers need to be managed with extreme care.

Heiman started his band with a splash. He rented out a hotel ballroom and catered an evening for wedding planners, hotel-venue managers, and others in the wedding industry to enjoy the band. That one event, along with an advertising campaign in bridal magazines and other publications, got him fifty-two bookings that first year. The point isn't that you need to spend a lot of money to start a wedding band, although that helps. Instead, remember that you need to win over the wedding planners and the hotel-venue managers. These are the people who can refer new business to you.

The High Society Orchestra gets all their gigs through word of mouth. They don't bother advertising anymore. In fact, they're completely booked for years ahead. Each wedding at which they perform gets them multiple new bookings from people in attendance. This is a key lesson: the better your wedding show, the more likely your band will be hired for additional bookings by other guests.

When it comes to putting on a great wedding show, Heiman gives the following advice:

- **The emcee is key.** The emcee should interact with the audience throughout the evening.

- **Focus on talent.** Many of High Society's musicians are members of such organizations as the Chicago Symphony orchestra or the Lyric Opera. Your wedding band should feature the best musicians you can find.

- **The set list is critical.** Heiman is constantly tweaking his set lists to provide an enjoyable variety of songs for his audience.

- **Don't lose momentum between songs.** The music should always be going unless the band takes a full break. High energy is key.

- **Stick to tried-and-true favorites.** Dancing songs, medleys, and sing-alongs are always sure bets with wedding audiences. Get people up on their feet and involved.

Corporate Shows, Bar Mitzvahs, and Other Special Events

The High Society Orchestra also does corporate shows, bar mitzvahs, and other gigs. But these are much more sporadic and difficult to get. Still, the secret to any of these other types of shows is again in the presentation of your materials, and in knowing who handles hiring the bands.

For corporate shows, the bookers can often be employees on a company events committee, or someone in the human resources department. Because these positions often rotate, it's hard to keep getting steady shows at each firm.

For other types of shows, your booking information on your Web site and the personal contacts that you make will be the best way to keep a steady stream of opportunities coming in.

Street Performances

The Brobdingnagian Bards started out playing in a park four days a week, for free. Eventually, after a year of playing, they had a hundred people showing up regularly to hear them. This group formed their initial fan network. When the Bards recorded their first album and played their first paid gigs, they already had an audience.

It's not always necessary to play formal shows—parks, streets, and other public areas are perfectly good alternative "venues." But keep in mind that most cities impose restrictions on public performances of this type, and you may need a permit.

SHOWMANSHIP

Musicians often argue the issue of "staying true to the music" versus "pandering to the audience." This might make an interesting debate over beers, but it's not useful when it comes to putting on a show. In the end, you're there to entertain the audience. Of course, you need to follow your aesthetic tastes—which might include a dark, brooding look or a screaming spandex serenade—but don't forget: *you are there for them*.

Having the attitude that your audience is "lucky to hear you" will *not* result in a good show. David Bloom, one of Chicago's jazz gurus, captured it best: "Don't reduce music to the size of your ego. It's a lot bigger than you. It was here before you, and it'll be here long after you're gone. Music is something to look up to." If you look up to music, the audience will look up to you. But if you look down at the audience, they won't be there next time you play.

Here's how to put on the best possible show for your fans and keep them coming back for more.

THE SECRET TO GREAT SHOWS

Think back to the most memorable shows that you've seen. They probably all had one thing in common: energy that you could reach out and touch. An electric current running between the performers and the audience.

In the best shows, the band and the audience connect.

Achieving this connection isn't as hard as you might think. It all depends on the energy that you put into your performance and, more important, where you put it. You need to direct it outward, toward the audience. Each musician has a different kind of focus when he or she plays. You enter a zone. You get out of your head and lost in the music, unaware of your surroundings,

But when you put on a show, direct your energies toward the audience, at least initially. When you do that, an amazing thing happens. People pick up on your energy and give it back to you, magnified. It begins a feedback loop, each side building on the other. It's an incredible feeling once this kind of thing starts. And when shows catch in this way, it becomes magic.

The one thing that's been consistent among our most successful shows is that energy. People always tell us that it looks as if we're having a ton of fun up there when we play. We are, and we share that enjoyment with the audience. We always get back many times what we put out.

To us, this approach is key to performing well, but ironically we've run into *very* few bands that actually get it right. One band that headlined after ours proved it to us conclusively. We did a huge finale to our short opening set and had people jumping and yelling and calling out for more. Then we tore down quickly to make room for the headliners.

"Um, wow," one of them muttered into the microphone. "Uh, thanks, Beatnik Turtle." Then they started their set with a slower number while staring at their shoes. The energy level in the room dropped. They kept looking at their shoes, song after song. Unfortunately, their shoes were not the ones they needed to entertain. The room emptied out pretty quickly, and the audience members who stuck around were in the back of the room, nursing their beers.

This is true no matter what type of music you play. Even quiet, contemplative music can create a connection between the musician and the audience if that connection is nurtured by the performer. And when it happens, it's magic.

START BIG AND END BIG

For ideas on how to put on a great show, learn from Hollywood. Take any successful action film. The films often start with a bang, literally, an explosion, or perhaps a gunfight or car chase. And no matter what happens in the middle, the film always ends with what Hollywood calls "the ticking clock," featuring a chase scene and heart-pounding stunts and sequences as time runs out. The Hollywood action-movie mantra is "Start big and end big!"

This formula *works*. You should use it whenever you perform. Beatnik Turtle always kicks a show off with a rocking song—usually one that uses the entire horn section. And we always end with an up-tempo number that gets the crowd jumping up and down and yelling. Even if you must start subtle, always, but always, end with a powerful song.

Think of fireworks displays. They always end on a big finale that fills the sky with lights and explosions. Your show should follow the same principle. People remember the ending best. They forgive problems in the middle of the set if you end on a strong note.

Our goal as performers is to have the crowd more red-faced and excited than we are when we finish. We usually succeed, because we close with wild, rocking songs that have choruses that get people jumping up and down as they sing along. The reactions we get from audiences after our shows are the reason we've kept playing all of these years. That's when you hear fans say, "You guys were *awesome!*" and you know they really mean it.

We don't know why most other indie bands fail to start big and end big, because it's a well-known axiom, and it just works. Almost every Broadway production, movie, and most pro bands understand this fact of show business. Remember it when you plan your set. What goes in the middle is just the creamy filling. You can do what you want in there as long as you follow this rule.

COVERS VS. ORIGINALS

There's an ongoing debate over doing cover songs versus doing originals. What you choose depends on your band.

First of all, don't worry about playing covers, even though someone else "owns" the song. See the "Your Rights" chapter for more on that issue.

Some purists wonder why anyone plays covers at all. With all that music easily available on CDs and as MP3s, you could play the songs by the original groups to your heart's content. The truth, however, is that people love live music (when it's played right). And if your band is creative, you can put your own spin on the covers. By performing a cover song, you also won't have to work as hard to prove yourself to your audience, because they'll already be familiar with the music.

If you do original songs, and you're still establishing yourselves, throw in some covers as well. Doing so will give your audience something to hook on to in between the unfamiliar songs. You can do this until you get established and your own originals become familiar. At that point, you'll be playing your older favorites as anchors for your fans as you introduce your new originals.

SOUND CHECK

The sound guy (and, yes, we call them sound guys even if they're women) can never make a bad band sound good. But one can definitely make a good band sound bad. The sound at a show is the most important part of it that you can't directly control. If you can't use, or don't have, your own sound guy, make friends with the one you're given. And, most important, *do not skip the sound check.*

Here's how to make the most of a sound check:

1. Get there in plenty of time.

2. Provide your microphone chart, so the sound guy can see where things go. For examples of stage plots, see IndieBandSurvivalGuide.com.

3. Designate one member to answer the sound guy's questions and tag along with him or her throughout the check to make sure things get resolved quickly and correctly. Every band has some oddities with its microphone setup, so it pays to have someone there to answer the sound guy's questions.

4. Be particular about the sound. If you need more volume or a different mix, take care of this now. It's impossible to change the monitors besides yelling "Turn it up" or "Turn it down" during the actual show.

5. Let each vocalist try his or her mic. If there are a lot of harmonies, make sure that each vocalist can hear the others during the check.

6. Have the member with the best ears stand in the room to double-check the sound. This is exactly where you can catch the mistakes of a bad sound guy.

7. Tell the sound guy about any instrument changes to expect. For example, one member of Beatnik Turtle plays sax, sings, then plays flute. He often gets one mic for saxes, and one for flute *and* vocals. When he switches between flute and vocals on that mic, he needs different levels.

8. Buy the sound guy a beer or give him a tip.

Make friends with your sound guy. Offer free CDs or other band merchandise. This gives him or her an incentive to make you sound good. Also, the sound guy is usually connected to other venues in your area, and that connection might just get you more shows. Sound guys can put you in touch with other musicians and otherwise expand your skill and opportunity networks.

In our experience, sound guys tend to be an unusual breed, and it's always interesting to get to know them. One of them would get drunk, hit on our female friends, and do a lousy job with the sound to boot. Another did great work, but posted a note facing the stage: "Do not play 'American Woman.'" Naturally, we announced that we were going to play it in the middle of a set. He made this hilarious hand-waving motion as if he were trying to get a plane to stop landing on a runway that was mined to explode. Of course, our audience missed the entire joke and just wondered why we wanted to play *that* song.

BANTER

We recommend a little small talk between songs because it can get the audience more connected to the band. But you should practice your banter. If you get some jokes or material ready ahead of time, it can make your banter much more effective. You should also have "stalling banter" prepared. This comes in handy when one of your band members breaks a string and has to fix it, if you need to tune, or something else happens that causes a delay. Have a story ready to keep the audience entertained during these inevitable breaks.

Other banter you should rehearse beforehand is your band introduction, an announcement about future shows, and a plug for your CDs, merchandise, and Web site. Some people are better at impromptu speaking than others, but it always helps to practice some of this material prior to the show.

REHEARSALS

The most difficult thing about rehearsals for most bands seems to be finding a rehearsal space. You should definitely get a permanent one rather than wander from place to place. It gives you a home base, which can help keep the band together. That said, a lot of bands have trouble finding a place where their music won't cause issues.

If you can't find a basement or garage to play in, you might try renting a space. We knew one band, the Hillbillies From Space, that rehearsed at night in a warehouse, during the off-hours when no one was working. It worked out well for everyone. You might be able to do this, too, if you know someone who owns a warehouse, perhaps flipping that person a little money.

Once you have a space, practice at least once a week. If you're just starting the band, you should try to practice even more often to make sure that everyone in the band is synchronized. Your goal is to get so good that you can recover from a train wreck onstage. Then you can drop back on practicing. We don't recommend practicing less than once a week (unless you're performing all the time) because you will start to get rusty and your band members will begin to drift into other activities. Cutting weekly rehearsals is a great formula for losing band members.

During your rehearsals, don't be shy about bringing up problems and tackling them. Rehearsals are not the time to dance around issues that might just fester for a long time. If anyone is too sensitive to handle working on his on her part, you'll probably lose that person eventually anyway.

Remember, the sound in the rehearsal room is nothing like the sound onstage. You can sound as great as you want in the practice room and never hit those same heights onstage. On a lot of stages, you can't even hear the other band members, so part of the reason for your rehearsals is to learn what the rest of the band will be playing when you can't hear them.

We recommend doing a full dress rehearsal before shows, and to use a timer for each song to get an idea of how long your sets are. Include the banter as well as the songs themselves.

END OF THE SHOW

Don't forget to thank the sound guy, and anyone else who helped you during the show. If appropriate, encourage your audience to buy more drinks and to tip the waiters and waitresses generously. Take one last time to plug your store and your Web site, then thank your fans.

When you finish a wedding, definitely thank everyone. George Hrab always thanks the maître d' and the caterers. Some have told him that, in years of working in the business, they've never had any other wedding bands thank them. They were grateful, and you never know when one of them might direct new business to you in the future.

In a smaller venue, pack up quickly and go talk to your fans. That personal relationship will keep them coming back. This is also another opportunity for you to sell a disc, give out a flyer, get people to sign up for the mailing list, and talk up your next show. Having Sharpies handy to sign albums is also a good idea.

Another idea to consider came from our friend Yvonne Doll from The Locals (localsrock.com), a Chicago band. They have a cute little doll named Danger Boy, and they take pictures of their fans with the doll for the Web site. They even have little cards to give out with the Web address explaining that the pictures will appear there. This connected the fans with the Website *after the show*, ensuring that they would bring other people to see their picture at the site as well as visiting it themselves.

Finally, if the people who hired you for the show are really happy with how you did, get a testimonial from them on the spot that you can use for your press kit and Web site.

POSTSHOW GAME TAPES

If you're heading out the door to a party, chances are you'll check the mirror to see how you look, straighten out your hair and clothes. If you're practicing for a show, it makes sense to record your performance to accomplish the same thing.

It doesn't have to be a high-quality recording to be useful. You can literally dig out an old cassette deck. If you have a laptop computer, or even a desktop that's in your practice space, you can buy a microphone at RadioShack and record directly to your computer, which would allow you to distribute the files more easily to the rest of your band.

For actual performances, ask someone you trust to watch the equipment and hit *Record* when the show begins so you don't have to worry about it. You can use audio recordings of your shows to find out how the sound people did and give them more specific feedback in the future on how to handle your music.

The best option for shows is to get your hands on a camcorder. Watch how your band moves during songs and presents itself during a show. Look at it from the point of view of a music fan who's come to be entertained. Is the banter smooth? Did you remember to announce your CDs? Did you say your band name enough times? Remember, at every show there will be people who don't know who you are, and some will walk in right after you finished that last song. Keep announcing who you are.

By studying recordings of your band in rehearsal and at gigs, you will learn a lot of surprising things, and some fixes will be as simple as straightening your hair before a party.

SHOW PUBLICITY

Once you have a show scheduled, you come to the fun part: promoting your show. You can do a lot of things to boost your draw and get the most people in the room. We'll talk about many of your options below.

POSTERS

You've seen them at every venue: posters for every band with an upcoming performance. When you have a show coming up yourselves, you should join them and get a poster up at least a few weeks ahead of time.

When you're a newer band, and not necessarily well-known in your town, you might doubt that a passerby would come to your show after seeing a poster. In truth, most won't. It's not a great way to get new people to come hear you play. So why bother?

The answer is simple: posters are one of the best places to imprint your brand on people who love music. While they may not show up at your gig because of your poster, over time, as they pass by your poster as they come and go to see other acts, your own name and logo will sink in. Eventually, when asked, they'll even say they've "heard of you." Get your name out there long enough, and there's a good chance some new people will check your band out, eventually.

The better your posters look, the more effective they can be. Get a graphic artist from your skill network to design one, assuming one of your own members can't do it for the band.

Brand every poster with your logo, your color scheme, your fonts, and make sure that your band name, Web site address, and the *correct* date and time of your performance can clearly be read. You may want to get your posters professionally printed ahead of time, in bulk, with a blank space in the middle so that you can write in the show information for each gig.

Hang your posters in these locations:

- *The venue itself.* Place them in front, as well as throughout. And don't forget the bathrooms—those posters actually get looked at.

- *Music stores.* Find CD and record stores in the neighborhood. At each store, give the employees free CDs and offer to leave one for the shop itself so they can play it on their PA system. These employees are your best advocates. If they allow it, sell your CDs on consignment at the stores, too.

- *Local shops.* Coffee shops are usually good about supporting local music. It's easy to figure out if they're friendly, because you'll see posters for other shows in the window or on the walls. Also, offer any of the workers or the shop itself free CDs. Again, they may recommend your band if they like your music.

- *Colleges.* Any schools near the venue are a good target. Local colleges are great places to get new fans.

Be careful about putting posters in your neighborhood, as local laws may prohibit you from postering public walls. Consult local regulations before you go nuts with that tape.

Janelle Rogers of Green Light Go publicity (greenlightgopublicity.com) puts up her bands' posters adjacent to posters for more well-known groups. This tends to give her posters more weight and a better chance of being seen.

DIGITAL POSTERS

Create digital versions of your posters as we mentioned in the "Your Brand" chapter. These will be used on your Web site. Remember that front page, the multimedia experience? You can easily include a poster. You will also use it on the social-networking sites as a comment.

You should also give it out to anyone that wants to "post it" so people can help you put it in places it should go. For example, sometimes you can put it in a footer for postings that you write to message boards.

FLYERS

A flyer given out at a show can be used to promote future shows, your latest album, your Web site, or all three. People often take flyers with them, which will remind them how much they enjoyed your band once they've sobered up.

If you want to boost your flyers' effectiveness, make them coupons for a special deal. Maybe a discount off a CD or admission to your next show or a free MP3 off your Web site. Your audience will be less inclined to throw your flyer out if they can get something by hanging on to it.

The more compelling the design, the better. We've posted glossy flyers from other bands to our refrigerators or near our desks because we liked the images as well as the band and wanted to remember both.

Don't forget a "call to action" when you're making your flyer. Tell people what to do, whether it's attending a show or visiting the Web site.

VENUE MARKETING

The problem with posters in bars is that no one gets a chance to hear your band. And it's hard to convince a bar to play your music, even if you give away your album to the bartenders.

Yvonne Doll came up with a solution to this problem. She put a little display up at a local bar stocked with free demo discs of her music, each labeled with the show information, as well as traditional flyers. This display brought in a lot of new audience members.

ANNOUNCING SHOWS TO MAILING LISTS AND
SOCIAL-NETWORKING SITES

Announcing your upcoming shows to your mailing list is probably the most important and effective publicity that you can do. Naturally, your fans are the people most likely to attend your gigs, but only if they know about them ahead of time. People make weekend plans weeks in advance, so give your fans plenty of lead time so they can schedule you in.

On social sites such as MySpace, your latest posts will appear on your friends' pages, so you can post your digital poster and effectively distribute it to your entire friends list. And, of course, mention upcoming gigs on your Web site and on any band blogs.

Depending on how often you play, you should also make an e-mail announcement the day before a show to remind people of where and when the show is. If you play several times a week, a weekly or monthly announcement should work.

Finally, if your mailing list includes regular mail addresses as well as e-mail addresses, it can be effective to send a postcard with your show calendar. The physical card can really help get more people in because, if you do a good enough job with the design, the recipients will want to put it up on the wall. This will keep them reminded about your band.

COLLEGE AND LOCAL RADIO

College and local radio are solid bets when it comes to promoting upcoming shows. Offer a ticket or album giveaway if they agree to mention the show. Most stations love free stuff to give to their listeners. Sometimes, you can leverage a giveaway into an interview the day of the performance, reaping even more publicity for your event. We talk about this in detail in the "Get Played and Heard" chapter.

NEWSPAPERS, MAGAZINES, WEB SITES, AND BLOGS

An upcoming show is a great excuse to send out a press release to local publications. Keep in mind they will only publish something if you have an angle. This does not include the headline "Indie Band Plays Show."

So if you're going to send a press release, make sure there's something special about the show. Maybe you're playing for charity, throwing a CD-release party, or doing your five hundredth performance. The easiest way to make your show special enough to warrant a press release is to play in another town. Ironically, it's harder to get publicity in your local area than it is when you travel, even to the next nearest city. Leverage this as much as possible if you're on the road.

Any show is also an excuse to write an e-mail to any blogs or Web sites that cover music or entertainment in the area. Again, this is especially true if you're playing outside your hometown.

You should always be thinking about new ways to publicize your band. This is especially true for shows, as your goal is to get as many new people to come see your band as possible.

LOCAL MUSIC STORES

Aside from putting up posters in your local music store and giving out free CDs to win over the employees, you can use music stores to help publicize your band in other ways.

One technique that has worked well for us arose as a result of a happy accident at our CD manufacturer. We got an extra one thousand CDs (discs only) for the cost of shipping due to a production error.

We packaged the discs in thin cases with a photocopied cover and little brochures about an upcoming concert. Then we went to record stores all over Chicago and offered to let them sell the discs. Before they could finish saying the word *consignment*, we added that they could sell the discs for a dollar and keep it. There isn't a local store in any town that will turn away free money.

We made a little display case for each store, and those discs were usually placed right next to the cash register—a pure impulse buy. Few people could resist spending an extra buck to get another disc. We didn't give the discs away for two reasons. First, it gave the store a reason to push them and place the display by the cash register. Second, people don't value things that are free. You're better off charging something nominal so they will value it more.

That show was one of the best attended we've had. And even years later, we've had people write us that they listened to the disc for years. If you have extra CDs, we highly recommend this technique.

This is just one of many possible ideas; you'll certainly come up with your own. Remember that local music stores have your perfect audience as their clientele. If you can think of other ways to get your band, your show information, or your logo in front of those people, you should make use of it. There's a reason why you see band stickers all over those stores.

SELLING AT SHOWS

Your shows are when it's most likely a fan will buy something from you. For one thing, there are no shipping costs. Also, you've just played live in front of them, and people like to support bands they've seen in person.

Always get someone to run the store for you. It's a fairly easy job, but it can be difficult to convince someone to do this for you. We once teamed up with other local bands and did an exchange program where we ran the stores at each other's shows. (And we promoted the other bands' shows as well.) You should do everything you can to get people to help out the band in this way. Offer your friends incentives such as free CDs and T-shirts, free shows, or anything else that would entice them to help you. The alternative is to sell from the stage, which is difficult and looks amateurish.

While onstage, remember one thing above all: *Don't forget to announce that you have music available for sale!*

Don't just announce once that you have music for sale. Do it many times throughout a show. Some people just need a reminder, that extra push to get them to make the purchase. Effective marketing is based on repetition. Don't repeat the message after every song, but definitely remind people in the middle and at the end of each set. If you feel embarrassed repeating yourself like that, remember that some people will have just walked into the room and don't know where they can buy your music. Radio stations aren't bashful about reminding listeners what station they're listening to, even if most already know. You shouldn't feel bashful about announcing your CD a couple of times each set.

A display for your CDs and T-shirts will help quite a bit. It can make your store look more professional. A more formal store also makes people feel better about buying your music, because they will feel that they are getting something of value.

Make your mailing list available at your store as well, and while making change, the person running the store should ask the customer to sign up. These are your most likely returning fans, so you definitely want them on your list.

You should also have your flyers available to hand to anyone who buys something.

CREDIT CARD SALES

Normally, sales at shows are cash only, but some independent bands do credit card sales. If you'd like the ability to do this at shows, we recommend using CD Baby's credit card program. For a little money, they give you a credit card swiper and some receipts. They take a small cut of every sale for handling the credit card transaction, but on the other hand these sales are tracked by Nielsen SoundScan.

People at bars often use all their cash to buy beer. We're all for that, of course! The problem is, that leaves them with nothing to buy your CD. A credit card swiper is a good way around this problem.

DIGITAL MUSIC AT CONCERTS

If you have someone to run your store and can provide a laptop, you can sell digital music, too. Tell your fans on your Web site and in your mailing to bring their iPods or MP3 players to the show. Then just rip your music to MP3 files and bring a USB cable and an iPod cable with your laptop.

You can afford to charge less than the price of a CD to sell your music this way because you don't actually have to duplicate any CDs. Doing something novel like this can also get even more people interested in buying your music. Some people bring their MP3 players wherever they go, so you might even be able to make sales to some walk-ins. These are not, of course, tracked by SoundScan.

POSTSHOW CDS

It's now possible to sell CDs of a show immediately after it's over. A dedicated engineer does a mixdown immediately after the show, then sends it to a fast CD duplicator. Usually only the larger venues have the resources to pull this off as of yet, but as the technology gets better, it will become more feasible for indie musicians. The Brobdingnagian Bards sometimes do this with a notebook computer at some shows. While it ties one of them up after a show, they've been able to sell copies of a just-performed show.

And don't forget that even if you can't make a CD immediately after your show, you can still sell the recording afterward to fans from your Web site.

MAILING LISTS AT CONCERTS

As we discussed in the "Your Network" chapter, you should have a mailing list at every show that you perform. If you can, you should have multiple mailing lists. These are the people most likely to come to your next show, so you will want to get their information while they are there. Most people are happy to sign up for mailing lists for bands that they like.

It's a good idea to ask for both e-mail and snail-mail addresses, in case you want to contact people in different ways. You may mostly use their e-mail addresses, but later decide to do a postcard mailing.

You should make sure that your mailing list is available at the show store, and you should also try to pass it around the room in the middle of the show. Your best bet is to get some helpers to walk through the crowd and hand people a clipboard so that they feel compelled to sign up. It's the best way to get a good response. Your floor people can also have a couple CDs on them for sale, and if you have a flyer, they should just hand them out to people. If you've ever walked down the street anywhere in Las Vegas and are over eighteen and especially if you are male, you probably know how likely it is that someone will take a flyer if it's handed to him or her.

MORE ON PLAYING LIVE

If you wish more in-depth information on booking and playing, we recommend *How to Be Your Own Booking Agent: THE Musician's & Performing Artist's Guide to Successful Touring* by Jeri Goldstein. Also, IndieBand SurvivalGuide.com lists venues in your area as well as lists of other booking resources and techniques.

CHAPTER 10

GET DISTRIBUTED AND SOLD

MOST BANDS want to know, how do we get our music on iTunes? How can we get our CDs distributed worldwide?

In this chapter, we'll cover everything related to selling your music, whether online, in stores, or in person. But, as always, you should be aware of, and do, some things before you start selling. We'll begin with those preliminary issues, then move on to the nitty-gritty of distribution.

PREPARING TO SELL MUSIC

SOUNDSCAN

SoundScan is the U.S. music industry's primary method for tracking music sales. The *Billboard* Hot 100 charts are all based on SoundScan numbers. The system is maintained by Nielsen, the same company that releases television and radio statistics. You need to decide if you care enough about these statistics to limit where your music is sold.

SoundScan statistics are reported by online digital distribution stores such as iTunes, Napster, and Rhapsody, as well as physical CD stores such as Best Buy. Unfortunately, plenty of ways to sell music are not tracked by SoundScan, most notably the indie musician's most successful sales method: selling at concerts.

The traditional music industry finds SoundScan statistics useful to determine which bands have gotten a significant sales volume. But for indie bands, these statistics are more useful for gaining legitimacy in the eyes of journalists. Since SoundScan is a third party, their impartial information can prove that people really are interested in your band.

If you really care about SoundScan numbers, limit your sales to channels that report in order to get your numbers as high as possible. Otherwise, you'll start regretting those show sales because, as far as SoundScan is concerned, they never happened. There are sometimes ways around this, though. CD Baby, for example, provides a method to sell music at concerts using credit cards, and those sales *are* tracked.

You need a UPC bar code for your album if you want your sales to register with SoundScan. Even if you're selling your music digitally, SoundScan requires the UPC to track the sales, because that's the unique code they use to identify each album.

Keep in mind that it's difficult to make enough sales to register as more than a blip on SoundScan. So it's usually not worth it for an indie musician to bother with the system, especially if he or she isn't interested in entering the traditional music industry. After all, music-buying customers don't really look at those numbers.

PROMOTING MUSIC SALES THROUGH YOUR WEB SITE

We'll discuss every aspect of getting your music through the sales channels, but if you don't promote your music on your own Web site, you're wasting your best opportunity to entice fans to purchase your music. Prepare this first, *before* putting the music into the sales channels, so that the material is ready to go when your album releases.

The best thing about having your own Web site is that you have full control. It looks pathetic when a band has to pitch its new album in between the ads on their MySpace page. When you have your own Web site, you can devote a page entirely to the album.

Your goal for an album page is simple: to get people to buy the music. If you have any aversion to plugging your own music, it's time to get over it quickly. You'll be making your album pages to really pump it. The text and images should all work toward that objective. Sampling and then buying the album should be as convenient and fast as possible. We'll talk about techniques for this below.

Song Samples

People want to hear music before they buy it. That's why radio has been such an important part of the music industry. People are willing to purchase a movie on DVD before seeing it. But they often aren't willing to buy music before hearing it. Perhaps this is because people spend more time listening to music, and they also listen to music repeatedly. Movies are viewed far less often.

Demonstrate that your music is worthwhile by offering actual songs or clips of songs for download. On your Web site, stream every single song on the album for customers to preview. On an online store, make clips available of as many songs as they allow. Put your music where your mouth is. Perhaps one of those songs is just the one that a fan is looking for. On iTunes, customers can listen to a short clip of every song, especially useful because you can purchase music by the track.

The digital music stores do a great job of making samples easy to listen to on their storefronts. But it's also sometimes possible to embed their Flash player in your page directly to make this even easier. Otherwise, you can do this with your own player, as we discussed in the "Your Web Site" chapter.

We stream entire albums from our site. It may allow some technically savvy and unscrupulous people to copy the music, but most just use it to get an idea of what the songs sound like. When it comes to music, "try before you buy" is the way customers prefer it.

Quotes

Feature favorable quotes about the band throughout your Web site, but most important, on your album pages. Getting reviews of your album before it's released is a good idea if possible. Otherwise, use reviews of shows or of previous albums. We talk about how to get reviews in detail in the "Get Publicized" chapter.

Think of the movie-listings page in your local newspaper. They're filled almost entirely with quotes from reviews, because people trust quotes most when it comes to spending money on a movie. Albums work the same way.

Other Text

Include the liner notes and lyrics on your album page. Since many people don't even bother buying CDs anymore, this might be the only place where they can find these. And if the notes and lyrics are particularly good, they may help make the sale.

Also, this text is useful in bringing more people to your site via search engines. The more text you have, the more often your site will pop up in searches for terms that appear within it.

Embedding an Online Store

The CD stores are there to help sell your albums, but don't wait for your fans to go to them. Link to the stores throughout your Web site. The goal of your site is to make album sales; it should be simple for people already on your site to buy your music. We provide links to buy our albums on every page of the Beatnik Turtle site.

Some CD stores allow you to embed a "shopping cart" on your own Web site, so that fans only leave your site when they're ready to purchase. We highly recommend doing this. Also, services such as Snocap.com, Hoooka.com, and Nimbit.com have embeddable widgets to integrate the store into your site. The iTunes music store provides a link that opens iTunes and goes either directly to an album or directly to a song. The more seamless the experience for your fans, the better. Since the methods differ, you should design your site around the store that best suits your needs and embed that store's functionality as much as possible into the album pages. You should embed both digital and physical CD stores into your site.

GRACENOTE AND FREEDB

Ever wonder how the album name, band name, and song names get filled in automatically in your MP3 player when you load a CD into your computer? The Gracenote Media Recognition Service (formerly CDDB) (gracenote.com) and freeDB (freedb.org) are the engines behind this. Both do exactly same thing, but Gracenote's service costs money for the software developer to license.

The companies that run these databases get listeners to do the hard work for them. When listeners load a CD that isn't already in the database, they often fill in the track info themselves so that they have it handy. Most music players have a simple submission button that allows you to upload this information to the database.

If you've released a CD, add your information to these databases yourself. Most fans, though they mean well, are not always the best spellers, and they sometimes get the information wrong. If you do it yourself, you can make sure it gets done right. To do this, simply load your CD into a player that supports each service. When you do, you will have an opportunity to enter the names of each track, and the other CD info such as band, album name, year, and others. Once you're done, make sure that you use the "submit" option in your application or else it will only be entered into your local library.

In general, iTunes works for Gracenote, while the free tool Audiograbber (audiograbber.com-us.net) works for freeDB. But you can also check their Web sites for other options.

SELLING OFF-LINE

SELLING AT SHOWS

We cover the details of selling at shows in the "Get Booked and Play Live" chapter. Show sales are not tracked at SoundScan unless you do credit card transactions with CD Baby, which we talk about in the "Get Booked and Play Live" chapter.

CONSIGNMENT

Most music stores, especially the mom-and-pop stores, will let you sell your CDs on consignment. This means that they will pay you after the album is sold, rather than before.

Consignment helps you even if you don't sell a single CD. As we discuss in the "Your Brand" chapter, you want to get your band name in front of as many people as possible. If music fans start seeing your CDs at stores around your area, they will begin to think that your band is significant (at least in the area) and are more likely to recognize your name the next time they see your poster.

Admittedly, this involves a lot of footwork for what might be only a small amount of exposure. And brick-and-mortar music stores are disappearing rapidly as people turn to online stores or big-box retailers, who are not interested in consignment.

As we've said, give free copies to workers at the stores where you sell your CD. If any of them like your music, they'll probably promote it to people walking in the door. Give an extra one to the store itself to play on the PA. People who work in CD stores are not doing it for the money; they love music and usually recommend their favorites to customers. Your CD, sitting in a consignment bin, won't sell itself. It needs to be heard and it needs other people to tell customers that it's worth buying. For inspiration, watch *High Fidelity,* then read this section again.

Oh, and while you're in the store, put up a poster for your album or upcoming show.

Sales will be tracked in SoundScan depending on the store. It's up to them to report sales of used or consignment discs.

GIRL SCOUTING

Every band member is a salesman. We employ a simple method called Girl Scouting, which amounts to sending your band members and friends out the door with a stack of albums to sell. We're not suggesting going door-to-door. Rather, use the same method that Girl Scouts do: leverage your personal network. When you mention your band to coworkers, friends, relatives, or your dentist, throw in that you've got copies of your latest album in your bag, in case they're interested. Throw in a "friend discount" and you'll probably have yourself a sale.

The "Your Network" chapter explains how important it is to credit everyone who had anything to do with your albums. This comes into play here, as anyone who is actually listed in the liner notes will usually agree to help sell the discs.

SELLING MUSIC ONLINE

ONLINE CD STORES

While some people want digital music, some still prefer physical CDs. Online CD stores are the best way to handle this distribution, unless you want to set yourself up as an online merchant and deal with packing, shipping, and handling orders.

When you evaluate online CD stores, make sure that the front page of the Web site looks like a *store,* and not like an ad for musicians to sell their music. When you enter the site, imagine that you're a fan, not a musician. Ask yourself where you'd go to buy music. If the online store's front page mostly brags about being a great place for bands to sell music, avoid it. They're probably just there to take your money.

The good online CD stores focus on selling music, not selling their service to musicians. If you use a store that seems indie-friendly, read the agreement carefully. Do not sign up for any services that take any rights to your music. The music store is there to sell your music, but they should not get any more rights to it than a grocery store gets to the breakfast cereals it sells. Some stores try to take advantage of you. Don't let them. Also, there's no limit to the number of CD stores that your music can be sold on. Don't agree to an exclusive deal unless you get a clear benefit from it.

Using Online Stores Effectively

Once you decide which stores to use, use the following techniques to get the most out of your new storefronts:

1. **Make comparisons.** List major bands with a similar sound in the album description.

2. **Feature quotes.** Make extensive use of good reviews in the description. These show your customers that people with acknowledged taste enjoyed your album. As we mentioned above, the movie-listings page of your newspaper is full of quotes for a reason.

3. **Offer samples.** Make song samples available if the store allows it. If they don't, put song clips on your site, then link to those clips from the description in the online store.

4. **Link from your site.** Put links to all your online album storefronts on every page of your band Web site to drive traffic and make it as easy as possible to buy your music.

5. **Link to your site.** Link back to your own Web site from your storefronts so that their customers can find more information about you and your albums.

CD Baby

In many ways, CD Baby (cdbaby.com) unleashed the indie music movement. They are by far our top suggestion for an online CD store. We've used them for years and are wildly happy about their services. Their price structure is simple: there is a onetime setup fee, and from then on, CD Baby keeps the first $4 of each CD you sell, and the rest goes to you. If you charge $10, you'll get $6 a CD.

Sign up on CD Baby. They'll get your music on all of the major digital music services, as well as offer worldwide physical-CD distribution. They are the most fair of any of the services we've found.

CD Baby was started by Derek Sivers, who created it to sell his own CDs. As a result, it's a musician-centric company. Here is a short list of CD Baby's advantages:

1. **Comprehensive service.** Physical-CD sales are seamlessly handled. CD Baby handles the credit card transactions, the shipping, the warehousing, and so on.

2. **Feedback from customers.** When customers buy a CD, they have the option to say where they found out about your music. This has been an invaluable source of information for us. You also get their e-mail address.

3. **Presence in major record stores.** CD Baby has agreements with stores including Best Buy and Wal-Mart. Your CD might not be available on the shelf, but it will be in their database if they search on it. This means that a customer can request to have your CD sent to the store for later pickup.

4. **Retail-store fulfillment.** CD Baby has linked up with a CD distributor, and if any retailers request your album, the distributor will ship it to them. (But it's up to you to generate the demand!)

5. **No paid favoritism.** CD Baby won't highlight an album just because they're paid to. They do feature bestseller lists, but otherwise they remain neutral.

6. **Helpful tips.** They offer suggestions on marketing and selling your music. Their regular e-mails feature surprisingly useful advice.

7. **Digital aggregation.** CD Baby is a digital store aggregator. They will convert your music to the innumerable formats required for each of the digital music stores and will handle the accounting and the setup for you.

8. **Partnership with Amazon.com.** If you sell your CD through CD Baby, it will also be listed at Amazon.com.

9. **Fully featured album pages.** CD Baby will provide song samples, statistics, and links to your Web site from your album pages.

There are many more benefits. Go to their site for more information. If you use just one online music store, CD Baby is the best choice.

For information on signing up, go to cdbaby.net. They don't clutter the main page with information for musicians. The front page at cdbaby.com is reserved for music fans, which is the way it should be.

All of CD Baby's sales are tracked through SoundScan.

Amazon.com

Amazon.com has a program for selling music from independent bands. Their deal is slightly less advantageous than CD Baby's, as they take a percentage of the sales price, rather than a flat fee of $4 per disc. But Amazon.com gets enormous amounts of traffic, so there's a good chance of making sales there. CD Baby has made an agreement with Amazon.com, though, so if you've contracted with CD Baby, your album will also be available at Amazon.com and you won't need to deal with them separately.

Amazon's sales are tracked in SoundScan.

Print on Demand

As mentioned in the "Your Albums and Merchandise" chapter, you can also print CDs on demand and sell them in an online store. See that chapter for details.

DIGITAL MUSIC STORES

Perhaps the biggest irony of digital music stores is that, even though they've opened their shelves to indies, they dislike dealing with them directly. You must use a digital aggregator service to get your music in stores like iTunes. These services can come and go quickly, though, so we suggest you use them with caution.

We have used CD Baby's program for many years now, and they have been a great choice. They make it simple for indie bands to get their music on all of the major services, and their cut is competitive with the others'. We suggest their program for everyone except those musicians who anticipate selling a high volume. For those musicians, we suggest using one of the services that allow you to pay a flat fee per year, letting you keep the rest of the digital sales for yourself.

Before you use these services, you should be aware of one problem with digital music stores. You often have no control about what date your songs become available to the public. You may want to have a release party and keep your album from being released ahead of time. Unfortunately, the only way to guarantee this is to submit your album to these services after your release.

DIGITAL AGGREGATORS

Digital aggregators differ in functionalities and features and price. Some of the ones that we recommend are:

- **CDBaby.com.** CD Baby charges a flat rate on each digital sale. In addition, there's an initial setup fee for each album. This is the most recommended digital aggregator as they are partnered with most digital music stores available.

- **Nimbit.com.** Nimbit takes a percentage of each digital sale. It also allows you to upload your MP3s directly into their system. Nimbit has a widget-based merchandise table that you and your fans can embed at your own Web sites.

- **TuneCore.com.** TuneCore charges a flat yearly fee for each digital music store in which you want to place your songs. If you achieve large enough yearly sales, it becomes economical to use this service. However, this service and pricing is designed for labels or big-name acts. For instance, Trent Reznor used this service when Nine Inch Nails released its album *Ghosts 1-N.*

WIDGET/APPLICATION-BASED STORES

These specialized digital music stores are usually compact embedded applications that you can easily add to your Web site. Even better, many of these services will allow your fans to insert your store into their Web sites as well. To encourage this, some of them will even share a cut of the sales with your fans. These stores often have additional features such as mailing lists, band bios, collecting e-mail addresses, playing videos, merchandise fulfillment. Some widget-based stores are Nimbit (nimbit.com), Hoooka (hoooka.com), and Snocap (snocap.com). Each one provides different services, so you should read the feature lists of each to see what they provide.

SELLING DOWNLOADS FROM YOUR SITE

If you wish, you can also create a store to sell your own MP3s from your Web site (or Web presences sites). If you decide to go this route, a number of different services are available. You should do a careful analysis of the associated costs and decide which is the best for your own band. For example, some charge different rates based on the number of items you have to sell, the number of sales that you get, or even the amount of MB space used by your digital items.

Most sites that sell digital downloads are made for people selling software rather than the low-cost, and low-margin, MP3 files. For example, you need to make quite a few sales of MP3s at $0.99 to meet a $25 monthly fee. Services bands have used to sell music include E-Junkie (e-junkie.com) and PayLoadz (payloadz.com).

LEARNING MORE

To stay on top of all the ways to get your music distributed and sold, visit IndieBandSurvivalGuide.com.

CHAPTER 11

GET PLAYED AND HEARD

WHEN YOU think about getting your music heard, the first thing that probably comes to mind is radio. But radio simply isn't the best method any longer. In the post-Net era, more ways to get heard exist than ever before. We're going to cover these methods below.

PREPARING TO GET HEARD

You should get together a few things before trying to get your music heard around the world.

PREPARE YOUR MUSIC

Have your music available in the following formats:

1. **MP3s.** Use these small, universally compatible files for free downloads on your own site, samples in your online store, submissions to music Web sites and social networks, and elsewhere around the Web. (For MP3 encoding instructions, see the "Your Web Site" chapter.)

2. **WAV files.** Use these large, high-quality files for podcasts, film, TV, and other mediums. They aren't as easy to share, but they offer the highest fidelity when it counts.

3. **CDs.** Have your music handy in physical form for selling online and at shows, marketing giveaways, and other publicity and PR opportunities. No band member should ever leave the house without at least a couple of CDs, just in case.

PREPARE YOUR WEB SITE

Before you begin your campaign to get heard, prepare your Web site as outlined in the "Your Web Site" chapter. As we've stated before, your Web site can make all the difference in converting a onetime visitor to a fan.

For example, we were once mentioned on a blog of office humor after releasing an album of sarcastic songs about office life. Samples from the album, easily found from the front page, were on the blog readers to listen to. If the songs hadn't been in place, that blog mention would have gone nowhere.

Some of the more effective ways to get heard are online. On the radio, the DJ might not even say the band's name. Online, listeners request the song and actively listen. All your information, and your online store, is at their fingertips. Your Web site is a part of this process.

Before starting a campaign, make sure that your music, your store, your contact page, and your press section are ready to go on your Web site. This is even true for off-line campaigns. Your Web site will be the first place people will go for more information once you get their attention.

HOW TO TAKE NO FOR AN ANSWER

You're about to submit your music for consideration. This may leave you feeling a bit vulnerable. After all, what if they say no?

If you submit a song somewhere and they don't accept it, move on. A venue or medium might not respond to your song for many reasons, such as it got lost, it didn't fit their format, or they forgot. The good news is that there are so many alternatives, and this is a numbers game. You can't control it, so move on.

What you can control is your submission. Make the best music and craft the best publicity materials that you can and send them as far and as wide as you can. Don't use rejections as critiques. If you want feedback, go to other musicians or producers.

Most important, follow up. Most places that accept music submissions don't even tell you if they've decided against using your stuff. Also, a well-managed follow-up can sometimes make the difference in getting your song played. Some of the methods we discuss in the "Get Publicized" chapter will come in handy here. Many of our follow-ups have gotten us plays, so don't skip this essential step.

REGISTERING YOUR SONGS WITH A PERFORMANCE RIGHTS ORGANIZATION

We suggest reading the "Your Rights" chapter on performance rights organizations (PROs) to learn how to get your music registered, so that the resulting plays on radio or elsewhere can generate income. Unless you're a big player, or you've gotten fairly well-known, it's unlikely that you'll see any income, but it still makes sense to get your music registered.

GETTING HEARD OFF-LINE

COLLEGE RADIO

College radio works the way that most people think commercial radio should work: you send them your music, and if they like it, they'll play it. It's wonderfully uncomplicated and far less expensive than dealing with commercial radio.

Students control access to college airwaves. They're the DJs. They select the CDs. They read the news. They play the dead air. They run the station. These are the people you need to convince to play your music. Best of all, college radio is inclusive. Students host shows that run the gamut of styles and formats. No matter what kind of music you create, there's a college radio show that will play it.

But this doesn't mean it won't take hard work to get your music played. It requires time, effort, and follow-up. The good news is that college radio is within your arm's reach. Before spending your time and money, however, consider what you're going to get out of a college-radio campaign. College radio has an undeniably smaller listenership than its commercial cousin.

Do You Need a College-Radio Campaign?

If your goal is to get played on the radio, a college-radio campaign is your best bet. But getting your music *heard* is more than just getting played on the radio, and a full-blown college-radio campaign might actually be a distraction from better opportunities that could spread your music further for the same effort. There are four major reasons to pursue college radio:

- Exposure
- Charting in *College Music Journal*

- Boosting concert-tour draws
- Performance royalties

Exposure

If your music is added to a station's rotation, you will potentially reach new fans. Most of the benefits of this airplay are somewhat indirect, however. Your song will get played, but will the DJ announce the title correctly? The band name? Will he remember to announce anything at all? If he doesn't, the radio play won't necessarily help you make new fans. Unlike with online mediums, you can't click on the band name to go to the Web site or instantly buy a track.

When listeners decide to buy your music, they'll have to do a Web search on how they *think* your band name is spelled based on how the DJ pronounced it. And there's no good way to determine how many times you've been played even if you do get added to the rotation. It could be thousands. It could be once. Stations have no obligation to tell you. In comparison to Web sites, which track all downloads, you have to listen to the radio station yourself to confirm if and when you get played.

Charting in College Music Journal

College Music Journal, or *CMJ*, is to college radio what *Billboard* is to Top 40 commercial radio. It's an expensive industry magazine that tracks what's "hot" on college radio. If your music is played often enough across multiple college stations, you have a shot at getting charted in *CMJ*. This can provide recognition by a trusted, objective authority that your music has momentum in the college market. This can generate interest in your band from the press and record labels. For many bands and labels, charting in *CMJ* is a major goal.

But charting for the sake of charting can be a distraction from what's really important: building your fan network. Many alternative outlets for your time, energy, and money can be more effective. Most campaigns that succeed at *CMJ* charting do so by paying radio promoters to perform the intensive promotional work and follow-up necessary to get airplay in multiple college markets.

Boosting Concert-Tour Draws

College radio listeners like attending concerts. Timing your radio campaign to your tour schedule can be a great way to boost your draws. If coordinated with a full-fledged publicity campaign, listeners in the area will become familiar with you and your music and will be more likely to check out your show.

For instance, posters on campus advertising your upcoming show are more likely to resonate with the college community when timed to coincide with your music on the radio. Offering complimentary tickets to the station to give away to listeners will increase their incentive to play your band's music on the air, announce and advertise your show, and have you come to the station to be interviewed and perform.

Performance Royalties

As discussed in the "Your Rights" chapter, one additional benefit of college radio airplay is that each play counts as a performance for the author/publisher. If you've registered with a PRO, you are eligible to earn performance royalties. Unfortunately, your handful of radio plays probably won't get caught in their surveys.

How College Radio (Usually) Works

We can't say how all college radio stations work, but there are some common elements. Naturally, most college stations restrict staff to current students to make sure that as many as possible have the opportunity to work in radio. This includes the DJs as well as the music directors who decide what goes into the station's rotations. Because the music directors are students, you need to keep their motivations and schedules in mind if you want to convince them to play your music. Getting in touch with them will be at their convenience. Generally, student music directors keep irregular office hours and, because they're students, might be at class or in bed with a hangover when you call.

Typically, students who take part in radio are genuinely excited about new music. Most of the ones we've met have unconventional tastes and prefer music outside of the mainstream—beyond commercial radio. Most love discovering something new—a new band, a new sound, a unique song—and sharing it with their listeners. Many are musicians themselves and love discussing music endlessly.

Many stations stick to a particular genre or style of music during daytime hours: alternative, rock, hip-hop, and so on. They play a rotation of preselected music. Typically, the music director determines what music to include in this daytime rotation, although some stations may let a committee of staff members decide. Like the music they play, music director's personalities run the gamut. Some share music decisions with the DJs and staff, while others can be dictators. In true tail-wagging-dog fashion, some decide based on what charts in *CMJ*.

DJs, however, also have a say in what music is played, although it's typically limited. College DJs can technically play whatever music they want as long as they meet a certain number of plays of the preselected music. For instance, at KRUI, where one of the *Guide's* authors worked, the station divided music into heavy, medium, or light rotation slots. CDs were physically labeled with red, blue, and yellow stickers corresponding to how often a particular song should be played during the hour. DJs were supposed to play a certain number of songs every hour, favoring the heavy-rotation songs, and going down from there.

Even so, the college radio DJ actually controls which songs air and when. Contrast this with commercial radio, where DJs are simply on-air personalities with no control over the music (despite frequent talk of a certain song being "requested"). Music on commercial radio is decided by music directors and is typically programmed into computers beforehand.

After the daytime college-radio rotation, evenings and weekends are usually dedicated to shows that focus on a particular niche. These generally focus on music radically different from the kind featured in the daytime format, such as a thrash metal show on a station that normally plays country. Latin, punk, folk, jazz, alt-country, bluegrass, ambient, or even children's music might be spotlighted.

Some of these are long-established shows that have been inherited and handed down through the years from student to student. Others are the original invention of a particular student who received approval from the staff for the format. The songs played on a particular show are decided by the student or students who control the show at that time. These shows tend to appeal to a limited, but targeted, college and college-community audience.

Running a College-Radio Campaign

The seven steps to running a successful college-radio campaign are:

1. Identify stations and shows

2. Make a list, and check it twice

3. Call in advance

4. Prepare your CD and press kit for submission

5. Send it in

6. Follow up to verify delivery

7. Follow up to verify acceptance

If the purpose of your college-radio campaign is to boost your draw for a tour, coordinate carefully to maximize the effectiveness of the campaign. This means planning ahead and building in enough time to get your music to each station, convince them to add your song, and if possible schedule an interview or performance in-studio well before you pull up on campus in the van. Because this will seriously affect your planning, determine if this is one of your goals early on.

Step 1: Identify Stations and Shows

Your goal is to send your music directly to those people who will actually play it. There are *stations* that specialize in your style of music and also *specific shows*. You must identify both for your radio campaign.

You can use two free resources to identify the stations. This includes the Web site for this book, IndieBandSurvivalGuide.com, and a directory listing found at Yahoo! (dir.yahoo.com/News_and_Media/Radio/Stations/College_and_University). You can also buy resources such as *The Indie Bible* and *The Musician's Atlas,* both of which list college radio stations as well as other resources.

For shows, you can use the books listed above, although it's hard to find a complete, up-to-date list, as those books can become outdated. You typically have to search each station's Web site for information on its shows, unless you live in the area and already know what those shows are.

You should submit your music directly to the person most likely to play it. To get in the general rotation, send it to the music director or the submission address they provide. If you want to get into a specialty show, find that DJ's address and send it directly.

Step 2: Make a List, and Check It Twice

Once you've identified the appropriate stations and shows, write them down. You need a comprehensive list of where and to whom you will be sending your music. A simple spreadsheet will do. Keep track of where and when you submitted your music and when you need to follow up. See the box below for our recommended headers.

INFORMATION TO TRACK DURING A RADIO PROMOTION CAMPAIGN

Since a radio promotion campaign takes weeks to pull off, you'll want to keep track of the following information for each station in a table or database:

- Name

- Address

- Submission guidelines

- Contact name

- Phone number

- E-mail address

- Notes about your call with the radio-station contact to help trigger your memory when you later call to follow up

- If touring, to time airplay to when you'll be in the area, your deadline for when you need to have the station add your song to the rotation

- When you mailed the CD and press kit

• When you need to call them to make sure the package was received and ask when the song might be added to the rotation

• When they tell you the song will be added to the rotation

• When it's confirmed your song was added to the rotation

Step 3: Call in Advance

Once you have your list, call to confirm the contact details, verify what kinds of materials they need, and hype your music. You may want to skip this step, but don't make that mistake. The key to any successful college-radio campaign is making direct contacts and creating a personal connection with you and your music. This will give you a leg up against bands that simply "submit and forget," and you'll also be competing for attention with radio promoters who do this for their clients.

We'll discuss radio promoters in detail in the next section, but know that these paid professionals always use a call to hype their client's songs because it's their job to get the station to add them to their rotation. Airtime is limited, and the difference between having your CD sit in a pile and getting it get added to the rotation is your ability to connect with someone at the station who will feel obligated not only to keep an eye out for your CD, but to make sure it gets added. How you do this is ultimately up to you. This is one of the times when the agent strategy we discussed in the "Get Noticed" chapter will come in handy.

Step 4: Prepare Your CD and Press Kit for Submission

Prepare your submission according to the station's instructions. Unfortunately, most college radio stations are still organized around the CD and don't accept MP3 or WAV files. So you'll have to do it the old-fashioned way and physically mail copies of the CD to your contact person's attention. Doing anything other than following instructions will probably result in your package being thrown out or, at best, seriously delayed as it's routed between radio station staff.

Suggestions for preparing your CD include:

- **Put it in a standard jewel case.** If your CD is not already in a standard jewel case, put it in one. In general, CD libraries at college radio stations are based on the size of the standard jewel case, so thin cases or paper folders are inconvenient for them. (If you haven't had your CD manufactured yet and you're planning a college-radio campaign, then this may be a deciding factor in how you package your CD.)

- **Remove the annoying plastic wrap.** If your CD is shrink-wrapped, remove it. Save them time and hassle.

- **Recommend two or three songs to play.** Label the case with the top two or three "radio-ready" songs you definitely want them to hear. You don't want them losing interest in your CD by track three when track six is the best song on the album.

Unless otherwise instructed, your press kit should be simple—do not spend extra time and money on this. We talk about press kits in the "Get Publicized" chapter. You can abridge the full kit for radio by limiting it to the bio and basic facts about the band (including the Web site address). They're evaluating your music, plain and simple, and probably won't be reading your press kit on the air. If you include a positive press article or review about your music, it might help, but the only thing they'll really be interested in is the CD.

Step 5: Send It In

With prep out of the way, it's time to mail your package:

- **Write "solicited material" on the envelope.** If you previously contacted someone at the station and were told to send in your CD, write "solicited material" in clear, easy-to-read print on the front and back of the envelope.

- **Write the date of your show on the envelope.** If you're touring and will be playing in the area, include the date of your show on the envelope. Adding a date tells the students that you're coming to town, which is an added incentive for them to promptly open the envelope, play your music, and contact you for an interview or on-air performance.

Be sure to mark the date you mailed the package on your spreadsheet, and mark the follow-up date appropriately (allowing at least a week from the mail date depending on your method of delivery).

Step 6: Follow Up to Verify Delivery

After all the work you've done, you won't want to neglect this important step. On the follow-up date, call your contact to confirm that the CD arrived. This is a second opportunity to hype your music and the particular track you'd like them to play. If they didn't receive the CD or if they've already lost it, you'll need to resend. If they did receive it, ask your contact when they're scheduled to evaluate it. Make a note of this date and mark it on your schedule.

Step 7: Follow Up to Verify Acceptance

As soon as the second follow-up date arrives, call your contact one more time to determine whether your music was in fact added to the station's rotation. This is not an odd question to ask. Stations receive this question regularly from radio promoters, who need to report back to their clients.

Being included in the rotation does not guarantee that your music will be played. Unless you actually listen to the station, you can never be sure if or when your music is played since, as we said, at most stations it's the DJs who choose what to play from the songs in rotation. If they don't like your song, regardless of how it's labeled, they will skip it.

Doesn't this seem like a lot of work? It should come as no surprise that an entire industry sprang up around orchestrating these campaigns.

Hiring a Radio Promoter

Eighty percent or more of the music you hear on daytime rotation at college radio stations is chosen thanks to the work of radio promoters. They offer three advantages over doing a college radio campaign yourself:

- **Existing contacts.** Promoters know the stations and shows and have the necessary relationships in place.

- **Comprehensive service.** Promoters do all the work promoting, following up, and verifying that your music has been added to the rotation.

• *Hype.* Promoters are good at schmoozing college DJs and music directors and convincing them that your music is "hot."

Radio promoters typically only accept clients whose music they feel is worthy of promotion. After all, their reputations are on the line when they try to get bands played. Promoters tend to be tenacious, with the capacity for barefaced promotion that the job calls for. And because they act as your agent, it's easier for them to hype your music as "the best ever."

One music director told us that, each week without fail, he'd get a call from a promoter describing the "hottest group ever" with "the best song," insisting it be immediately added. Every week the promoter would have a new "best song ever." And although the tactic didn't work on this director, it always seemed to work with his junior music directors, who would approve the new song for rotation. They loved the attention this promoter gave them and how important it made them feel.

If you have the money, a radio promoter may be an option for you. Fees can range anywhere from $2,500 to $40,000 or more depending on:

• The scope of your campaign (there are a lot of college radio stations out there)

• The services you want (they'll charge you less if you do all the grunt work and mailing)

• The duration of the campaign

One word of warning: promoters get paid to try to get your music into rotation, not to actually get it played. Once your campaign is over, all they'll owe you is an invoice and a report on which stations they contacted: "talked to so-and-so," "left message," "will review CD."

If you're going to spend money to promote your music, as an alternative to a traditional radio promoter, whose campaign will be limited in time and scope, calculate what you would spend and take that money to hire someone on your own. Find someone in your skill network with the right personality and skills to handle this. One individual calculated that, for the amount of money he spent on a radio promoter for six weeks, he could have financed his own promotions person for six months. And unlike a radio promoter, who has to allocate limited resources among many clients, a part-time promotions person works for you alone. Of course, your promotions person won't have the established relationships in place that a radio promoter already has, but with a little research even a newbie can be effective in this role. Just remember that your new hire will be competing against people who do this for a living.

Live-Music Shows and In-Studio Performances

If you're touring or have a gig within a station's broadcast area, you should see if they have a live-music show. Live-music shows typically run during the day and feature in-studio performances and interviews with bands and musicians performing in the area that night or weekend.

Most stations are more than happy to have bands come in the afternoon before a show and play a few songs, give away a few tickets, and get interviewed by the DJs. Beyond actively promoting your show and boosting your draw, doing in-studio performances is an excellent way to cement your relationships with the station staff and get to know them face-to-face.

Even if the station doesn't have a live-music show, they may still want you to come in to do an interview, play some songs off your CD, and give away some tickets. If you're on tour, you'll need to coordinate your radio appearances with your shows.

COMMERCIAL RADIO

As we discussed earlier, commercial radio does not work in the idyllic way still portrayed in some television shows. Generally, they don't accept unsolicited submissions. A commercial radio campaign can cost anywhere from tens to hundreds of thousands of dollars. Part of that money goes to independent promoters who control access to the stations and block other music from getting added to the playlist. A radio promoter is different from an independent promoter. While a radio promoter tries to get music added to the rotation, an independent promoter acts as the gatekeeper and tollbooth for each station.

Even the major labels will often try to chart on *CMJ* before doing a commercial-radio campaign. As we explained above, it might be best to start with a college campaign even if your goal is to eventually get played on commercial radio. A *CMJ*-charted band has a big leg up to get an "add" on commercial radio.

Getting Played on Commercial Radio

Your best bet for getting into a commercial radio station's rotation would be to hire a radio promoter who specializes in commercial radio. But this isn't economically feasible for most indies.

The amount of effort you would need to invest to get your music on commercial radio would probably be sufficient for you to become a professional radio promoter yourself. This is why most indie bands avoid commercial radio altogether.

Local Music Shows

Although it's difficult to get added to a commercial radio station's rotation, there are a few other opportunities. Some commercial radio stations have shows that feature local artists, such as WXRT's *Local Anesthetic* with Richard Milne in Chicago. Such shows will accept submissions from any local band. They can be a good way to get heard because they usually have large audiences, and they love promoting local shows because it's something happening in their backyard. It helps to listen to these shows before submitting, since show hosts often prefer a particular genre or style.

Submitting to these shows is usually easy. Follow the submission guidelines on the station's Web site. Local music shows are usually flooded, so make sure you obey the guidelines carefully, and as with college-radio campaigns, follow up on your submission.

Commercial Specialty Shows

Some commercial stations air syndicated specialty shows that accept submissions. These commercial specialty shows are similar to local music shows in that the show host typically decides what to play. Unlike the local show, syndicated shows span multiple markets and have larger listenerships. Examples include *Little Steven's Underground Garage* and the long-running *Dr. Demento Show*.

Talk Shows

Talk shows are another way to get played on commercial radio. If one of your songs is on a topic being discussed, they might just play it if it's brought to their attention. A play on a talk show helps make your music stand out more than one in a standard music rotation. This happened to us when we sent our version of the Irish song "Tell Me Ma" in anticipation of St. Patrick's Day to Jonathon Brandmeier who has a morning show in Chicago.

Of course, no formal submission guidelines exist for talk shows. You will often have to find their contact information from their Web site. Sometimes the producer is a good person to approach. Other times, getting your music directly to the hosts works best. It helps if you're personally familiar with the show, allowing you to tailor the message. When Jonathan played our song, all we had done was e-mail the show and send an MP3.

PUBLIC RADIO

Public radio is a great way to get your music played because the audience is much larger than that of college radio and it isn't as gated off as the commercial-radio market.

A National Public Radio station will play the general NPR news feed and then add their local news at the end. Then, throughout the day, they will alternate local shows with some national ones.

Each program has a producer of its own who makes decisions about the stories and music that are included.

Getting Played on Public Radio

We suggest the following steps to get your music on public radio:

1. Identify all of the programs that you want to target (it's best to start with the local ones). Add each one to your spreadsheet, as discussed above.

2. Go to each program's Web page and find the producer's contact information and any submission guidelines.

3. Craft and send a pitch that's tailored to each show's content. (Note that sometimes you can get phone numbers or fax numbers. But other times you need to be content with an e-mail.)

4. Follow up!

We got our debut album played on WBEZ, Chicago's public radio station, using this method. We found the e-mail of the producer of *Eight-Forty-Eight,* a program on WBEZ, and sent a CD at their request. They played it on their show.

Keep in mind that producers may not get back to you, even if they play your music. A friend of the band once claimed to have heard us on public radio. Skeptical, we searched the radio station's site and discovered that, lo and behold, our song had been played after all—despite the fact no one from the show telling us.

SATELLITE AND CABLE RADIO

Satellite radio works like satellite television, the signal being beamed from orbit rather than from local towers. Satellite radio receivers are still mostly built into cars, but some portable devices are also available, and satellite channels are also available to subscribers over the Web.

Satellite radio has been chipping away at terrestrial radio's listenership, but it's still lagging far behind because it requires special equipment and a subscription fee. Initially, satellite held a lot of promise for indie bands, but the format has became less friendly as it's matured. Although they haven't adopted the independent promoter system of terrestrial radio, they still aren't easy to approach with unsolicited music.

Although some satellite providers have "indie music" stations, those stations aren't attractive to listeners. People look for genres such as country, hard rock, or classical. Your goal is to get played on the genre that fits your music.

NONRADIO OPTIONS
Theater and Comedy Groups

Theater and comedy groups provide many opportunities to get played that are often neglected by bands. They can be a particularly good way to get heard. Audiences at a theater show are really paying attention, as opposed to fans at a concert, who are usually shouting or spilling beer on each other.

For a theatrical performance, you can perform live as part of the show or get your recorded music played for a scene or sketch.

The best part about getting your music played in a theater is that your band will get mentioned in the program. Your band name will appear with your Web site address on a piece of paper that some people will take home. It's an instant flyer. You may also get an opportunity to present a mailing list and sell your albums.

If you're interested in getting your music in a theatrical performance, hook up with the local theater community, improvisation community, or sketch-comedy community. (These are three distinct communities, if you can believe it, although there is always some crossover.) Many local artists are putting on their own shows, and you never know who might be looking for music unless you get involved.

We used this to good effect when we hooked up with a sketch-comedy group and got a run of shows at the famous Second City, partly because they were able to promise a band with the sketch comedy (which made for a bigger show as well boosting the draw). The comedians turned out to be wonderful contributors to our skill and opportunity networks. Years later, they used our recorded music as part of yet another Second City show and then later for a TV show called *DVDGeeks* they developed. These plays have been great for our band résumé.

Music at a theatrical performance of any kind stands out, just as actors would at a concert. We've found that these shows often have an easier time getting critical attention and mentions in the paper. It's a good way to get publicized, and a good excuse for a press release.

Film and Television

Both independent and studio films are opportunities for indie bands. So are television shows. In fact, film and television production companies are starting to work with indie bands more and more because they are less expensive, easier to work with, and easy to find, thanks to the Internet. To get played on film and television, you just need to make producers aware of your music.

Fortunately, everything you do to get your band noticed contributes to this goal. Still, you can maximize your likelihood of getting your music on the small or large screen via:

• **Your Web site.** Mention on your Web site that your music is available for film and TV use. That way, your site might come up in a search for "film music." Although it should be obvious that music can be used for anything at all, sometimes you have to draw producers a map. You might just give them an idea.

• **Film and TV schools.** With the Internet, you can make your music available to any film school in the world. If you have any film or TV schools in your area, you can hook up with them more directly and provide your music for their use (usually just for exposure rather than money). And if the film takes off, it may create a lot of interest in your work.

• *Creative Commons.* Sites based on the Creative Commons license make music available to many types of creators, including film producers and television show producers. See creativecommons.org and the "Your Rights" chapter for information about this.

• *Community television.* Some community-television stations have shows that need music. Given the copyright obstacles with using major-label music, they are always on the lookout for precleared alternatives.

• *Music aggregators.* TV, film, and commercial producers sometimes rely on music aggregation services that act as middlemen between musicians and producers. We talk about this in the "Your Rights" chapter.

MUSIC CONTESTS

From battle-of-the-bands to songwriting contests, countless places exist to "compete" against other musicians to get your music judged and heard. While we have never seen music as a competitive activity, competition can motivate some people. Below are a few of the opportunities that may come as a result of these contests. Some of these options cross into online options as well, but we'd rather keep all of the contests in one place.

Battle of the Bands

Battle-of-the-bands contests are usually live, although many are appearing online by pitting a band's recorded music against that of other bands. Some of these contests require a fee to participate, but others are free. It's a simple enough concept: there are usually a bunch of bands, a way to judge the "best," and a show that gives all the bands a chance to perform. If held online, the "performance" is usually a Web page with the band's posted songs.

If you win one, you can publicize it. But even if you don't, you can at least expose your music to new listeners. So although these are seen as competitive, they can be worthwhile, whether you win or lose.

Songwriting Contests

Some contests focus simply on your ability to write songs. Songwriting contests have been around for quite a while and often require an entry fee to participate. That's the way a lot of these contests make their money—from the musicians.

There are innumerable songwriting contests you can enter, with perhaps one of the most famous being the John Lennon Songwriting Contest (www.jlsc.com). Some lists of songwriting contests can be found at Muse's Muse (www.musesmuse.com/contests.html) and the Craft of Songwriting (www.craftofsongwriting.com/contests.htm). Many of these songwriting contests offer prizes for first place, including recording gear, instruments, and, for some reason, record-label contracts.

One notable and free songwriting contest that occurs weekly online is Song fight! (songfight.org). Songfight typically posts a song title or titles on their Web site. Musicians have one week in which to write and record a song based on that title and e-mail it in. Songs are made public for visitors to stream and download so they can vote on their favorite. The prize for winning is bragging rights for the week. If you enjoy a creative challenge, we recommend Songfight.

Album Challenges

The goal of an album challenge is write, record, and produce an entire album in one month. Most album challenges were inspired by National Novel Writing Month (NaNoWriMo.org), which challenges authors to write a 175-page (fifty-thousand-word) novel within the month of November. And like NaNoWriMo, there's no contest or prizes at stake.

Three of the major album challenges that you can participate in are the Record Production Month Challenge (rpmchallenge.com), February Album Writing Month (http://www.fawm.org), and National Solo Album Month (www.nasoalmo.org). The RPM Challenge and FAWM occur in February, while the NaSoAlMo occurs in November alongside NaNoWriMo. Each is free to participate in.

A surprising number of musicians take part in these challenges. According to Christopher Grenier and David Karlotski, two of RPM's organizers, they've had musicians from all seven continents (yes, this includes Antarctica!). Karlotski states one of the purposes of the RPM Challenge is to "get musicians back to why they do music in the first place: to create music for the sake of music and not focus on whether it's commercial or not." In fact, that's what we found when we participated in the RPM Challenge ourselves. We had a blast writing the music and got an album out of it, to boot. We also connected with other musicians on the RPM Web site and discussion boards and even met a bunch of them in person at the Chicago celebration party, which was held simultaneously with parties in many other cities all over the world.

One notable participant in RPM was Bob Boilen of the band Tiny Desk Unit. Boilen is a host and director of National Public Radio's *All Things Considered*. As a participant he highlighted RPM and some of the bands that participated on his show. Best of all, sites such as RPM make their participants' music available free to the public year-round on an online jukebox. So, it's yet another place to be heard.

GETTING HEARD ONLINE

As we mentioned in the introduction to this chapter, the online opportunities to get heard are often the most effective because they link directly to your Web site. The exciting thing about getting heard online is that any Web site at all can put your songs on its pages, not just music Web sites.

Ironically, music Web sites are probably the worst places to get played. They tend to be overcrowded and lack the necessary coherency to be a good place for listeners to find new music. We'll present many alternatives to music sites below.

FIND OUT WHERE THE PARTY'S AT

The difficult part about deciding where to spend your time and energy on the Web is determining whether a given Web site is popular. Most don't display their statistics, so you'll need to rely on other methods.

But just as important as the size of the audience for a particular Web site is the kind of audience. If you write songs about beer, for example, you'll want to target the most active Web sites and message boards about beer to promote your music. Even a modestly popular Web site can have a dramatic effect if its audience is mostly people who would probably enjoy your music for one reason or another.

Who Is the Audience?

The first thing to do with any Web site is to figure out what the audience is like. This comes into play in the indie music arena more than most. For instance, lots of sites out there say they're a great place for indie music to get heard, declaring all these benefits right on the front page. The problem is, as a listener, you wouldn't stay on a page that speaks directly to bands.

Amazon.com, on the other hand, devotes its front page to selling to customers, although links are on there as well for setting up your own store. YouTube also does a good job of balancing their front page between featuring the latest cool videos and explaining how to submit your own.

Think twice about signing up on any site that doesn't strike this balance. Most likely, the sign-up agreements aren't fair to the musicians, because these sites aren't making their money off listeners, and it's coming from somewhere.

Google PageRank

One of the quickest ways to judge a Web site's popularity is to install Google Toolbar (toolbar.google.com), available for Microsoft Internet Explorer and Mozilla Firefox. After installation, browse to any page to see its Google PageRank on the green bar in the middle of the toolbar. Page Ranks range from one to ten and are based on the number of sites that link to a Web site together with a host of other constantly shifting criteria.

PageRank is generally a good way to judge the popularity and trustworthiness of a site. A four or five is quite good, although these numbers change whenever Google tweaks its methodology. Keeping up with the latest changes to Google's PageRank on blogs about search engine optimization (SEO) will help you interpret the numbers more effectively.

Searches

You can use search engines to find out who is linking to a particular site. For instance, in Google, enter "link:www.beatnikturtle.com" to see every site that links to ours. It won't take long to learn if a site is a scam, as posts complaining about it will be in the first few pages of results.

Design

Often, it's possible to tell how good a site is simply by how well it's designed. If it has a lot of bad links or looks too simple, it probably won't be worth your time. People have to spend money to make sites look good, and this is a good indicator of how seriously they take the endeavor. If they've gotten a slick design, they've almost certainly spent some money doing SEO work to boost their Google PageRank, which generates traffic. (See the "Your Web Site" chapter for information more on SEO.)

MUSIC WEB SITES

While music Web sites come to mind first for getting heard on the Web, they're often the least effective online outlet. Most of them don't take a stand on what music is good, accepting songs from anyone who signs up for an account. These sites are often enormous, undifferentiated piles of music. Even a terrific song won't stand out in a chaotic mess like that.

Beware of music sites that feature terrible agreements for the musicians, requiring them to give up rights to their songs in return for the slight possibility that someone might actually listen to their music. Read any agreements carefully before signing up. There's often a provision stating that the agreement can change with almost no notice, so negative terms can be added later or positive ones removed.

Also, remember to make sure that the site is targeting listeners and not indie bands. We've rarely seen the trade-offs to be worth the trivial exposure that you can get from music Web sites such as MP3.com. Be careful if you decide to use them.

Part of the reason for the popularity of these sites (with musicians) is that they promise to generate interest in your music just by your signing up. In our experience, interest comes from sending your music directly to the people who might be interested in it: reviewers, bloggers, podcasters, forum members, and so on.

That said, a few sites that we've seen many musicians use to share their music (besides MySpace) are Virb (virb.com), SoundClick (soundclick.com), Alonetone (alonetone.com), and GarageBand (garageband.com), which give you a band page, a player to show off your music, and other features.

NONMUSIC WEB SITES

There's an entire Web full of sites out there, and any of them can easily incorporate music. Rather than catalog Web sites by the kind of content they normally feature, categorize them by topic.

We're not suggesting that you pitch just any site. You need to find the most popular ones whose topic is most directly related to your music. A post to the right message board or a mention on the right blog can mean a lot of listens for your songs.

To give you some ideas, as we mentioned previously, a few mentions on the starwars.com message boards for our song "Star Wars (A Movie like No Other)" brought a lot of people to our site. Our song "Were All These Beer Cans Here Last Night?" was mentioned on Cheapass.com and generated over thirty thousand song plays. The song "I've No Pants" found a home on NoPantsDay.com. And "Why Don't You Drive?"—about those slow drivers that won't get out of your way—found its place on a popular trucking Web site.

Categorize your songs by topic, then find the most popular Web sites on each topic and figure out ways your music might fit in. Most sites have blogs, and bloggers are always hungry for content on their chosen topic. Other sites have message boards you can post to. Still others have a news feed. Submitting your music may involve some sleuthing to find an e-mail address, and once you find one, the submission itself should be informal, along the lines of "You might like this song about snorkeling." If you can be on-topic to that extent, that's often all that you need to do.

Using a Web Flash player, you can give them the HTML code to embed your song directly in their blog rather than sending them a file. This has the advantage of letting you see the listening stats and may make it easier on someone who has a site and doesn't know how to play music from it. See the "Your Web Site" chapter for details.

You should ask any site owner that does play your music to provide a link back to your own Web site, so that people who like the song can find you.

While this is one of the more informal ways of getting your music heard, because you are piggybacking on the popularity of each Web site and are using its interest in the topic to make your music heard, this can be one of the most effective tools at your disposal.

WEBCASTING

Webcasting uses the Internet to stream your music to people connected to an Internet radio station using a multimedia player. Unfortunately, it's been regulated into obscurity. The fees charged by the major music owners, as well as the rules and reporting requirements that Webcasters have to deal with, are so prohibitive as to shut down most stations. Most Webcasters today are terrestrial radio stations that are simulcasting their feed on the Internet. The other ones are usually affiliated with larger organizations, such as Live365.com, which handles the paperwork, some of the cost, and the requirements that regulations have imposed on Webcasting.

Webcasting started out unregulated, like most new technologies. The idea that ordinary people could basically create their own radio stations created a groundswell of interest in this new media. Unfortunately, the major copyright owners got together and set rates that were in many cases higher than those charged to terrestrial radio, along with difficult reporting requirements. These regulations quashed the initial excitement and put a stop to technological innovation.

A new agreement has since been put in place that raised the rates so significantly Webcasters will not be able to make a profit.

Webcasting stations cover every genre. Many of them are friendly to indie bands. Submitting your music to Internet radio stations can get your music played, and the payola problems present in commercial radio are largely nonexistent.

Some Internet radio stations are explicitly devoted to indie music. While those stations are fairly easy to break into, we suggest you focus on stations that specifically cover your style of music. Because Internet radio is not closed to indies, why not try to get played alongside more popular songs in your style? The listeners who prefer indie-band-only stations are the listening avant-garde, a much smaller audience than the general listening public. People often forget that indie music is not a style, just an indicator that a band is not on a big label. There are indie bands in classical music as well as power punk, but the two don't necessarily mesh well on a radio broadcast. You're better off finding a station that matches your style to get your music heard by those who would probably like it.

Some sites to check out for Internet radio information are Live365 (live365.com), SHOUTcast (shoutcast.com), and Radio Paradise (radioparadise.com).

PODCASTS

Because of the burdens placed on Webcasting, podcasting has become the radio of the Internet. Podcasts are some of the best places for an indie musician to get played.

And people are listening. The growth of podcasting has been stunning. If you'd searched Google on September 28, 2004, for the term *podcasts*, you would have gotten twenty-four hits. On September 28, 2005, the term got 100 million hits. Today, there are vast numbers of podcasts, and the momentum and excitement over this new medium has only continued to grow.

Because podcasts are audio files, music and podcasting are a natural fit. Better still, the Recording Industry Association of America (RIAA) actively denies podcasters the right to use its music. What does this mean for you? Podcasters are in need of music to play.

Podcasting is good for listeners, too. It provides a viable alternative for music fans tired of the increasingly homogenous music on radio. Podcasts are a place where music lovers and independent bands meet.

Understanding Podcasting

At its heart, podcasting is a simple concept. Named from the enormously popular iPod, podcasting evolved thanks to the rise of blogs, the ubiquity of the MP3 format, the popularity of portable MP3 players, and the cheap and easy availability of audio recording software.

To podcast, people record an episode of their show, upload the MP3 to the Internet, and create a link to the file from their blog. Thanks to the power of Really Simple Syndication (RSS), which we discussed in the "Your Web Site" chapter, the podcast episodes can then be automatically downloaded and enjoyed by subscribers as new ones become available.

Pros

- Podcasters are always looking for music

- Free and easy to submit music

- Unregulated by the music industry

- Dedicated, niche audiences

- On-air mentions and hyperlinks to band Web site

- Episodes are indefinitely archived

Cons

- Smaller audiences than radio

- Less professional sound quality and shows

- No set rules for submitting music

- No set schedules for shows

- Podfading; i.e., podcasts stopping production on a whim

Understanding the Podcast Audience

Podcasting is "radio on demand." It's easy, it's prevalent, and most important, people are listening. Podcast audiences tend to be small and, at this early point in the medium's development, tech-savvy, but also dedicated to the topic of the podcast or the personality doing the show. That said, some podcasts, such as *Keith and the Girl* (keithandthegirl.com) and Adam Curry's *Daily Source Code* (dailysourcecode.com) have consistently large audiences.

Podcasts put the audience in control. People can listen to episodes on their schedule—not when they're broadcasted. Also, since episodes are simply audio files, people can listen anywhere on their portable MP3 players: in their cars, while working out, or while commuting to work. They can pause a show and come back to it later without missing anything or listen again at a later date.

Plus, since podcasters generally leave their old episodes up at their Web site, new listeners who discover a podcast can easily download earlier episodes. Best of all, listeners don't have to hunt around for the latest episodes—thanks to RSS their computers grab the new ones automatically.

Understanding Podcasters

Podcasters are mostly amateurs, producing shows in their free time and with a shoestring budget simply for the love of it or for love of their subject. As a result, you'll find few rules or formalities when dealing with podcasters.

Production values vary greatly as well. Some podcasters use state-of-the-art recording and production techniques, with results that wouldn't sound out of place on the radio, while others sound as if they recorded their show with a cassette recorder while cooking dinner. Some maintain rigorous schedules, updating their shows at the same time each week, while others upload new podcasts "when they get around to it" or disappear all together ("podfade") due to lack of interest or more pressing commitments.

Thanks to copyright laws, most podcasters are not only happy to hear from indies, they are often in desperate need of "legal" music to play.

Podsafe Music

Many podcasters want to play music, but most popular music is controlled by the RIAA. Rather than allow podcasters to play their music, they have instead scared these potential advertisers away with legal threats. In other words, they have basically shut themselves out of this new music medium. Considering that indies are usually locked out of every area that the music industry is in, this is a great opportunity. Since podcasters are not supposed to use major-label music unless they pay to license it, they have generally turned to indie bands for music instead.

That's not to say that indie music isn't copyrighted—it is. It's just that indies are more likely to relax certain copyrights and allow podcasters to play their music. Some people think that podcasting works like radio when it comes to copyright, but that is not the case. Because podcasts are downloadable audio files, there's no legal distinction between downloading a podcast with an RIAA song or downloading the song itself from a digital music store such as iTunes.

Radio, on the other hand, is "streamed" over airwaves, and copyright law has grown up to allow it special statutory exemptions to play music without even talking to the copyright holder of that music. Radio stations just need to pay performance rights organizations for this privilege. But podcasters need permission from all of the copyright holders. While some podcasters, either out of naïveté or contempt for the RIAA, use whatever music they want despite the legal consequences, many prefer to do the right thing and avoid problems.

Unfortunately, obtaining permission to use a particular piece of popular music is not easy or cheap. As you know from the "Your Rights" chapter, a podcaster needs to clear a variety of rights from various copyright holders. Not only does each copyright owner likely want money for these rights, but the process takes weeks of effort, time better spent creating new episodes, grouting tile in the bathroom, or, really, doing just about anything else at all instead.

To facilitate the use of music for podcasting, podcasters created the concept of "podsafe" music. In essence, they ask musicians to license their music under a specific podsafe license—a license that makes a few exceptions to the default copyright setting of "all rights reserved" in order to allow podcasters to use the musician's music legally (and freely) in their podcasts. Issuing music under a podsafe license also protects musicians as well, because it limits the rights that are granted.

It should come as no surprise that indie music makes up most of podsafe music. After all, indies can license their music any way they choose. With the right podsafe license, you have the ability to grant podcasters a small exception within your umbrella of copyrights for a particular song. You can continue to sell your song and license it to others, all while letting podcasters freely play it to give you more exposure.

There are multiple podsafe licenses, but our favorites are issued by the Creative Commons (creativecommons.org), which are free to use and easy to understand, even though they are written by lawyers. They are flexible with regard to what rights you want to allow.

No matter which podsafe license you use, you should fully understand the rights that you are granting and those you are reserving. As with all legal matters, you should contact an attorney with any questions.

Podsafe Collectives

So, let's say you're a podcaster. You're aware of the legal issues of using copyrighted music in your podcast. You decide you want to add some podsafe music to your show. Great! Now, where do you get it?

Podsafe collectives are sites that host thousands of podsafe songs. Podsafe collectives are where musicians and podcasters meet. Musicians upload their music and get a profile page with an embedded player so podcasters can sample their stuff. Podcasters can then download and use whichever songs they want.

Podsafe collectives are a great way to make your music available to podcasters worldwide, but note that each uses different licenses. Some collectives are based on licenses that are subject to change at the collective's discretion. We prefer podsafe collectives that use Creative Commons licenses, such as PodsafeAudio.com.

PODSAFE COLLECTIVES

Use these sites to make your music available to podcasters for use on their shows.

- PodsafeAudio (podsafeaudio.com)

- Podsafe Music Network (music.podshow.com)

- Opsound (opsound.org)

- ccMixter (ccmixter.org)

- Magnatune (magnatune.com) ♦

Submitting music to a podsafe collective is a passive way to get your music heard. It's easy to do, and we recommend joining one. But to really get exposure, you'll need to actively submit your songs to podcasters.

Music Podcasts

Unlike commercial radio stations, music podcasts are usually happy to accept unsolicited music from independent bands. Most podcasters will announce the band name in the episode. The more professional ones will also post the band, album, and Web site for each song in their podcast notes so that listeners can easily find and purchase the music. For this reason, getting on a music podcast can be even more effective than getting played on the radio. And because podcasts are archived, the episode will likely be accessible for future listeners for some time—the medium continues to promote your music long after it has been released.

These music podcasts offer excellent exposure for indies because their listeners are, by definition, fans of new music, and podcasters are always hungry to find the freshest stuff for their audience. This doesn't mean that they have low standards. The best music programs are typically particular about what they will play, depending on their tastes. So if you submit a song to one and don't get chosen, don't get discouraged. Whether a particular podcaster finds your music appropriate is not something you can control. What you can do is make the best music you can make and get that music to as many different podcasters as possible to increase your chances of connecting with people who will enjoy it.

A few examples of well-known music podcasts include, C. C. Chapman's *Accident Hash* (accidenthash.com), Phil Coyne's *Bitjobs for the Masses!* (bitjobs.libbyn.com), and Brian Ibbott's *Coverville* (coverville .com).

The Universe of Niches

Given that affordable and easy-to-use hardware and software have made podcasting accessible to the masses, it's no surprise that podcasts cover any topic you can imagine: politics, comedy, education, religion, sports, self-help, and so on. Almost every human interest is addressed by a podcast. It's hard to imagine a *radio* show about, say, crocheting, but a search on Podcast Alley returns over twenty podcasts, with titles such as *Crochet Unraveled*, *CrochetCast*, and *Crochet for Men*. The same holds true for music podcasts. Name a genre and there's a podcast that covers it—and ones that cover its subcategories. Best of all, they're all looking for music to play. The podcasting world is a universe of niches, and no niche is too small.

But podcasts aren't only talk shows. Sometimes podcasters produce a short-run series of podcasts on a particular social, political, charitable, or other cause. Another trend is for authors to podcast their books in serial form. Notable authors who have done this include Scott Sigler (scottsigler.com), J. C. Hutchins (jchutchins.net), Tee Morris (teemorris. com), and Mur Lafferty (murlafferty.com). Once these podcasts run their course, the podcast ends. And yet all of these, as we will discover, need music.

Podcasts are an effective way to get heard today because listeners *request* to listen. While there is certainly something to be said for getting your music played on the radio and in other mass media, audiences actively download a particular podcast because of their interest in its subject matter or the personality delivering it.

Applying the Standing-Out Strategy

As we discussed in the "Get Noticed" chapter, the standing-out strategy tells us that submitting your songs only to music sites or, in this case, only to music podcasts is not the best way to get noticed. Getting your music played on a nonmusic podcast such as a talk show about football, or a comedy show about politics, can introduce you to potential new fans in a more effective way. Think creatively about your music in relation to the podcasts that are out there. If your song fits a particular topic, it may be the exact music a podcaster wants to round out a show. Again, since podcasting is unburdened by formalities, it's all about asking—whether a podcaster adds your song is entirely at that creator's whim. You have to take that chance.

Just remember that some niches are large, such as the board-game niche that we mentioned previously, which had a Web site with more than six hundred thousand unique visitors a month. Creative thinking about how your music and talents fit the needs of podcasters can get your music heard by many new ears. For indies, the lack of set rules and boundaries is an advantage.

Podcast Theme Songs

Podcasts often have a theme song (or should). This identifies the podcast, establishes the brand, and gets listeners pumped about the show. Some podcasters turn to indie bands for a song the band has already recorded. Others request a new song be created especially for them.

If you have a knack for this type of songwriting or have a song that naturally fits, most podcasters are happy to receive an e-mail from a band that wants to write a theme song just for them. Some bands do this for money, and others will do it for exposure. The likelihood of a podcaster choosing your band to write a theme song is, of course, greater if you offer to do it as a favor.

If a podcaster uses your theme, you're likely not only to get a great mention (or multiple mentions over time), you'll also get a reciprocal listing of your band's site on the podcast Web site as thanks. (It never hurts to ask for this just to make sure.)

We've done quite a few theme songs, and each of them has given us a lot of great exposure. You can get an idea of the diversity of the audiences from this partial list of podcasts:

- *Playing for Keeps* (playingforkeepsnovel.com), a podiobook (book read by the author in a podcast) by author Mur Lafferty. The first episode had more than four thousand downloads. By the end of the book, she had fifteen thousand.

- *Buffy Between the Lines* (buffybetweenthelines.com), a serialized podcast fan-fiction audio drama written, produced, and created by fans of *Buffy the Vampire Slayer.*

- *The Gigcast* (gigcast.nightgig.com), a Webcomic podcast.

- *Give Us a Minute* (www.joemurphymemorialfund.org), a charity podcast for the Joe Murphy Memorial Fund, to combat leiomyosarcoma and cancer in general.

When we do themes, we are constantly overwhelmed by the amount of thanks and exposure we get, including many great comments in the podcasts' discussion boards and in person from fans. As you can imagine, this also generates theme-song requests from other podcasters.

Incidental Music, Beds, and Bumpers for Podcasts

Listen to any commercial or public radio format and you'll notice that music—typically instrumental music—is used in a variety of ways to grab the attention of the listener and keep the show moving along. It's also used to introduce particular segments. Incidental music works well in radio but is often ignored in podcasts. And yet this kind of music can really help a podcast sound more professional. If your existing music lends itself naturally to incidental music such as beds (music played underneath talk) and bumpers (music played before or after talk), or you enjoy writing instrumental music, it's worth reaching out and exploring this option.

Your Music as a Special Guest

Saturday Night Live is a popular, long-standing sketch-comedy show, and yet, on each episode, they have a guest band perform twice. It breaks up the monotony of the sketches and gives the audience and talent a break from the format. Similarly, many "talk" podcasts will feature a song or two, either because it's related to the subject or simply to break up the dialogue. We have gotten tens of thousands of podcast plays of our music in this way.

As we discussed earlier, nonmusic podcasts are an effective way to get your music noticed—more so than music podcasts, since yours is likely to be the only music on the show. Better still, nonmusic podcasters aren't inundated with song submissions and are usually excited about playing your music if it's a good fit for the show. Tapping a podcast in the right niche can build a strong connection with a lot of potential fans.

Finding Podcasts to Play Your Music

So now that we know how podcasters use music, it's time to find some to play your songs. There are a number of good podcast directories. Most podcasters voluntarily register with these sites because they want to advertise. See the box below for directories that feature a search engine as well as a category-based listing. Categories are a good way to find podcasts suited to your music.

In addition, some podcasters have organized networks of podcasts where they share resources, pool audiences, and collectively market to the public. Examples of such networks include FarPoint Media (farpointmedia.net) and PodShow (podshow.com). We suggest going to these network sites and finding podcasts that your music is suited for, because these tend to have large listenerships. We've noticed that getting played on a podcast within a particular network usually leads to other opportunities with additional podcasts within that network as word spreads about our band.

So what's the best way to approach a podcaster with the idea of using your music? For those podcasts that post submission guidelines, the approach is simple: just follow the instructions carefully. We talk about the best ways to send music to podcasters below. The ones that don't have a formal procedure for submitting music are trickier. But remember, podcasters are just people. So all the common sense you learned while growing up continues to hold true here: being friendly, and brief, usually works great.

If you have the same hobby or interest as a podcaster, it's best to start by pointing out your common interest and your admiration for their show, and by commenting on the particulars of a prior episode. Follow that by mentioning that you're a musician and that you have some songs they might use on their show. They are often happy to accept at that point.

PODCAST DIRECTORIES

The following links have podcast directories that can help you find the podcasts that may be a good outlet for your music.

- Podcast Alley (podcastalley.com)

- Podcast Pickle (podcastpickle.com)

- Podcast Net (podcast.net)

- The Podcast Directory (www.podcastdirectory.com)

- The iTunes Music Store (iTunes.com)

- Podiobooks (podiobooks.com)

- IndieBandSurvivalGuide.com ♥

Preparing and Submitting Your Music to Podcasts

Podcasters vary in how they want music submitted, but one guideline is clear: they want it fast and convenient—through the Web, not sent through snail mail on a CD.

1. Make a quality recording.

2. Choose the appropriate track.

3. Encode the audio file correctly.

4. Name the file using your band name and song title.

5. Input ID3 tags in MP3s.

6. Choose a license for the music.

7. Follow the podcast's submission guidelines.

8. Send a sample e-mail to the podcaster.

9. Follow up.

Step 1: Make a Quality Recording

One submission guideline that is nearly universal for any quality podcast (and any band that takes itself seriously) is to use a quality recording of the song you are submitting. Everything that we talk about in the "Your Albums and Merchandise" chapter holds true here.

Step 2: Choose the Appropriate Track

For music podcasts, you'll want to promote the song that would have the most appeal for listeners to that particular podcast. After all, you want them to be wowed enough to check out the rest you have to offer. Also, don't hold back your "best tracks" from podcasters. Think of it like radio: would you want anything but your best track to be played?

Step 3: Encode the Audio File Correctly

One way to completely mess up the first step is by encoding your audio file improperly. Bands often overlook this important step. Since a podcast will ultimately be made available in MP3 format, it's imperative that your audio file be encoded at the highest bitrate possible. Not all podcasters understand this point either. Some will happily add a band's MP3 to their show, only to compress the song a second time when they convert the finished podcast to MP3 format.

This has the unfortunate effect of adding digital pops and glitches (called artifacts) that distract and annoy listeners—no one wants to listen to an audio file that sounds as if it were being played in between stations on an AM dial. Worse, although it's not technically the band's "fault," the low quality of the audio reflects badly on the band.

Therefore, send an uncompressed WAV version of the song. These files are large, so use a large file-transfer service such as YouSendIt (yousendit.com) or zUpload (zupload.com) to avoid clogging the podcaster's in-box.

Step 4: Name the File Using Your Band Name and Song Title

Always name your audio files consistently. Although you are only submitting them to a particular podcaster, you never know where they may show up. Some podcasters may ask to make the song available directly from their Web site, and it may end up in a huge folder of other song files. As a result, you want to make sure the file name is tagged correctly as outlined in the "Your Web Site" chapter.

Step 5: Input ID3 Tags in MP3s

As we discussed in the "Your Web Site" chapter, the MP3 format comes equipped to handle a variety of information about the song through a tagging mechanism called ID3. You should fill in this information as we suggested there.

Step 6: Choose a License for the Music

As mentioned above, we suggest using a Creative Commons license for your music to make it podsafe. A smart podcaster may ask about the license, so be clear from the start which one you're using for the track.

Step 7: Follow the Podcast's Submission Guidelines

This rule is simple: read each podcast's submission guidelines and follow them carefully. You don't want your music ignored just because you didn't follow their instructions. Most music podcasts have a preferred method of delivery, file format, and information they need about the band (such as Web site address, bio, etc.). Some want songs sent through e-mail. More sophisticated or long-standing podcasts have FTP servers or other mechanisms. You don't want to start off on the wrong foot by causing more headaches for the podcasters. Follow their instructions. And when it's not apparent what to do, ask for clarification *before* sending.

Step 8: Send a Sample E-mail to the Podcaster
Include the following:

- Band name and Web site address

- Song title (and album title, if applicable)

- Brief band bio and description of your music

Always keep this info short and to the point, but be personable where appropriate. Be sure to spell the name of the person properly, as well as the name of the show. If a podcast has played your music before, remind them. You've passed their quality test before, so they'll be more likely to play you again. This is especially important with music podcasts because they're inundated with submissions. When you wrap up, be sure to thank them!

Step 9: Follow Up
Keep track of every podcast you submit to. Track the name of the podcast, which song(s) you sent, and the date of submission. Then follow that podcast to see if it plays your music. Some never alert the musicians that they've used a particular song, so it may be up to you to see if you get played.

If you are played in a podcast, send a thank-you e-mail! Relationships with podcasters are valuable, and maintaining a collaboration is the best way to keep getting played. For instance, one podcaster has featured our music a dozen times and continues to ask for more.

AUDIOBLOGS OR MP3 BLOGS

Audiobloggers, or MP3 bloggers as they are often called, are essentially freelance music reviewers. The main difference between MP3 bloggers and traditional music journalists is that the former often provide the MP3 of the song being reviewed.

MP3 blogs are often distrustful of anything that seems like self-promotion. Although some accept submissions from bands, others are geared toward people who've discovered some music that they would like to talk about. If you find an MP3 blog that accepts submissions and reviews music in your genre, and you can get a review, this can be a great source of quotes for your press kit and Web site. Readers of MP3 blogs are always looking for good new music, so a positive mention can get you some good exposure.

A good place to find audioblogs is to look through the site Hype Machine (hypem.com), which posts the latest audioblog entries from all sources in one place, or head to IndieBandSurvivalGuide.com.

PLAYLIST SUGGESTION AND SHARING SITES

People use the Web to share many aspects of their personal lives, and their musical tastes are part of this as well. Playlist sharing has become as much a part of social networking as microblogging. Multiple sites do this type of sharing, and the most surprising part of these sites is that they all work very differently from one another toward the same goal: to introduce people to new music. We're going to cover three below, explaining their similarities and differences, as well as how to use them as a band. These applications are constantly evolving so we recommend keeping on the lookout for new tools when they appear.

Last.fm (last.fm) shares the playlists of its users and provides a way for the users to discover new music based on artists that they enjoy. While you've probably seen quite a few sites that suggest music, this one uses the playlists that it collects to make the suggestions rather than going by genre or some other method. For example, if a lot of people who listen to They Might Be Giants also listen to Beatnik Turtle, Last.fm will make a connection. When people type *They Might Be Giants* into their "Find Music" search bar, they might get a track of ours in their player.

There are two ways to use this as a musician. First, you can sign up for a Label or Artist account, which allows you to upload an image for your band, create a profile, and upload your own music to let people discover it. We highly recommend doing so, as this site can expose your music to many new fans. The second way to use it can be even more useful. When you search on an artist in Last.fm, it will give you how many plays of that band have been recorded, and it will also show you the profiles of people who have listened to that band. You can basically find out who your listeners are, and other bands they listen to. In many cases you can even use it to contact them. This is invaluable research and can allow you to directly connect with your fans.

Pandora (pandora.com) also tries to make suggestions to its users based on a search bar where you can list a band that you're interested in, but it does it differently from Last.fm. It's based on the Music Genome Project, which attempts to group music into hundreds of musical attributes to capture the unique musical identity of a song.

Pandora only works from albums that it is aware of, so you won't find your albums in Pandora unless you send them to it. The site only accepts actual CDs mailed to it, not MP3 files. Your CD must also have a bar code. You can find the submission instructions in their help section.

Imeem (imeem.com) is a playlist-sharing social-networking site. You can upload songs, videos, or other media to share with friends. As a band, you can of course upload your own music to share. Users can create groups and share media among the groups.

Naturally, the more you appear on sites such as these, the more chances someone will recognize you. And if you participate as a user, you can increase the chances of getting your own music noticed. As we've said throughout this guide, you need to question how much you'll get out of each opportunity to decide where to spend your time. We do suggest at least exploring these types of sites.

MUSIC ARCHIVES

If you wish to give away some songs to get exposure, you may wish to use music archives to share your music. The most famous music archive is Archive.org (www.archive.org/details/audio). They make it especially easy to license your songs under a Creative Commons license, should you want to use one. We recommend that you create an account just to check it out.

The downside to this service is that they tend to scale back the sound quality to save space, and you may find that the songs that you upload do not sound good, so it's not a particularly good place to *highlight* your music.

LIVE-MUSIC ARCHIVES

A long tradition exists of trading live-music performances recorded by fans. Naturally, with the Internet, the practice has gone online. Live-music archives allow people to freely trade recordings of performances that fans attend.

These live-music archives have some unique characteristics. First, they tend to be picky about sound quality and prefer music files that use lossless encoding. Second, they often insist that any files traded in their networks be made freely available to all, and for nonprofit purposes only. And finally, they are usually careful to only trade music from bands that allow it.

Perhaps the most well-known-live music site is Etree (etree.org), which has software, resources, and information about live-music archives. If you're interested in finding out more about Etree, we suggest using their wiki (wiki.etree.org) to get the latest information, or to learn how to encode your own band's performance so that you can add it to this archive.

Etree's wiki has an interesting page that you should consider visiting called the Trade Friendly page (wiki.etree.org/index.php?page= TradeFriendly), where they provide lists of bands that allow the recording and trading of their music. For example, one such place that you can register your band is Bands That Allow Taping (btat.wagnerone.com). It's easy to create an account and register your band at BTAT if you want to encourage your fans to tape you.

INTERNET CONCERTS

Want to go on a worldwide tour without leaving your basement? All you need is a webcam, a decent microphone, a fast Internet connection, and, of course, a computer. Internet broadcasting sites make it possible to give people a concert no matter where in the world they are.

Treat a broadcast concert just as seriously as any other gig. It's possible that you'll get even more people watching than you might at a live show, especially since most Internet broadcast services archive what you record for later viewing. This kind of performance can be just as important as your other live shows.

Plan for Web broadcasts exactly as you would any show, with the same level of attention to publicity. This technology represents a wonderful opportunity to play for thousands of people all over the world. Recommended resources to use are Ustream TV (ustream.tv), Mogulus (mogulus. com), and GoTo Webinar (gotoWebinar.com).

PLAYING MUSIC FROM YOUR WEB SITE

As we discussed in the "Your Web Site" chapter, your Web site is one of the best ways to distribute your music. On your own site, you have complete control over how the music plays, which of your songs and albums are featured, and what other information visitors see while they listen.

Often, people will link to your Web site from a blog or message board. Your music must be available on your site so that new visitors can listen immediately. Also, someone might hear one of your songs elsewhere and come looking for a further taste of your music. This process should be as smooth as possible. Incorporating an "E-mail a Friend" feature would help further spread your music by allowing visitors to easily send a link to a particular song or album page to one or more friends.

FILE-SHARING YOUR OWN MUSIC

The music industry tended to view file-sharing as rampant piracy causing lost sales, but for indies, it was an inexpensive way to get their music heard by new audiences. We recommend that you file share your own music to get more exposure.

Even if you're file sharing your music already, you may want to take a more structured approach to it. There are multiple file-sharing networks, so you will need multiple programs to share your music on all of them. You will want to find programs to get you onto, at a minimum, Gnutella and eD2k, but file-sharing networks can appear and disappear without warning in the ongoing war between the file sharers and the industry. To see the latest networks, programs, and techniques visit the companion site to this book, IndieBandSurvivalGuide.com.

LEARNING MORE

To keep up with all the new places and techniques to get your music heard, head to IndieBandSurvivalGuide.com.

CHAPTER 12

GET PUBLICIZED

*Isn't it funny? One type costs everything and means nothing, and
the other costs nothing and means everything.*

—*James Ernest*, PRESIDENT AND FOUNDER OF CHEAPASS GAMES
ON THE DIFFERENCE BETWEEN ADVERTISING AND PR

THE WORLD appears completely different when you look at it through
publicity-colored glasses. You start thinking about the press angle for everything you do as a band. You see potential press releases for every
achievement. You'll start thinking about everything your band will do three
to four months from now, because that's the lead time most media outlets
need.

Every form of entertainment relies on the media to get people interested
in it. While it would be great to just focus on playing music, musicians don't
have that luxury if we want to get our music heard by as many people as
possible. As Ariel Hyatt of Ariel Publicity (arielpublicity.com) said, "I
don't care what business you're in, big or small, unless you spend forty percent of your time on promotion and marketing, you're dead in the water."
Although the Internet has made it much easier to communicate and get
some attention, it's really only added another layer to your publicity campaigns, one you can worry about a little closer to the event itself.

Publicity can be a large and mysterious world, so we're going to cover
the parts of it that are important for musicians and break it into steps so
you can conquer it.

THE MYTH OF THE "MAGIC BUZZ BUTTON"

By now you should realize that getting your band and music heard takes work and perseverance. Publicity works the same way. And yet, some musicians still think that there's a shortcut. Jim DeRogatis, music editor for the *Chicago Sun-Times* and cohost of National Public Radio's *Sound Opinions*, said, "There's this perception that there's some mystery button that gets pushed, and buzz starts. It's this magic, elusive thing that every group is trying to get. But buzz just means that people are excited about the band and are talking about it."

But initial publicity and chatter about a band is rarely organic. It needs a push to get it started. Money and orchestrated PR campaigns are usually the only way to speed this process. Below, we'll talk about how to wage these campaigns yourself. Eventually, you can get to a point where people have heard of you, and buzz will grow organically.

THE TRADITIONAL MEDIA AND THE NEW MEDIA

The Long Tail doesn't just apply to music. It's changed everything that delivers content. In journalism, the Web has enabled more coverage of topics outside the mainstream, or ones that weren't as appealing to advertisers. Citizen journalists can cover subjects unhindered by political or financial influence or by a specific publication format or schedule. Web-based reporters have short-circuited the process of journalism, forcing the older model to play catch-up.

Some people distinguish between "new media" and "traditional media." We will offer a definition here of each term, but keep in mind that the Long Tail is a continuous spectrum, not a set of discrete camps. That's why you should always research your media outlets carefully before submitting and never take their requirements for granted. We will refer to press contacts as journalists whether they have a radio show, podcast, TV show, blog, or magazine or newspaper column.

PUBLIC RELATIONS

If you have the notion that reporters find stories by pounding the streets and investigating, you need to change your thinking before going forward with your campaign. You should also drop any illusions about journalists covering you just because you're playing good music. Although they occa-

THE TRADITIONAL MEDIA
AND THE NEW MEDIA

Media	Submission Guidelines	Examples
Traditional media	Generally have formal submission guidelines, prefer press releases, and require three to four months of lead time.	Newspapers and newswires, televised news and talk shows, radio programs, and magazines.
New media	Generally have informal submission guidelines, prefer personal messages to press releases, and don't require long leads.	Blogs, podcasts, video blogs, and other Web sites.

sionally do find stories the old-fashioned way, in reality most of the articles you read are based on press releases.

What this means is that, if you want the traditional media to pay attention to you, you should get the stories directly into their hands via releases. It also means that you will be competing with professional PR people who do this for a living. It probably sounds tough. And it is time-consuming, but you *can* do this yourself. You do have one thing going for you: journalists are always looking for a good story, and you can give it to them.

GOALS OF A MEDIA CAMPAIGN

If getting press is so difficult, is it even worth the effort? It's a question you have to ask since you could definitely be doing other worthwhile things with your time—including working on music. Overall, though, we think it makes sense for bands to invest the effort in coordinating a full-scale press campaign or to spend the money on a good publicist.

Here's what a press campaign can do for you:

- Boost your draw for your upcoming performance or tour

- Bring more visitors to your Web site

- Get your music played

- Sell albums and merchandise

- Establish your band with the media, who will not only share your story with the public, but also be more likely to write about you in the future

- Generate press clippings that will help you get better venues and more attention in the future

All of these benefits help everything you do as a band. And since a band's worth is often measured in popularity, a press campaign is a natural tool that can get it for you. Certainly, labels understand this and spend a lot of their money for big album launches on publicity.

Finally, consider what the movie industry does when it wants a film to succeed. Marketing budgets equal to half or more of a movie's production costs are not unusual. For example, *Spider-Man 3* cost $258 million to make and had a marketing budget of $150 million. This marketing budget went toward advertising the movie on billboards, buses, television, radio, and magazines—all of it coordinated to display just before the release. While you don't need to spend half of your money and efforts on PR, this should give you an idea of how important it is to plan a comprehensive publicity campaign for your band and follow through with it.

PR CONCEPTS

Think publicity, always. Everything your band does should be considered material for press releases. When you're planning anything from a performance to an album launch, ask yourself, is this sufficiently newsworthy? If necessary, alter your plans to make your new project even more press-friendly. While some musicians just focus on music, remember that music is entertainment. And entertainment and publicity go together like peanut butter and chocolate.

Not all press releases have to be about momentous events. Some announcements we've sent out include:

- Our music video getting five thousand views

- Hitting the halfway point in our Song of the Day project

- Launching a new album

- Releasing a song about *Star Wars* near the first film's thirtieth anniversary

Each announcement has a decent angle, but some are obviously juicier than others. For instance, we sent out a press release announcing that we'd reached the halfway point of our Song of the Day project knowing that it probably wouldn't be covered as a story. But, by talking about the project, we gave journalists a reason to anticipate the press release we would be sending when we finished it at the end of the year, a story we did want them to cover. In other words, the press release was more about priming the journalists than the story itself. When we sent out the final press release, the journalists were already familiar with who we were and the story.

You may also wonder how a press release about getting five thousand views of a video is newsworthy. First of all, the press release might just make someone curious enough to actually play it (and this kind of press release is usually just an e-mail, so the link is right there). Second, we used the announcement as an excuse to mention other projects that we were working on at the time, including the Song of the Day and our forthcoming album, which we were going to send an official press release about the following month. Third, the release creates yet another impression of our band name and logo on the recipient. The more familiar the press is with our name, the more likely it is that they'll cover us in the future.

PR IS AN ICE PICK

Remember as you're putting together your campaigns that each release should send a *very* targeted message to each audience. Don't try to be everything to everybody. This is true not only for PR, but in marketing your band and your music everywhere.

Bob Baker (bob-baker.com), whom we consider to be *the* music-marketing guru, said it best: "You need to find your most defining aspect. You need a sharp focus. If you try to break through a wall, you can't get through if you use a board. But you can if you use an ice pick."

When you market yourself to the media, fans, or on Web presences, you should take a stand and sharpen your message to focus on just one defining feature in order to break through.

PR IS A CROCK-POT, NOT A MICROWAVE

The Internet has made us impatient. We expect information, and gratification, immediately. Unfortunately, PR takes place in people-time rather than Internet-time. Even successful PR campaigns take months, even years. The goal of your campaign is twofold: getting coverage for your upcoming event, and spreading the word about your band in the long term.

The first press write-ups in a PR campaign are hard to get because you have nothing to build on. But once you have some press clippings, it gets easier to get more stories. This means you need to start small. For your first campaigns, target local newspapers, blogs, and anything else that seems to be within your arm's reach. Use those initial press clippings to get mentions in more widely read or prestigious outlets.

IT'S STILL ABOUT WHO YOU KNOW

Press coverage conveys two benefits. One is the clipping itself, and the other is a new press contact who now knows you, liked your story, and is likely to cover you in the future. Always send thank-you notes to journalists who mention you, and do your best to get to know them personally. Professional publicists personalize press releases to some journalists because, by establishing a personal connection, they can get more of their stories covered.

IF THE MEDIA DIDN'T COVER IT, IT NEVER HAPPENED

The media are like a public memory. If you had an event and the press never covered it, it's as if it never happened. Because of this, you should try to get at least some kind of clipping about every major event that you do, even if it's only a mention on a blog. It's the best way to establish a public "memory" of the history of your band.

TIMING IS EVERYTHING

Traditional media aren't generally interested in something that has already happened—they want to know about the news before it happens, so that they have the necessary lead time to break the news the moment it does.

Traditional media outlets such as news shows and magazines generally have articles slated three to four months ahead of time. This means that, if you want the press to pick up a story, you need to give them a press release early enough to allow them to cover it.

Say you plan to release an album. To ensure enough lead time, you'll need to send a press release more than three months before your CD-release party. Since you'll need to include your new album with the press release, back up from *that* date when you determine the production schedule. By this point, your CD-release party is probably occurring a minimum of five months from the start of the entire process. For tours, send the press release as soon as details are available.

New media outlets, on the other hand, tend to publish news immediately. They don't keep a backlog of stories. Writing to bloggers about an event three months in the future doesn't make sense to them. They want to know about an event just before it happens, or on its release. Put the dates you plan to approach both traditional and new media outlets on your band calendar.

THE TWO WAYS TO GET COVERAGE

A PR campaign boils down to a two-pronged strategy: sending out press releases to try to convince journalists to write a particular story, and making it as easy as possible for the press to cover you if they decide to do so. You can do a few things to increase the likelihood that journalists *spontaneously* write stories about you:

- Write clear press-contact information on your Web site, so it's obvious whom reporters should ask about interviews and so on. Also, provide all the tools they would need to write a story, such as bios, fact sheets, and images.

- Get blogs to write about you. Both traditional-media and new-media journalists watch blogs for story ideas.

- Piggyback on events that are already being covered by the press. For instance, you might offer to perform at a noteworthy charity event.

- Add "If you are a member of the press and want a free CD, write to us at …" to all of your Web presences, to welcome journalists to get your music.

- Brainstorm and execute projects that are unusual or interesting.

When we began our Song of the Day project, we only announced it to our fans. But word about it spread as people blogged about it, generating a lot of interest and sending more people to the site. In another instance, Todd Martens at *Billboard* magazine wrote about our band because he read about us on Lawrence Lessig's blog (lessig.org), and Caryn Rousseau of the Associated Press wrote about us after reading a short blurb about us in a Chicago-happenings blog called Gapers Block (gapersblock.com). None of these stories began as a press release, but they weren't entirely spontaneous because the seeds were planted in other media.

A JOURNALIST'S SECRET PLEASURE

If there's one thing that journalists love to do, it's to be the first to break a story. Giving a journalist the scoop on what your band is up to, before sending the press release to others, works especially well if you know a journalist personally. Keep in mind that this can also work against you, because sometimes other outlets will lose interest if the news was already released. If you do this, keep track of which stories are under wraps and which have been released. This is a technique for more established bands since what they do tends to be newsworthy.

IMPROVING PRESS RELEASES A THOUSAND WORDS AT A TIME

While you might be tempted to simply send text, your press releases will be more much effective if you add images. Janelle Rogers of Green Light Go Publicity has more than twelve years of experience as a publicist, ten of which were spent working for major labels. Her advice is that "people make decisions visually first, before listening or reading."

CONSISTENCY AND PERSISTENCE

Rogers says that the most important qualities of a media campaign are consistency and persistence. Both of these qualities will establish you as a serious source of news for journalists. So, you need to send quality press releases regularly. Once you develop relationships with the press, you can send more direct and informal messages.

But Rogers warned us that there's a fine line between persistence and pestering. Journalists in both new media and traditional media can become annoyed when someone gets on their case to write a story. Rogers gave us some rules of thumb to help avoid stepping over that line:

- *No means no, but . . .* If you get a no, accept it, but remember that it just means they won't print *this* article at *this* particular time. They might still pick up a future release, so don't take them off your list.

- *It's the second e-mail that counts.* According to Rogers, one journalist told her that he would only start paying attention after the second e-mail, even when coming from a professional publicist. So when you e-mail press releases, wait a week, then send a follow-up if you don't hear back. You always have an excuse: spam filters sometimes eat e-mails, so it's acceptable to confirm whether they received the first e-mail.

- *Never send an old story.* Persistence does not mean sending reworded versions of old stories to the same outlets. Make sure that every new release covers new news. It's okay to refer to older events in a new release, as long as there's new content or a new angle.

TWO STEPS FORWARD, ONE STEP BACK . . .

When you get major press coverage, your site will immediately get a huge number of visitors over a short time, perhaps a day or so. And after that initial burst of traffic, your site will go back to normal, but with a slightly higher number of regular visitors. People will often read a news story or find a link on a bulletin board and click through for a closer look. After checking that one page and satisfying their curiosity, most will leave. Only a few will be hooked enough to stick around.

You will see this behavior again and again as you do your publicity campaigns, so don't be surprised when you get these bursts, then a drop in traffic afterward. Your best bet for keeping people coming back is to have constantly updated content, as we discussed in the "Your Web Site" chapter.

Jonathan Coulton had this experience throughout his "Thing a Week" project as certain songs got coverage. For instance, he recorded a unique cover of the song "Baby Got Back," which had him deluged with listeners. The majority just downloaded the song and went on their way. But after the visits cooled off, his Web statistics indicated he'd gained a few more regular visitors. We noticed the same trend with our Song of the Day project.

FOLLOWING SUCCESS

One of the simplest ways to figure out where to get coverage is to study bands with similar music to yours who are a step or two ahead of you in terms of popularity and success. Simply perform a Web search on those bands to find out where they've gotten press. Read the articles and look at the angles the media took. Note which particular journalists covered them and make a list of potential press contacts. These journalists are much more likely to cover your band than the ones found in entertainment-writer listings. You might also consider adding search-engine alerts for new entries, so that you can jump on opportunities when they appear.

Also, don't forget to piggyback off the other band's name in your subsequent press releases.

THE PRESS KIT

When a journalist receives a press packet from you, he or she will ask two questions: Who are these guys? What do they want from me?

The press kit answers the first question. Your press release answers the second. The good news about your press kit is that you can use it over and over with any release that you send out.

ONLINE PRESS KITS VS. PAPER PRESS KITS

Paper press kits have been a mainstay of publicists for years, and they do still come in handy from time to time when you want to send someone a CD. But your online press kit will be used far more often.

You will need a press section of your Web site to hold your online press kit, organized in a way that makes it easy for the press to get your information. Think of a journalist on a deadline who wants a photo of your band or needs a fact such as the date your band was founded. Make it easy for that person to get those basic facts quickly and without hassles.

We recommend turning each part of your press kit into PDF documents, which are the easiest type of files to read and print. You should also put up all of the content as Web pages, so that visitors can read it quickly when they visit your site.

We suggest hosting this on your own Web site, but sites such as Sonic-bids (sonicbids.com) specialize in hosting an online press kit and also provide methods to submit your materials directly to talent buyers, bookers, and more.

MAKING A PRESS KIT
Press Kit Ground Rules
Here is your basic strategy for a professional press kit:

- Keep the format consistent for all pages of the kit.

- Use your logos, stories, images, and letterhead you created in the "Your Brand" chapter.

- Studies have shown that you only have about six seconds to hook someone's attention with your press kit. It should be visually arresting and should give journalists the information they want quickly.

- Put your contact information on every page. Include the name, e-mail address, phone number, and Web site address for your press contact.

Don't ignore the last rule. Whoever is reading your kit should be able to contact you at a moment's notice. Should journalists print out or get a paper version of the kit, they may lose the front page, so put your contact information on every single one.

Press Kit Components
Here are the components of a press kit:

1. Band bio

2. Band photo

3. Press clippings

4. Info sheet

5. Song samples (online press kit only)

6. Press releases (online press kit only)

We are going to talk about each of these components in separate sections below.

Band Bio

You can create two kinds of bios: one for the press, the other for bookers. These differ.

The band bio for the press should always fit on one page and feature a picture of the band. This bio should tell a story that tickles the readers' interest, giving them just a flavor of the rest of your press materials. Don't make this a history of the band. The band bio for bookers should provide a history of the band, as well as each musician, so that a potential booker can see how much experience the band collectively has.

We have posted examples of good band bios at IndieBandSurvival-Guide.com to give you a place to start.

Band Photo

Visuals can decide whether a kit is read or tossed. The best photos tell a story and stay true to the band's image. Avoid the standard pictures of the band in front of a brick wall; try to stage photos that are distinctive and memorable. According to Janelle Rogers, who has seen countless press kits, some of the most effective band photos have been candid shots taken by one of the band's friends. Journalists will often look at the band photo before listening to the music, and it can color their perceptions of what they hear.

Band photos should be 8.5" by 11" in size. For an online press kit the photo should be in JPEG format at 300 DPI (dots per inch) resolution. At your Web site, you should provide thumbnails of your band photo at your Press/Booking page so that people don't have to download each large-image file just to see what it looks like. If you can, provide multiple photos, because different circumstances and promotions call for different types of shots. What might work for a booker might not be appropriate for publication in a newspaper.

Press Clippings

Nothing in your press kit is more effective than press clippings. They provide real-world, objective validation of your band's success. Also, journalists hate missing a story, and the right clippings can make them feel as if they've been missing out on something great. Use these guidelines to make your clippings sheet:

- Choose the best of the best.

- Your clippings page should be no more than two pages, front and back.

- Take the best quotes or snippets from the clips, and put them in a list on the sheet.

- Feature articles should be included whole. (Which could make the clippings longer than two pages, but a feature article warrants it.)

- Reviews and fan quotes are both fair game.

Info Sheet

Since your bio is a story about your band, you will need a separate info sheet that lists details such as when your band was founded, your discography, what your music sounds like, and other details journalists might need for their story. This should be no longer than two pages.

Here's a list of everything that you should consider adding to fact sheets:

- **Blurb.** A one- or two-sentence blurb about your band and its music.

- **Basic information.** Band name, Web site address, genre, bands you sound like, date founded, hometown.

- **Discography.** List each album, the date released, and a descriptive blurb. For our info sheet, we include thumbnail images of our album covers.

- **Band members.** Instrumentation and list of band members.

- **Radio plays.** If you have any radio play, indicate where and when.

- **Live-show info.** List venues where your band has played live, and any tours you've done.

- **Press.** You may wish to list in one place all the media outlets that have covered you. Unlike the clippings page, this is just a list of the outlets, articles, and dates.

- **Upcoming projects.** You should list the projects you are currently working on.

This info sheet takes longer than you'd think because it calls for brief, targeted writing. The trickiest part is keeping the information up-to-date. Review your info sheet monthly, and add to it as you get more press, plays, and exposure.

Song Samples (Online Press Kit Only)

Pick three of your strongest songs and add them to the online press kit. Use an embedded Flash player so people can just hit play if they want to hear what you sound like. If you have multiple pages in your online press kit, keep the player on the left or right side of every page.

Your goal is to give the press samples of every type of media you create: text, photos, music, and video. Find the best of what you have of each, and put it on your pages to give them a taste. Do not set music or video to play automatically on these pages, because you don't want to annoy people who just want your bio or photo.

Press Releases (Online Press Kit Only)

You should include your prior press releases in your online press kit so the press can reference what you've done before.

THE TRADITIONAL MEDIA

Traditional media are still rooted in formalities, and these formalities distinguish a traditional-media campaign from a new-media campaign. Because the rules for approaching traditional media seem obscure and difficult, many musicians don't even bother trying for coverage. It's true that the new media are getting more and more effective for getting the word out, but a good media campaign should embrace both kinds.

Traditional media will need an official press release and your press kit. Informal e-mails that tickle their interest will, at best, get them interested enough to ask you for the full package. But the good news is that they are now usually willing to accept an e-mailed submission. The only time you will need their physical address is when you send them a CD.

THE FITTING-IN STRATEGY

The key defining factor of a traditional-media outlet is its target demographic. Outlets are acutely aware of who their audience is, and what it is interested in. This isn't surprising, considering most of these media companies make their money from advertising, and their success rests on their advertisers knowing what demographics are being targeted. This means that traditional-media outlets are looking for perfect-fit stories for their demographic.

While we talked about the standing-out strategy in the "Get Noticed" chapter, when you deal with the press, the goal is to fit in. You need to break out of thinking how the press should pay attention to you and instead concentrate on solving problems for each journalist. Journalists are interested in:

- *Finding relevant stories.* Journalists are always on the lookout for interesting stories that will be appropriate for their demographic. People buy kickboxing magazines to read about kickboxing. People check the local newspaper when they want to do something fun, such as see a band over the weekend.

- *Hitting deadlines.* Journalists are tasked with filling a certain amount of space before their deadline. To be safe, they usually build up a three- to four-month buffer of stories.

- *Getting the facts.* Journalists need all the information to flesh out the story, including facts and photos. Research takes time, and if it takes too much time, they may cut their losses and skip the story altogether.

- *Capturing the zeitgeist.* Journalists want to write stories of the moment, identifying and articulating the latest trends.

The more you can meet journalists' needs, the more coverage you will get. This might mean that you write targeted press releases to particular media outlets based on their focus and demographics. If you send a general press release, keep the above goals in mind when you write it, and give outlets enough story hooks to take your story in different directions for their own needs. And always consider piggybacking on a story that is big at the moment.

NEVER MAKE THEM WAIT

Never make a journalist wait if they get in touch with you for a story. They have deadlines. If they are calling you about a story, they need the information now. If you make them wait, you might miss out on a chance for publicity.

THE NEW MEDIA

The new media are informal, fast, and usually inconsistent in quality. These online outlets are mostly run by people who are simply covering what they personally love. Generally, they won't write their stories or record their podcasts ahead of time the way traditional media do. In fact, they often don't have a regular release schedule. New-media journalists are usually skeptical of the traditional media and love to cover topics that the traditional media won't. That is a big reason for the existence of the new media.

And of course, one of the topics that the traditional media ignore is indie music. Many new media proponents argue that traditional media are keeping good indie music from the people who want to hear it. (And who are we to argue?) In short, being an indie band is an advantage, not a disadvantage, when it comes to new media.

Ironically, new-media journalists have a special disdain for anything that looks like promotion. For example, here's the start of a blog review of our fifth CD, *All in a Day's Work*. We sent an e-mail to the Office Humor Blog (officehumorblog.com) because the album seemed to be a perfect fit. Indeed, the writer liked it. But take a look at how the writer started the review: "Last week I received an email from a person representing a band called Beatnik Turtle—a band that apparently has an office-themed album coming out August 7. Normally I'd write off such an email as some sort of spam, but I decided to check out the Beatnik Turtle Website to see what they have to offer and I'm glad I did."

The traditional media would *never* start an article admitting that an e-mail from a representative of the band caught their attention. But in this case the writer was not only telling the story of how he found out about it, he was also disclosing, in the interest of transparency, that he found out about it from the band itself.

So the traditional media expects you to send them unabashedly self-promoting materials, but usually ignores them. The new media, on the other hand, would love to write articles about you but *doesn't want to get anything that seems like promotion!*

That's not the only irony. The traditional media write supposedly neutral or unbiased articles based on these press releases. The new media, in spite of rejecting outright promotion, usually take a *personal* or biased point of view of news, events, and entertainment (most are even written in the first person just like the above blog).

HOW THE NEW MEDIA WORKS

Unlike the traditional media, the new media often don't feel as obligated to please their audiences because they aren't usually trying to sell anything to them. They cover topics because it's their passion, not because they are trying to hit a particular demographic or drive sales for their "advertising department." This gives the new media an authenticity that is lacking in the traditional media, and that is often the appeal for their audience.

The new media don't usually have a backlog of news and don't feel pressured to meet deadlines. They often cover stories immediately. But because they print news whenever they want, they often have a bigger appetite for news than the traditional media.

The exceptions, of course, are the largest and most popular examples of blogs and new media. They tend to act more like the traditional media, lining up stories ahead of time and possibly receiving press releases.

THE FITTING-IN STRATEGY (REPRISE: THE NEW-MEDIA REMIX)

Just as you have to fit in to the traditional media's needs, you will also have to fit in with the new media to get covered. But the process is entirely different.

New-media journalists want stories that are personally interesting to them. Their interests are easy enough to discern by looking at the topics covered by their site. Most bloggers and podcasters find their stories on their own. The best way to convince them to cover you is to encourage them to make the story their own and find their own unique spin.

In general, the new media love covering niche stories, ones outside the mainstream. They love poking fun at the traditional media and also glom on to stories about bucking the system. As an indie, you will often have these stories. For instance, one of our fans blogged about how he was frustrated by the digital rights management (DRM) restrictions that Napster imposed on his music and used our album as an example. This was a number of years ago, when the music industry did not release any of its digital downloads in DRM-free formats. We disliked DRM as well and only made our music available on Napster through CD Baby, which put us on every digital music store. So, we sent the blogger DRM-free versions of all of the songs he'd bought. Naturally, the blogger was pleased with our response. We blogged about this and sent a link to our blog entry to Stanford law professor Lawrence Lessig. That we were giving our music out without restrictions was highly relevant to him. He picked up the story, and then so did other blogs.

While traditional-media pitches need to be formal, the opposite is true for the new media. Some do accept press kits, but sending one is usually a mistake. If you're *lucky*, they'll ignore it. If you're not, they will publically criticize you for your shameless self-promotion.

Here are a few ideas for getting new-media coverage:

• Send a short e-mail consisting of nothing more than "Hey, I thought you might like this," with a link to a blog entry or song, using a nonband account.

• Get someone else, preferably a fan of the site who has suggested material in the past, to send an e-mail on your behalf.

• If the site accepts comments or features a message board, find a way to relate your song or story to the discussion at hand. Since site owners usually read their own Web site's comments, this is an authentic way to give them the idea for a story.

• Tell the site owners that you're with a band, and that you love their blog or podcast or video show. Add that you think that they may like your song, album, or story. While this is self-promotion, it's also a meeting of equals that new-media types sometimes appreciate. This also opens the possibility of cross-promotion, which we talked about in the "Your Network" chapter.

Remember that the new media will cover stories soon after they learn about them. Some will post stories within a week, some the same day. And, of course, some are unreliable and won't cover a story even if they say they will.

WRITING PRESS RELEASES

Press releases are mostly used with traditional media, but while you are unlikely to send the new media your releases, they may end up going to your site to research you and read them.

Press releases work best when they incorporate current trends in pop culture. It's easier for journalists to sell their audience on a story it is already familiar with rather than a completely new one.

Press-release writing can be difficult. You might find yourself laboring over each word. We find it to be the most demanding kind of writing that we do. Here are the basics:

- *Length.* It should be short—one or two pages.

- *Contact information.* Add your publicity contact information at the top of each page. Include a name, phone, and e-mail and Web-site addresses.

- *Release date.* If there's a date that the story should be released (such as the release date of an album), put it at the top. Otherwise, add "For immediate release."

- *Headline.* The headline, often written in all caps, should be designed to catch the journalist's attention. It's a good idea to use salting here.

- *The lead.* This is the first sentence or two of the press release. There are two types. A news release should answer the questions who, what, when, where, why, and how. A feature story should have a hook that is attention-grabbing or amusing.

- *The press release text.* Tell your story briefly, succinctly, and make it as compelling as possible. Aim it at your audience's interests as you write it, and read it out loud several times to make sure that it's punchy. Use small words and subject-verb-object sentence construction for more impact.

- *Call to action.* Your story should have a call to action.

- *Mention recent and future projects.* Near the end of a press release, it's a good idea to mention recently finished projects as well as future ones. You never know what the press will pick up on.

- *Envelope teasers.* When you mail the press your materials, write further information on the envelope itself. For instance, Carla Ulbrich, folk musician, always writes a special note if she'll be in town, such as "Playing in your area at the Riviera on March 12!"

If you'd like model press releases to start from, we've posted some examples at IndieBandSurvivalGuide.com.

INTERVIEWS

If your press release hits home, you might be called for an interview. How well your interview goes will depend partly on your personality and partly on preparation. Interviews are much like stage performances: you need to practice for them just as you'd practice for a show. The difference is, you will never be exactly sure what questions you'll be asked. Here are some techniques that will help you prepare.

WHAT TO EXPECT OUT OF AN INTERVIEW

By the time you're contacted to do an interview, the journalists usually have an idea of the story that they want to tell. Most of the time, they are interviewing you to fish for original quotes that will match their story and perhaps fill in some details that weren't covered in your press release or press kit. It's rarer to get a feature story, where a journalist will interview you to learn what you're really about. Your goal during the interview is to give journalists what they're looking for while subtly blending in the points you want to get across. It's a delicate balance.

In a written piece, you'll be lucky to see more than two actual quotes from a one-hour interview. Clearly, you don't have much control over these stories, except for how you answer questions and the points that you manage to squeeze in. After your first interview or two, you will probably be frustrated by the errors—most journalists get at least one thing wrong in every article. They will misspell your name, get your Web-site address wrong, get the story out of order, or take something you said out of context. Combat these problems with talking points, sound bites, and other techniques we talk about below.

Talking Points

Talking points are just a list of the points you want to cover, with short, paragraph-length statements ready to go for each point. You will usually have two types of talking points handy for interviews. One consists of answers to basic questions such as "Who are your influences?" and "Where do you get your ideas?" The other includes points that you want to introduce to the interviewer, such as your latest projects and anything that your band will be doing over the next few months. If the interview seems to be getting off track, you should try to pull it back to the talking points, because that will be the strongest material.

Sound Bites

Soundbites are short packaged quotes, no more than three or four sentences long. The shorter they are, the better. You want to prepare sound bites before interviews because print journalists are looking for them. But they're especially useful for radio and TV interviews. If you give journalists a good sound bite, they are more likely to use that than something you said off-the-cuff that might not reflect positively on you.

Fact Sheets and Follow-Ups for Interviews

We talked about the fact sheet in the press-kit section, but it comes into play again after an interview. Journalists often wait until the last minute to get in all the little details, such basic information as the date you were founded, your Web-site address, the number of band members, and so on.

If they have to look it up, they may get the information wrong. Your fact sheet is the best way to help them get the facts right.

Offer to send journalists a fact sheet once the interview is finished in case they don't have one. Also, send up a follow-up e-mail after every interview to thank them, and to clarify anything that you think was unclear. These two steps may save you a lot of grief in the future. It will also help cement your relationship with them, which is an even more important objective.

Anecdotes and Stories

Janelle Rogers from Green Light Go Publicity says that one of the most important things to prepare for an interview are stories about the band. Be specific and engaging with these anecdotes, as it gives journalists hooks to write about. For radio and television, it's the stories that can make an interview truly memorable.

PRESS CAMPAIGNS

Press campaigns can be as simple as sending out a press release, and as complicated as a highly orchestrated mailing campaign simultaneously promoting a tour and a new album. No matter what you are trying to do, stick to these steps:

1. Determine your goal.

2. Prepare a targeted press list.

3. Plan the timing.

4. Update your press kit.

5. Write press releases.

6. E-mail press releases.

7. Snail-mail CDs.

8. Send e-mail to new media close to deadlines.

9. Send follow-up e-mails and use trackback.

10. Send thank-you messages.

Step 1: Determine Your Goal

Your most effective press campaigns will have well-defined goals. Goals help determine which media outlets to target and how to best schedule your campaign.

Some example goals include:

- Get articles written about a CD-release party.

- Get a review of your album.

- Get coverage of a big charity show.

- Get attention for a music video.

- Increase your draw for an upcoming tour.

These are, of course, just examples, but the point is that they don't always have to be big goals. Any goal will help determine the later steps.

Step 2: Prepare a Targeted Press List

Each media outlet will respond to different aspects of your stories. Music journalists will be concerned with your music and your influences, the local paper will want to know about your latest shows, and so on. You may need different press releases for each of these targets, and they will each have different deadlines, so plan carefully.

Your press list is simply a list of the submission contacts at each outlet. If you haven't worked with that outlet before, you will have to research to find the right person. This is where publicists have an advantage, because they have already gathered a large database of contacts and can put together press lists for new campaigns quickly. Many publicists will send an e-mail with personalized notes to each contact to raise their response rate.

As you generate your list, keep in mind that you shouldn't send every press release to every outlet. Some of your press releases will go to just a handful of outlets.

Step 3: Plan the Timing

Once you have a press list, figure out what the normal lead times are and plan your campaign accordingly. If media need a three-month lead, and you know that your CD-release party will take place on a certain date, you'll know when to send them your press release. If you're targeting new media, you can probably send messages out just a week or so before major events, and immediately after the release of an album.

Step 4: Update Your Press Kit

Before you send out your press materials, it's a good idea to look over your fact sheets, bios, clippings, and other materials. Details change quickly with bands, and it's worth your time to make sure everything is up-to-date. Often, we'll find that our fact sheet mentions future events that have already taken place. We also often find new information to add, such as new places where our music has been played.

Step 5: Write Press Releases

As discussed in the section above, write press releases. The press releases should be targeted for each type of outlet to be most effective.

Step 6: E-mail Press Releases

Most outlets prefer e-mail press releases. You can improve the chances of getting your e-mail read by creating a compelling subject line, and a punchy lead. The subject line might be the only thing a journalist reads before deleting your e-mail. Again, we recommend salting your subject line to create an expectation that can only be met by reading the body of the message. Provide links to your online press kit in the press release. Links to songs, and especially videos, are also recommended.

Step 7: Snail-Mail CDs

You should only spend the money to send a paper press release when you have a CD to promote. You'll need paper versions of your press kit, your press release, and a pitch letter. The pitch letter should summarize the press release, salted just enough to get the journalist interested in reading more.

Step 8: Send E-mail to New Media Close to Deadlines

As we said, you'll get better results out of the new media when you contact them close to the event that you want covered. This will likely go out months after you send materials to the traditional press.

Step 9: Send Follow-Up E-mails and Use Trackback

Remember our lesson: some journalists won't even read your release until the second e-mail. Wait about a week, and send a second e-mail to any journalists who haven't already responded (use the spam-filter excuse!).

After your campaign begins, track your progress by searching for your band name in search engines and watching the referrers page of your Web-site stats.

Step 10: Send Thank-You Messages

If you get a story covered, send a thank-you, but don't expect a reply. You want to use each successful article to build a relationship with the press. The more you know them personally, the more articles they are likely to write about you.

PRESS CAMPAIGN TIPS

Your Expected Response Rate

According to Janelle Rogers, you can send a hundred e-mails out for a campaign and get only ten responses, or less. Publicity, unfortunately, is a numbers game. You'll need to take the responses you do get and do as much with them as you can.

PR Newswires and Press Services

Newswires accept all types of press releases and blast them out to all of their subscribers. Many publications rely on these wires as sources of fresh stories. When we were covered by the Associated Press, for example, the story went to many publications, and newspapers in different parts of the country picked it up. Newswires are a particularly good place to get coverage because of this.

Some newswires are free to submit to, such as the Music Industry News Network (mi2n.com), while others are for pay. Whether to use them depends on what your goals are. Newswires want press releases. There's no need to send the full press kit. Any press releases sent on a wire should have a call to action to reach your press contact for more information.

For a complete list of current free and for-pay newswires to use for your publicity campaigns, head to IndieBandSurvivalGuide.com.

The Two Magic Words

When it comes to any physical mail you might send, there are two magic words: *solicited materials.* Use them when you can.

If you get in touch with a journalist and he or she tells you to send your materials, that's an invitation to use those magic words on your envelope. These words will move your press release to the top of the stack since it's expected. If you do send a press release that was solicited, be sure to write this on the envelope and in the cover letter.

Web Trackback

One problem with the press is that they rarely tell you they've written a story about your band, even if you sent them a press release. The only way you'll know is if you discover the story yourself.

To track mentions of your band, you should use the Web trackback techniques that we discussed in the "Your Web Site" chapter. After a press release is sent out, you should do regular searches on your band name in the major search engines. Then, you should track your Web statistics and watch the referrer list carefully. You might discover articles that have linked to your Web site that the search engines have missed. Even better, you will be able to see how many people have come to your site from each link, so you can learn which articles are the most effective.

INTERNET CAMPAIGNS

As we discussed in the "Your Web Presence" chapter, the Web has evolved from a broadcast, to a conversation, and finally to a collaboration. While publicity is usually about *broadcasting* a message to as many people as possible, it doesn't have to be limited to that.

DIGITAL POSTERS

Make a digital version of your posters as you can "post" these in many places on the Internet. The most common use is as a comment on My-Space. Again, think of it like a billboard on a busy road. Colorful posters get people's attention more than a plain text message.

After creating a digital poster, upload it to your Web site, then link to that image within your post to a message board, wall, or comment since many boards don't allow you to upload images, but will let you insert one that is hosted elsewhere. This has the added bonus of allowing the image to be tracked in your Web statistics, so you can learn which posts and posters are the most effective.

NEWS AGGREGATORS

As stated in the "Your Web Presence" chapter, sites such as Slashdot, Fark, and Metafilter are key targets for Internet campaigns. The best part about these sites is that they don't only post news stories. They can, and often do, post links to songs, videos, or whatever link takes their fancy, especially if it's related to one of their interests. They are always happy to send their users to something entertaining.

Although many of these sites choose stories from user-submitted links, it's ultimately an editor who decides what gets posted. It's never possible to tell exactly why an editor picks what he or she does, because most of these editors are fickle. Your best bet for getting a mention is to find an angle that would appeal to the editors. Follow each news aggregation site for a while before submitting until you've gotten a feel for their interests.

FAN-NETWORK CAMPAIGNS

Your fan network is the most persistent and genuine way to get your press campaign under way. If your fans are willing to help you, they can put your name in places that you haven't even thought of.

The Brobdingnagian Bards found their fans to be an effective part of their campaigns after they'd been given a little direction. The Bards gave their fans three simple steps to follow to help get the word out:

1. Post the band name and URL around the Web.

2. Link to our blogs.

3. Tell a friend. Or, even better, a couple friends.

HIRING A PUBLICIST

Now that you've been on a tour of what you need to do to publicize your band, you might be feeling overwhelmed. As we discussed in the "Your Network" chapter, do-it-yourself does not mean that you have to do it alone. Publicity is one area where finding or hiring someone to help makes a lot of sense. Publicists can provide some of key services, such as:

- Help you assemble a press kit and bio.

- Brainstorm, plan, and implement press campaigns.

- Find angles to your stories that fit with what the media are looking for.

- Write press releases.

- Give you ready-made press lists appropriate to each press release.

- Send your press releases under their letterhead, which gives it a better chance of getting noticed.

- Put together your press clippings for your press kit.

- Follow up with media after your campaigns.

- Set up and coordinate interviews.

But publicists can't do everything. Do the following to get the most out of publicists:

- Tell them all of the events that you have planned for the next year at least. This includes CD-release shows, major concerts, and anything else that will need a lead time for the traditional press.

- Inform them of any newsworthy event. Remember that these can be small things, such as a music video getting viewed over five thousand times.

- Give them all of the press contacts you've developed on your own. They will make better use of every connection that you have.

- Make sure that they have copies of all of your press materials.

- Give them high-quality MP3s of your best songs. The media outlets that accept music will sometimes ask for an MP3 before the entire album.

- Make sure to give them enough lead time for any story that has to go to the traditional press. If a story misses the deadline window, there might be nothing a publicist can do for you.

LEARNING MORE

If you want to learn more about publicity, we recommend *Public Relations for Dummies* by Eric Yaverbaum, Robert W. Bly, Ilise Benun, and Richard Kirshenbaum, and *Guerrilla Music Marketing, Encore Edition* by Bob Baker. Additional information and resources can be found at IndieBandSurvivalGuide.com.

CONCLUSION

WHEN WE wrote this *Guide,* we hoped to achieve what one reader of the original online version e-mailed us to say: "I get it. A dog-eared copy in every battered instrument case, eh?" That image stuck with us throughout the writing of the book. It kept us focused on our goal to write a book that real musicians like ourselves would use in the real world and would refer to often.

No one knows where the music industry is headed. As Jim DeRogatis said, "If anyone says they know what it will look like in five years, they're lying." And he's right. But no matter what happens to the industry, we do know one thing: musicians will always be able to do it themselves. New opportunities to connect with fans and get your music out there are appearing daily. The amazing thing is that they are within your arm's reach.

We hope that the *Guide* will help you to recognize when these new opportunities appear and to take advantage of them for your music. But know that you're never alone. We'll be keeping up with these opportunities as well as all the latest tools, sites, and resources at IndieBandSurvivalGuide. com, where you can join us and a community of motivated musicians.

We'd love to hear any suggestions, ideas, and comments. You can get in touch with us by mailing contactus@IndieBandSurvivalGuide.com or going to the Web site and using the contact form.

But enough reading about music. Now go out and make it.

After all, there's no better time to be a musician.

ACKNOWLEDGMENTS

No book is created by just the authors, and this book is no exception. We'd like to thank our agent, Rick Broadhead, for realizing our potential. We wouldn't be writing this if it weren't for him. Thanks for all the guidance and encouragement.

Thanks to all at St. Martin's Press for their help, knowledge, and support in bringing this *Guide* to life. Special thanks to our editor, David Moldawer, for believing in the work in the first place and for turning a couple of musicians into authors who write good.

We'd like to thank everyone involved in Beatnik Turtle. Without the band, there'd be no book. In no particular order, we'd like to thank everyone involved in the band and with TheSongOfTheDay.com: John Owens, David Hallock, Chip Hinshaw, Tom Susala, Mike Hernandez, Mike Combopiano, Chris Joyce, Ryan Lockhart, John Lisiecki, Matt Scholtka, Caroline Bruno, Cheyenne Pinson, Dana Huyler, Ted ("Hi, my name's Ted and this is my song about ants") Blegen, Alison Logan, Steve Owens, Dugan O'Keene, Eric Elmer, Jerry Waggoner, Danielle Wetle, Tom Hordewel (and his alter ego Tom Beeyachski), Mike Holmes, and everyone else who has been a part, past and present.

We'd like to especially thank Tom Roper for picking up and running with TheSongOfTheDay.com when we had to turn our attention to researching, doing, interviewing for, and writing the book. Sure, we'll write a book and do 365 songs in the same year, what's so hard about that?

Many who helped make this *Guide* a reality don't know it. These have been our advisers and mentors—people who have helped pioneer the areas that made it possible for musicians to do it themselves and inspired us. These include, in no particular order, Lawrence Lessig, Derek Sivers,

Janis Ian, Eben Moglen, Bruce Schneier, Richard Stallman, Steve Albini, and Eric Boehlert.

We also want to thank everyone we interviewed for the *Guide*. In no particular order, we'd like to thank Chris Anderson (thelongtail.com), Derek Sivers of CD Baby (cdbaby.com), Jim DeRogatis (jimdero.com), Todd Martens, Fletcher Lee (leeproductionsinc.com), Mur Lafferty (murlafferty.com), Patrick Faucher (nimbit.com), Matt Scholtka (scholtkadesign.com), Michael Freeman, Ariel Hyatt (arielpublicity.com), Bob Baker (bob-baker.com), Mike Dolinar (getmadbaby.com), James Ernest (cheapass.com), Scott Alden, and Derk Solko (boardgamegeek.com).

We'd also like to thank all the great indie musicians we talked to: Grant Baciocco of Throwing Toasters (throwingtoasters.com), Andrew McKee and Marc Gunn (thebards.net), George Hrab (www.georgehrab.blogspot.com), Carla Ulbrich (carlaulbrich.com), Peter Shukoff of Nice Peter (nicepeter.com), Jonathan Coulton (jonathancoulton.com), Brad Turcott (bradsucks.net), Brett Ratner, and Yvonne Doll of the Locals (thelocals.net).

Additionally, we'd like to thank the editor of the first online *Survival Guide*, Brad Weier, for his excellent work, as well as Erik Balisi for his initial help. We'd also like to thank all the musicians who e-mailed us after reading the online *Survival Guide*. Their advice, insight, and questions helped make this *Guide* all the better.

And lastly, we'd like to thank everyone who has been part of Beatnik Turtle and TheSongOfTheDay.com past and present, as well as the friends, family, and fans of Beatnik Turtle.

RANDY WOULD LIKE TO THANK . . .

I want to give my heartfelt thanks to my parents, Glenn and Susan Chertkow, for their support. Thanks to the GamesNight people for keeping the games going during my absence. Also thanks to my D&D group for taking on an entire army without your cleric.

Thanks to my sister and brother-in-law Heather and John Cumings, and niece Chloe. Thanks also to Grandma Alaine Klein and Grandpa Eddie Klein for the encouragement. Thanks to my good friends Tony Downing, Heidi Downing, Dana Huyler, Steve Levy, Jay Kline, and Bradley Trenton Malloy Quinn for the personal support. Also, thank you to the

Pegasus folks for the research, banter, distractions, and senseless violence, including Shannon Prickett, Andrew Crawford, Tom Shekleton, James Tripp, and Jessica Firsow.

I want to thank everyone who has worked with me in music, David Bloom, the perfect set group, and Berklee College of Music. And especially my departed and much missed sax teacher, Frank Schalk. And Paul Maslin at PMWoodwind (pmwoodwind.com) for his excellent saxophone advice. Also, thanks to New Trier's music department, especially James Warrick and Jim Thompson.

I need to say a special thank-you to Quinn Obermeyer for his understanding while I wrote this book. And also to Zin Fooks, for his wisdom, camaraderie, and for helping me get through this major project. *Spasibo*. Also, thanks to the rest of the team at my day gig for filling in and for mostly mocking me while I wrote this book: Jim McCafferty, Dan Noah, Shawn Delaney, David Matuszewski, Matt Obermeyer, Scott Soto, Andy Franklin, and Tommy Carter.

And thanks to Jason for cowriting this. Working with you on this project, as well as all of the others, has been a pleasure.

And, finally, to Peggy: I'm sorry. You can have Jason back now.

JASON WOULD LIKE TO THANK...

First and foremost, a big thanks is owed to my wife, Peggy Mahoney, for all her love, support, encouragement, and understanding as I put long hours into the *Guide* and Beatnik Turtle. I'm lucky to have a wife like you, and Liam is lucky to have you as his mom. I love you both.

Everything in this *Guide* stems from Beatnik Turtle. And everything about Beatnik Turtle stems from my parents, Jim and Jean Feehan, who, for some reason, allowed me to build a home studio years ago in their basement. Little did they know their decision, made on a whim, would result in countless musicians traipsing through their home at all hours of the night, instrument cases banging up their walls, and a never-ending stream of Beatnik Turtle music sound-tracking their lives as they struggled to complete the crossword, do the dishes, or watch TV. Despite their inconveniences, they've constantly worried more about us than themselves ("Did you guys eat?"). Although they may still have no idea what the hell we're doing with Beatnik Turtle or the *Guide*, they certainly are proud nonetheless. And I'm proud to call them my parents. Thanks, Mom and Dad. I love you.

I'd like to thank the rest of my family, including my brother, Jared Feehan, my cousins John and Jeff Franzen, and my grandparents William and Ester ("Sick of Sandwiches") Grommes. I'd also like to thank my fun and supportive in-laws, Joe and Collette Mahoney, as well as Chris and Moria Waldron for all their support, advice, and encouragement throughout this process.

Lastly, I'd like to thank everyone at work for their understanding and encouragement throughout this project. That includes Jim Citrin for unknowingly inspiring me to do this and everyone in my department—Dave Rasmussen, Tricia Spence, Terry Thornley, Heath Brewer, and the law clerks, Doug Reisinger and Marcella Hein, who agree with me that "What We Need Is Some Interns in Here." Also Tim Schmidt, who specifically asked to be acknowledged, though I'm not quite sure why....

Lastly, I'd like to thank Randy for cowriting this. As always, we not only did it, we came up with a hundred other ideas we now have to do.

ABOUT THE AUTHORS

RANDY CHERTKOW

Professionally, Randy Chertkow is an information-technology specialist with over fourteen years of experience in enterprise-class Fortune 100 companies. He has a bachelor's in business administration in information systems from the University of Iowa and a master of science in computer science, data communications, with a secondary concentration in artificial intelligence, from DePaul University, where he graduated with distinction. Randy has played music all his life, including jazz, rock, and classical music. His instruments include baritone, tenor, alto, and soprano saxophones, flute, B^b and bass clarinet, guitar, bass, and anything else he can get his hands on. He started at the challenging New Trier High School jazz program and went on to study jazz at Berklee College of Music, then completed a Perfect Set course at the Bloom School of Jazz. He writes, records, and performs with Beatnik Turtle as well as performing with theater companies around Chicago. Randy also writes sci-fi and fantasy (dreamofanotherworld.com) and about computer topics (effectivemonitoring.com).

JASON FEEHAN

Professionally, Jason Feehan is a practicing corporate attorney working for a multinational executive-search firm. He plays guitar and keyboards, sings, records, engineers, and produces. He founded Beatnik Turtle in 1997, growing it from a four-piece band into an eight-piece rock machine with a full horn section and a recording studio all its own. Unfettered by a formal music education, he often learned to play instruments as he wrote the music, using nearly anyone in arm's reach who could play or claimed to be able to play a musical instrument. He is a prolific songwriter and has written close to a thousand songs, three of which are actually not too bad.

BEATNIK TURTLE

The authors' band, Beatnik Turtle (beatnikturtle.com), is a horn-powered pop-rock band based in Chicago. They have recorded eighteen albums, released over four hundred songs, and successfully completed a song-of-the-day project where they released one song for every day of 2007 at the Web site TheSongOfTheDay.com. They've written music for TV shows, commercials, films, podcasts, theater (including Chicago's Second City), and have licensed music to Disney/ABC Family.